"**H**ere we go, Roger," I shouted as I twisted the motorcycle-type throttle on the H-5 as far as it would go and pulled in full power on the collective. The 450 horses in the Pratt and Whitney engine barked loudly into the black Korean night, and the Sikorsky H-5 helicopter leaped off the ground and climbed skyward like a homesick angel.

Then all hell broke loose. It was like the Fourth of July on Coney Island: glowing red fireballs and explosions everywhere. There was no point in trying to take evasive action: the stuff came from all directions. All I could do was hold full power and hope for the best. The North Koreans were throwing everything they had at me, and I mean *everything*.

I suddenly realized why. When I'd climbed up from 9G at full power, there had been a stream of fire shooting out of my exhaust stack at least six feet long. The enemy could see it for miles; it made a perfect target.

I could hear the sound of lead and steel piercing the Sikorsky: *Ping! Pow! Plunk!* Then the controls began to feel strange, and at the same time my bird began to shake badly. I could almost feel the helicopter beginning to disintegrate around me. . . .

WAR PILOT

True Tales of Combat and Adventure

Richard C. Kirkland

PRESIDIO

BALLANTINE BOOKS • NEW YORK

To my wife, Maria,
whose help and encouragement
were my inspiration.

A Presidio Press Book
Published by The Random House Ballantine Publishing Group
Copyright © 1999, 2002, 2003 by the Smithsonian Institution

www.ballantinebooks.com

ISBN 0-345-45812-5

This edition published by arrangement with the Smithsonian Institution Press.

Manufactured in the United States of America

First Edition: April 2003

OPM 10 9 8 7 6 5 4 3 2 1

Contents

INTRODUCTION

A War Pilot's Journey
The Violent Decade:
1943–1953

One day shortly after the fiftieth anniversary of the end of World War II, one of my sons dropped by and asked me to attend an air show with him. He knew I'd be interested since there would be some warbirds on display. As it turned out only one showed up, but it was a beautifully restored P-38, which was very nostalgic for me.

When I stepped up for a close look, the young pilot who had flown it to the show asked if I was familiar with the Lockheed Lightning. I replied yes, I had flown it in combat against the Japanese Zero in World War II.

I was surprised at his reaction and of those standing nearby, who, overhearing me, crowded around and began asking questions. I wouldn't have thought these young people would be interested in something that happened more than half a century ago. "What was it like?" one of them asked me. He hesitated, then added: "I mean what was it *really* like?"

On our way home after the air show, my son and I stopped off at a pub for a beer, and I admitted to him how surprised I was at both the genuine interest and the depth of the questions that were asked.

"Ya know, Dad, you have firsthand experience in the events and personalities of a period in history that changed the world. You ought to put it in writing. Just the way it was, just the way it happened . . . with fifty years' perspective of someone who was there."

I thought about my son's comment that evening and realized he was right. I'd had some unique and exciting experiences as a war pilot during that historic decade from 1943 to 1953. I was an Army Air Corps fighter pilot tangling with Zeros in life-and-death dogfights over the South Pacific. I was an Air Force rescue pilot after the war and a radiological pilot on the atomic bomb tests. Then I went off to Korea, where my combat flying was the antithesis of my World War II experiences: I was flying an unarmed helicopter, under fire, while trying to save lives.

As you might imagine, I took some razzing in Korea, from my old World War II fighter-squadron buddies who were flying jets. They laughed at me and my "windmill" . . . until a few of them were snatched from the jaws of death by that windmill.

I hadn't previously thought much about the historical implications of those events or the personalities involved. In retrospect, it seems that destiny laid a rather extraordinary itinerary out for me. It wasn't the result of any conscious effort on my part. It just happened that circumstances put me at the right place at the right time—or the wrong place in some instances, depending on how you look at it.

I had flown combat missions with some of America's great aces, including Gerald Johnson, Tommy McGuire, and the ace of aces, Richard Bong. I had also flown a combat mission on Charles Lindbergh's wing and, in Korea, joked with the real Hawkeye Pierce at the 8055 MASH. But could I tell it the "way it really was," as the young spectator at the air show had requested? The idea intrigued me.

After thinking about it awhile, I decided to give it a try by writing a series of short stories not only about my involvement in those events, but that of my squadron mates and others. I revisited the action of air combat duels with the Japanese Zero; of flying with some of the great combat aces; of my involvement in the fascinating first days of atomic bombs and the giant B-36 bomber built to carry them; and finally, of my adventures and action in the Korean War, where the enemy shot at me but I had no guns to shoot back.

To give the reader as realistic a picture as possible, including a taste of the ambiance and the jargon of the time, I decided to use dialogue. The challenge was for me to create the chatter of a life-and-death dogfight, and the out-of-cockpit interaction between the characters, including myself. And it *was* a challenge, and at the outset I was concerned that I might not have the recall to accomplish my objectives. But when I got into it I was pleasantly surprised. After reading my old diary, notes, and letters, and looking at the paintings and sketches I'd done during that decade, the memories began to tumble back.

I also got some good help from a few World War II and Korean War buddies such as Ralph Wandry, Charlie DuPont, Pierce Myers, Jerry Pouhlin, Bob Ferry, and Baylor Haines. And I gleaned some data from *Protect and Avenge,* by S. W. Ferguson and William K. Pascalis (a history of the 49th Fighter

Group), and from military archives in Washington, D.C.

I counted on my half-century's perspective to add depth to the recollections and perhaps a little philosophical reflection. But I didn't want to stray from my goal of staying in the trenches and telling it the way it was. So I didn't philosophize much about war. I think we all know that war is a nasty, destructive business that disrupts lives and gets a lot of good people killed. Other than a few war lovers, the vast majority of us hated it and counted the days till we could go home. But we all knew why we were there and what we had to do. In retrospect, I can only marvel at how all those young pilots climbed into their warplanes, day after day, took off, and faced the enemy.

But I don't think that young people have changed all that much today. Although our social behavior has gone through some dramatic changes, I don't believe that our human emotions have. Back then we acted and reacted, talked and laughed, loved and hated about as we do today.

I selected stories that I believe will give the reader a glimpse of the action and the personalities involved in the distinctively different types of flying in the two wars, which, incidentally, required a fundamental shift in technique as well as emotion. An aerial duel to the death at speeds and altitudes that never a Spad or Fokker ever flew was a world apart from scooting across the battlefield at treetop level to medevac a wounded GI, or zipping across enemy lines to rescue a downed pilot.

I improvised a little where memory and research failed, but the stories are true as I remember them and the events and places are as historically accurate as I could make them. I used the characters' real names, except in a few sensitive cases, where it seemed best to use fictitious names. I'm pleased with the results. I believe I've told it the way it was.

Richard C. Kirkland
Vienna, Virginia, 10-15-02

CHAPTER ONE

To Shoot Down a Zero

It was a long time ago in a faraway place, yet the vision remains so clear that it seems only yesterday when I glanced through the canopy of my P-38 fighter and saw my first Zero. He was coming in fast, slightly above me and heading in the opposite direction, so I actually only saw him for a few seconds. But even a half century later, I vividly remember the hypnotizing sensation that gripped me and the strange feeling that it was all happening in slow motion.

I'd had enough aircraft-recognition classes to identify it as a Japanese Zero by its sleek aerodynamic lines, rounded engine cowling, bird-cage canopy, and tapered fuselage, all clearly registering as though my brain were taking slow-motion pictures. Then a flash of intense color drew my eyes to the aft fuselage and that huge red ball—the insignia of the rising sun.

It was a brilliant red, painted on the side of the earthy green fuselage and wings, creating a startling color contrast. American pilots called the insignia the meatball, derisively, of course. But I suspect that most pilots saw the rising sun on the Japanese fighter as I did: no joking matter. And I saw that red ball many times during the 103 combat missions I flew in the Southwest Pacific during World War II.

There were several different types of low-winged, single-engine Japanese fighters, generally referred to as Zeros. Probably the best known was the Mitsubishi A6M. To simplify things, I'll refer to all of them as Zeros. Even before I completed Army Air Corps flight training, I'd heard stories and read reports about this famous fighter's performance against our fighters in aerial combat, and they ran the gamut from invincible to a piece of cake. I wasn't sure just what to believe. When I was finally sent overseas and assigned to the 9th Fighter Squadron of the 49th Fighter Group, I found out what to believe—very quickly.

The squadron was encamped on the northeast coast of New Guinea in the steaming jungle, at Dobodura. On my first day in the "Flying Knights" squadron, I was assigned a cot in one corner of a GI pyramidal tent with three "ol' heads," pilots who had been in combat for a while and knew the ropes. Wearing shiny new silver wings and an equally shiny gold bar, I felt somewhat intimidated by first lieutenants who were experienced combat pilots. But they were about my age and seemed like just ordinary guys. That night at dinner, I listened intently to their conversations, hoping to hear some good war stories. But strangely, they didn't talk much about that. They wanted me to talk about what was going on back home in the States.

I wasn't scheduled to fly the next day, but I rode down to the airstrip in a jeep with my new tent mates and watched them roar off the steel-thatched jungle runway in their P-38s, headed for a place called Rabaul—which, I subsequently found out, was one of the hottest targets in the Southwest Pacific.

When they returned later that afternoon, I hurried down the jungle path to our tent to hear about the mission. When I rushed in I saw one of my tent mates sitting on his mosquito-netted cot, smoking a cigarette and cleaning his .45 pistol.

"Hi Ralph!" I greeted eagerly. "How did the mission go?"

He glanced up at me for a moment. "Okay. We got in a fight with a bunch of Zeros," he said in a kind of distracted tone of voice, the cigarette dancing between his lips as he spoke.

"Well . . . uh, how did you make out?"

"I think I got one."

"You shot down a Zero?"

He nodded and turned back to cleaning his gun.

"You really got one, huh?" I probed.

"Yeah. But I won't get confirmation unless the gun-camera film shows it, and that's about a fifty-fifty shot. Those damn things don't work about half the time."

"They don't?"

"No."

"Well, can't one of the other pilots confirm it for you?"

"No."

I hesitated. "Uh . . . why not?"

He glanced up again as he reached into his sweat-soaked khaki shirt pocket and pulled out a fresh cigarette. "You can't confirm what you don't see."

"Oh . . . no one saw it?"

"Only me, and that don't count."

"Gosh, you'd think your wingman or someone else would've seen it, wouldn't you?"

He stuck a fresh cigarette between his lips and lit it with the butt of the old one. "We try to retain our two-ship element in combat, but, as you will learn, Kirk, once you get into a dogfight with a Zero it often ends up being you and him. And he is one tough son of Nippon."

"The Zero is a tough opponent, huh?"

A nod.

"I've heard stories . . . uh . . . how did Frank and Jim make out?" I looked across the tent at the empty cots of my other two tent mates.

"They got shot down."

For a moment I just stood there in the musty GI tent in the musty New Guinean jungle, not sure what I'd heard. "They got shot down?" I finally croaked.

A nod.

"Jesus."

Another nod.

"By Zeros?"

He glanced up at me and frowned. "What the hell else?"

In the jungle outside the tent, one of those long-beaked birds let out a loud screech. Ralph picked up the clip to his freshly cleaned .45 and slammed it into the chamber. He got up from his cot, walked across to the tent door, stuck the gun out, and fired twice.

"That'll shut his ass up for a while," he muttered.

Returning to the cot, he chain-lit another cigarette and started the gun-cleaning process all over again. I stood rooted to the moldy wooden tent floor, with my thoughts racing as I desperately attempted to put some kind of a rational spin on this earthshaking development. If two of my tent mates, who were experienced combat pilots with several victories to their credit, had both been shot down by Zeros on a single mission, then how was I going to . . . "Uh . . . Ralph?"

"Yeah?"

"Could I have one of your cigarettes?"

He looked at me curiously. "You out?"

"I never smoked before," I admitted.

He nodded and tossed me the pack. "Sure. Two things we ain't short of around here is cigarettes and Zeros."

Now you can sort of understand my reaction when I saw my first Zero, live and in full color. Actually, during that first encounter, I saw several rising suns coming from every which way. But I was so busy trying to stay on my element leader's wing that I never even fired my guns. His instructions had been simple: "Stay on my wing. If you don't, a Zero will flame your ass."

During the next couple of weeks I flew several milk runs, as we called a combat mission when no enemy resistance was encountered. But I was still in "Zero shock" and stuck to my element leader's wing like glue. Needless to say I also became an overnight chain-smoker, like everyone else in the squadron. We even had one kid from Texas who could roll his own cigarette from a sack of Bull Durham with one hand while flying formation with the other. If you've never rolled your own Bull Durham or flown tight formation in a fighter, you may not appreciate what a feat that was.

Then came the day when I finally tangled with a

Zero. My squadron was flying a target of opportunity mission: a fighter sweep up to the big Japanese base at Wewak on the northwest coast of New Guinea. I was in the number-four slot of green flight, which made me tail-end Charlie of a sixteen-ship flight. Intelligence had said we'd probably encounter enemy fighters on this mission, so we were all primed and ready for action.

As we got near the target area, our squadron leader gave the signal to clear guns. That meant fire a short burst to make sure they worked, tighten up the formation, and sharpen the watch for enemy aircraft. I had just completed the procedure when radio silence was broken with: "Bogeys! Bogeys at three o'clock high!" And an instant later: "Drop tanks, now!" On the longer missions we always carried external fuel tanks, which we dropped off if we got into a fight.

I saw my element leader's external tanks drop off, spewing fuel as they tumbled away. I quickly flipped the arming switches on mine and punched the salvo button. About a half second later, a stream of tracers arched across our flight path from a V of three Zeros that came screaming down through our formation. I followed my element leader into a steep left bank, just as both my engines quit. I knew instantly what had happened: in my excitement, I'd forgotten to switch the fuel selector from drop position to internal tanks.

Although both Allison engines roared back to life quickly after I'd switched the fuel valve, one did it a little sooner than the other, which caused an unequal surge of power—and now, among other things, I found myself flying upside down. When I got the fighter right side up again, I glanced around and saw airplanes—both Zeros and P-38s—going every which way, all around me. I was looking wildly about, trying to find my element leader, when I suddenly realized there was a Zero directly in front and slightly below me. There he was, with those huge red balls plainly visible on the top surface of his wings.

I was agonizingly aware that my clumsy mistake had caused me to break formation. But there was nothing I could do about that now, and there was the enemy, a Zero. Shoot him down!

I rammed the throttles to full power and dove after him. He went into a right diving bank, but I stayed with him and closed the distance rapidly. Within seconds his silhouette filled my gunsight, and I jammed down hard on both the 20-mm cannon and the .50-caliber machine-gun firing buttons. The guns roared and my nostrils stung from the acrid smoke that always sifted into the P-38 cockpit, since the gun compartment was just forward in the pilot's gondola.

I saw my tracers falling behind the Zero, so I pulled back on the yoke to gain some lead. But about that time I guess he saw me, because suddenly he reversed his direction into an incredibly tight left bank. I couldn't believe any aircraft could turn that quickly. Instinctively I slammed into a left bank and reefed back on the yoke with all my might to try to stay with him, but all I succeeded in doing was pulling a solid black curtain down over my eyes.

I shouted and shook my head violently, trying to fight off the blackout, as we had been taught to do in training. Then, through the blackness, I remembered my element leader's caution: "Don't try to turn with a Zero, whatever you do." I slammed the yoke forward, which, in turn, slammed my head against the top of the canopy. Now I saw stars in my blackout.

The Lockheed P-38 was one the of great fighters of World War II: it was fast and had deadly firepower. But the cockpit was small and would not accommodate a pilot much taller than five feet nine, and I was six feet tall. But this wasn't the usual Army snafu. I had wanted to fly the P-38 so badly that during my cadet physical exam, I had managed to shrink down when they measured my height. I paid for that little deception—in spades.

Anyway, with the G forces relieved, my sight began to return. As soon as I could see I glanced around, but the Zero was gone and so were all the other airplanes that had been there a few seconds earlier. Despite all the chatter on my radio, I seemed to be all alone in the skies over Wewak, New Guinea. Or at least I thought I was, until I realized that those red things flying past my canopy were 20-mm cannonballs made in Japan.

I looked back and sure enough, there he was: the black engine cowling shining in the sun, and those big black wing guns blinking fire. "If you get one on your tail, dive away quickly: you can outdive a Zero." My element leader's words rang in my head at about the same time as I saw pieces of my airplane spewing off into space.

I'm not sure how, but I managed to put my rapidly deteriorating aircraft into a power dive at full throttle. And I discovered that it was true, fortunately: the P-38 could outdive the Zero. But there was a complication, which I remembered when I saw the needle on my airspeed indicator spin past the number six, and the aircraft began to shake. "The pilot should monitor airspeed closely in a power dive to prevent compressibility." The folks at Lockheed had written that in the flight manual.

I jerked the throttles off and tried to pull back on the yoke. I might as well have been pulling on the Empire State Building: it wouldn't budge. Then I remembered another little scrap of timely information: "In compressibility, use the trim tab." The P-38 hadn't been designed to break the sound barrier, so when it approached that speed, it went berserk. We called it compressibility.

I guess that pulled me out of the dive, because the next thing I knew I was wandering around the skies over Wewak trying to find somebody to fly with. Then, loud and clear over the radio, came, "Kirkland! Where the hell are you?"

It was great to hear from someone, even if it wasn't a very friendly voice. "I'm here, sir," I replied.

"Where's here?"

"Uh . . . well, I—"

"Is that you trailing smoke from your left engine?"

I glanced out at my left engine. Yes, it was trailing smoke, all right, a lot of smoke.

"Yes sir, that's me."

"Well, you better shut it down and get your ass back in formation."

A lot of World War II pilots thought the twin-engine fighter was no match in combat for a single-engine fighter, because of less maneuverability. And to some degree, that was true. But then no American fighter could outturn the Zero anyway, so the P-38 lost nothing, and it was superior in other ways. For example: that day I shut down my smoking engine, feathered the prop [stopped it from turning], and got back in formation. I'd like to see a single-engine fighter do that.

My baptism under fire had been somewhat of a disaster. I'd made several bad mistakes and nearly got myself killed. The airplane was shot full of holes and one engine was ruined. I caught hell for breaking formation, and I would have caught even worse hell if I'd told my element leader all that I'd done wrong.

But there was a plus side too, in that at least I'd fired my guns. And even though I'd probably still been in my Zero-shock phase, I had tangled with one. And now, strangely, I found myself wanting to meet him again and get it settled, one way or the other. I got my wish about a week later.

This time my squadron was escorting B-24s on a bombing mission to Hollandia, which was another big Japanese base on the coast of New Guinea, north of Wewak. We picked up a group of Liberators from the Ninetieth Bomb Group at the rendezvous point, about an hour out of the target. I'll always remember it because it was my first mission escorting B-24s, and, although it was kind of an ugly duckling on the ground, the Lib had long, thin wings that gave it a graceful look in the air. And I was fascinated with the tail markings of this group: big, white skulls and crossbones on the two vertical stabilizers. They called themselves the Jolly Rogers.

The four flights of my squadron flew at different levels above the bombers, while doing lazy S turns to watch over them and at the same time keep our speed up in case of attack. When we reached the target and the flak came up in thick black clouds, we swung out wide to avoid it, as much as possible, while still keeping a sharp watch for enemy fighters. The rationale was that there was no point in our flying through the flak unless the bombers were attacked. In this instance no Zeros came up, so we watched the bombers do what they had to do, which was to bravely fly right through that stuff to drop their bombs on the target. And they did that, and they plastered it good.

When I heard one of the leaders of the bombers say, "Good job, Jolly Rogers, let's head 'em for the barn," I sort of relaxed, stretched my legs as best I could in that tiny cockpit, and got ready for the long flight home. I wanted a cigarette bad—by this time I was hooked—but my flight was top cover, and we were still at altitude and on oxygen. When I saw my element leader pull his oxygen mask off and light one up anyway, I decided to do the same.

I didn't get it lit before someone shouted, "Bogeys! Bogeys! They're after the bombers!"

It caught everybody off guard, as the Zeros usually attacked before a raid, not afterward.

"Captive flight! Captive flight! Don't drop your tanks over the Jollys!" screamed the voice of Capt. Gerald Johnson, our squadron leader. (Captive was the 9th Squadron's call sign.)

"Three o'clock high! Three o'clock high!"

"Look out! There's another bunch at nine o'clock!"

"Red Three! Red Three, you got one on your tail!"

"Tighten up Jolly Rogers! Tighten up!"

"Jesus Christ, they're all over the place!"

As it happened, my flight was off to one side of the bombers, so we could jettison our tanks quickly. This time I remembered to switch the fuel-selector valve before I punched the salvo switch. And I was right on my element leader's wing when he rolled into a steep bank and started after a pair of attacking Zeros. They fired at one of the bombers, then broke off in a diving turn, with us after them.

"Captive Green Four, take the one on the right," instructed my leader as we closed the distance on the two Zeros, who were flying in loose formation about 50 yards apart.

"Roger wilco," I replied, watching the Zero assigned to me mushroom in my gunsight. With my finger on the gun switch, I suddenly felt confident. I had him this time: he would not elude me with that quick-turn stuff or anything else. He was in my sights and I would hold my fire until there was no escape, then shoot him down!

He flipped the Zero on its back and split-S'd (rolled over and dove away) so quickly I never even got off a shot. He was simply there one instant and gone the next. It infuriated me! I slammed the Lightning over and split-S'd right behind him, even though I knew that was a no-no. He was going straight down a couple hundred yards ahead of me, but I closed the distance quickly. Then, just as I was about to squeeze the firing switch, he pulled out of his dive and I hurtled past him so quickly he was just a blur.

Like most aerial dogfights, this one had only lasted a few minutes. It was over by the time I pulled out of my dive and got back up with the rest of the squadron covering the bombers.

As we headed for home, there was quite a bit of radio chatter going on about who'd shot down what, and who'd seen what. Apparently none of our bombers or fighters had been lost. And the bomber gunners claimed one Zero, and our fighters claimed two, one of them nailed by my element leader. "I got mine. Did you get yours, Green Four?" he asked when I joined back up in formation.

"No. I didn't get him," I answered disgustedly.

"But you scared the shit out of 'im, huh Kirk?" someone else piped in.

I couldn't help but grin, there in my P-38 cockpit. "Nope, I didn't even scare him," I admitted.

That got a laugh over the radio from several in Captive flight.

That night my tent mate, Ralph Wandry, broke open a bottle of Stateside scotch he'd been saving. He'd scored the other victory that day, his fifth confirmed kill, and that made him an ace. I wasn't much of a drinker, but I drank that night.

My problem was that I had become frustrated. I realized that a few beginning mistakes were normal. But I also knew, now, that the Zero was a formidable opponent in the business of aerial combat, and that my quota for mistakes was probably running thin. After a couple canteen cups of scotch and rainwater, I came right out and asked Ralph what he thought I was doing wrong.

"Aw, you're doin' all right, Kirk," he drawled. He'd had several cups of scotch and rainwater too. "You just gotta remember that Zero is a great li'l fighter, and those li'l bastard Nip pilots will whip your ass every time if you play the game their way—" He took another drink of scotch.

"And you two new guys better listen to this too," he added, glancing across the tent at the replacement pilots, who were watching and listening, eyes wide. "You got the speed on 'em, you got the firepower. But you can't dogfight with them. You run up their ass and shoot them down. And if you miss, you get the hell out and come back another day. If you remember that, you'll do okay. If you don't, you're gonna end up bein' a li'l American flag on the side of a Zero cockpit. Got it?"

All three of us nodded. (Actually, the Japanese pilots didn't indicate their victories in any way on their aircraft.) About that time a couple of the other pilots showed up, and, after they'd had a couple scotch and rainwaters—and there was plenty of rainwater there in the jungle—we all sang one of the squadron songs . . . well, it was more like howling:

Oh, I wanted wings till I got those goddamn things
And now I don't want 'em anymore
Oh, they taught me how to fly and they sent me
    here to die
I've had a belly full of war

You can save those Zeros for your goddamn
    heroes
Distinguished Flying Crosses do not compensate
    for losses
Oh, I wanted wings till I got those goddamn things
And now I don't want 'em anymore.

It was a kind of feeling-sorry-for-yourself song and good for harmonizing, but no one really meant it. The next morning, those same pilots roared off to meet the Zeros without a second thought.

I had resolved that I would heed Ralph's advice, and on my next mission where we tangled with Zeros, I finally fired my guns and hit something—but not the way Ralph had instructed. It happened while we were escorting B-25 "Billy Mitchells" on a low-level strafing mission.

Although the B-25 is probably best remembered as the bomber that Jimmy Doolittle used to bomb Tokyo in the early days of World War II, it was also a deadly strafer. I've seen them with twelve .50-caliber machine guns and a 75-mm cannon, all firing forward. And when they went across an enemy installation in a V of three at treetop level, there was nothing left standing, only a swath of utter devastation.

On that day, a group of about twenty Zeros jumped the B-25s. My flight leader and I went after two Zeros, and when they saw us coming they split up and went in different directions. We closed in on the nearest one, who held an almost straight course. I don't know why the Zero pilot didn't split-S, like they always did when I was chasing them. But he didn't, and, after the first volley from my flight leader's guns, the Zero exploded into several pieces that flew in all directions, leaving trails of fire and smoke in crazy zigzag patterns, while half the fuselage and one wing spun wildly down into the jungle below. It was an awesome, gripping sight.

"That's a confirmed," he said over the radio.

"I'd say so," I replied.

But while watching the Zero's death plunge, we weren't watching our backside. And the next thing we knew, we were in a hail of fireballs from two Zeros that dove on us like banshees. There was nothing to do but dive away, which we both did. But since we were at low level, it was a short dive with an immediate, hard pull out that blacked me out cold.

When I could see again, I was a bare 20 feet above

the jungle. I rammed the throttles to the fire wall and went into a 250-mph high-speed climb, which I knew the Zero couldn't match. Fortunately there were thunderclouds all over the place, as usual, and I stayed close to one so I could duck into it if another Zero dove on me from above. I called my flight leader but there was no answer, so I just hugged the clouds and kept climbing.

Then I saw another aircraft. He was ahead of me and barely visible in the distance. I could tell from the silhouette that it wasn't a P-38, which meant it was probably a Zero. You couldn't miss the distinctive silhouette of the P-38: that had both pluses and minuses in combat. Everybody knew who you were, both friend and foe.

I knew the dogfight was still going on because of the chatter on the radio, but I couldn't see any other aircraft. I told myself that I should find my element leader and get back in formation. As I glanced at the Zero again, it was evident he'd not seen me. I decided to go after him.

I went to full power and pointed the Lightning toward him. I was a good 500 meters (a bit over 500 yards) from being in position to fire when he did see me, and he quickly headed for the closest cloud bank. Now it was going to be a horse race to see if he could get to the cloud before I could fire. I had great position on him, which he obviously recognized, so flying into the cloud was his best option.

I rammed on full "war emergency" power, so now it was just a matter of trusting that my engines wouldn't blow before I could get into range. I was closing fast and, as his silhouette began to fill my gunsight, my finger tightened on the gun switch. Just a little more, Mr. Zero, and you're mine, I said to myself. And then I could see that he was going to make it. He was only seconds from the cloud, and I was still out of firing range. He was going to win the race, all right, and we both knew it.

And then he did the strangest thing. As though to kiss me off, he went into a series of aerobatics, alternately snap-rolling one way and slow-rolling the other.

There was one outside chance. I pulled the nose up high for a second, then jammed down on both firing buttons and held them. I could see my tracers arch across the distance just as he entered the cloud. The instant he disappeared into the mist, my tracers went in after him. It was a case of miraculous timing and trajectory. The Zero had disappeared, but I saw the explosion. The inside of the cloud glowed bright red orange for an instant, then dissolved into a gray mist.

I let out a shriek, there in the cockpit: "I got 'im! I got 'im!" I'd finally shot down a Zero! I was elated. I knew now that I could win the contest. My Zero shock was over. Yet deep down, I had the strangest feeling . . . it had been so close. He'd been so close to winning the race and escaping. I almost felt sorry for him . . . almost.

As it turned out, the Flying Knights squadron chalked up several confirmed victories on that mission, and mine was not one of them. My gun camera worked like a charm that day. But all it showed was me shooting a long burst of fire into a big, beautiful cloud. Because I'd had the nose up so high to get the right trajectory, you couldn't see the Zero or the explosion, just the clouds.

"Hey Kirk, you sure shot hell out of that big

cloud," said one of the pilots with a laugh when we looked at the film. And there was more on the downside of that mission: my flight leader crashed and killed himself doing his victory roll after the mission.

The combination of things was pretty distressing to me, and I guess our commanding officer [CO], Captain Johnson, spotted it, because the next day he told me he wanted me to fly on his wing for a while. Capt. Gerald Johnson was an excellent commander as well as one of the great fighter aces of World War II. His final score was twenty-two confirmed aerial victories. He ran a tight ship and took a personal interest in his pilots. But he was a bit of a hard-ass and was not taken to mincing words. "Stay on my wing and watch me," he instructed, as we prepared to take off on an eight-ship fighter sweep up the north coast of New Guinea.

We'd been flying along the coastline at about 20,000 feet for a little over an hour when Johnson spotted a pair of Zeros that no one else saw. He signaled for me to follow, and, since we weren't carrying drop tanks that day, down we went.

The Zeros were at least 5,000 feet below us, and I never even saw them until we were practically on the tail of one, who was trailing the other about 50 yards. I'm sure neither Zero pilot saw us, either. Johnson didn't open fire until he was practically chewing up the Zero's tail. And when he did fire, one wing flew off instantly, and seconds later the Japanese fighter disintegrated in a fiery explosion.

I found out after the war that the early Zeros did not have self-sealing fuel tanks or pilot protective armor, as we did. But then any fighter would disinte-

grate, ours included, when struck with such a fusillade of firepower.

"That is how it's done, Kirkland. And I expect to
see you do it the same way from here on out," he advised over the radio, then turned his head and
grinned at me across the short distance between our
fighters.

"Yes sir," I replied, grinning back.

But I didn't have the opportunity for a while, because Fifth Fighter Command of the Fifth Air Force
decided to switch our squadron to the new Republic
P-47 single-engine fighter. We were distressed over
the switch, because we were all twin-engine fighter
pilots and wanted to stay that way. There was a saying among fighter pilots in New Guinea: "Once you
pull up your landing gear, you're a dead man until
you put it down again." If you went down in the jungle, the crocs, headhunters, or mosquitoes got you. If
it was the Bismarck Sea, the sharks did the job. So we
worked on the theory that "two fans are better than
one."

But headquarters didn't see it that way, and we all
checked out in the Jug, as the P-47 was affectionately
called. We also called it "the big-ass bird," not in a
derogatory sense, because it was indeed big, and it
was tough. And it mounted eight .50-caliber machine
guns. But it only had one fan, and we didn't like that.

Fifth Fighter Command sent Col. Neel Kearby
over to convince us that the Jug was as good as the
P-38. We listened, but we did not believe. So Kearby
went out with his own P-47 and shot down six Zeros
on one mission to prove his point. What could we say
then?

But for the next couple of months, fighter command assigned us milk-run patrols over the Markham Valley, where they had moved our squadron. We were anxiously waiting to see how the big bird would make out in our first tangle with Zeros. But we saw few enemy aircraft during that period.

We did get into a few dogfights while flying the P-47, and it performed well. And I did score a probable victory in one of those engagements. My gun-camera film showed big chunks flying off the Zero from those eight .50-caliber machine guns. But his wingman bounced me before I could finish him, so I had to break off, and it was called a probable.

I liked the big bird because it was rugged, with a roomy cockpit and a highly dependable engine. But it wasn't as fast as the Lightning, and, although more maneuverable, it was still no match for the Zero. Unfortunately, Colonel Kearby found that out the hard way. Although he had twenty-two confirmed aerial victories, a Zero turned inside him one day and shot him down.

About that time I was promoted to first lieutenant and made a flight leader. I flew one mission, came down with malaria, and spent the next several weeks in the hospital at Port Moresby and then a rehabilitation center in Sydney, Australia, (where I fell madly in love with a beautiful Australian girl, but that's another story).

Shortly after I returned from Australia, the squadron was equipped with all new late-model P-38s. We were one bunch of happy campers over that turn of events. To celebrate, Maj. Wally Jordan, our new CO (Gerry Johnson had been promoted and transferred to group headquarters), broke out a couple cases of Aussie beer. But not only was it not cold beer, it was hot. So we put it in one of our new P-38 drop tanks, and I took it up to 30,000 feet for a few minutes, then dove back down. Now we had ice-cold beer. Another of the great features of the Lockheed Lightning: it could go to high altitude and get there in a hurry.

On one of my first missions in a new Lightning, I had the opportunity to fly with Maj. Richard Bong, who was the Flying Knights' leading American ace at that time, and who at the end of the war was the leading American ace of all time, with forty confirmed victories—and a lot more that weren't confirmed, for one reason or another.

Dick had been on leave for a while, and I was anxious to see him in action. He claimed that he was a terrible shot, and, since I was having trouble with my shooting too, I figured I'd watch him and maybe discover his secret. I knew pretty well, though, from what other pilots had told me, that his secret was getting close.

I'm not sure where we went that day, but it was a flight of eight P-38s on a fighter sweep, and I was leading his second element. We had been airborne about an hour when he suddenly spotted a bogey that no one else saw. I discovered later that that was one of his secrets: he had the eyes of a hawk. He could see an enemy aircraft before anyone else.

When I finally saw what looked like a Zero off in the distance, we were still out of range and on a parallel course. I couldn't believe what Bong did. The Japanese aircraft was a good 500 meters away when he opened fire on a 90-degree deflection shot. One second the Zero was an airplane, and the next it was a plummeting ball of fire. It was an incredibly long deflection shot, and here I had expected to see him close to point-blank range before firing.

After we'd returned to base and landed, I complimented the major on his remarkable shot. Dick wasn't a big talker, but he grinned and said, "Yeah, that was a good shot, all right. But I'll tell you, Kirk, that was also the luckiest shot I ever made."

"You sure made it look easy," I said, hoping he would elaborate, because I knew his normal procedure was to close to point-blank range.

"Aw, I just wanted to try that deflection shot and got lucky. Actually, nothing has changed. The best way to win over the Zero is use your superior speed and firepower, and get close."

Well, I hadn't learned anything I hadn't already known, but it was special coming from America's "ace of aces."

It was not long after that when I had my most memorable and remarkable experience in combat with the Japanese Zero. We were on a sixteen-ship fighter sweep to Manokwari, on the northwest coast of New Guinea. I was leading Red flight, and it was one of those long missions where we'd been in that tiny cockpit for more than two hours before even reaching the target area.

As we approached we went through our usual procedure: clear guns, set the drop-tank switches, turn on the gunsight, and cinch up the seat belt and crash straps. I had barely completed that when the squadron leader, Major Jordan, squalled, "Bogeys! Bogeys at twelve o'clock. Drop tanks!"

There were about a dozen of them: Japanese Navy pilots, and this group was very aggressive. They dove at us in a head-on pass, which was very unusual.

Most Japanese pilots would not take on a P-38 that way, because four .50-caliber machine guns and a 20-mm cannon firing straight forward from the nose of a Lightning was murder. However, in this case we all met head-on, with every gun that would bear blazing away on both sides. A few seconds later it was one big aerial melee, with Zeros and P-38s going in all directions.

A Zero appeared in my sights and I blazed away, but, as usual, he whipped into a tight turn. Despite an urge to follow, I let him go and went into a high-speed climb. "Nine o'clock! There's one at nine o'clock, Red leader!" shouted my wingman.

I glanced over and saw him coming. He was already firing, but I could tell from the angle that he didn't have enough lead. I turned in to him, and he broke off. I swung back into my climb, and when I glanced over my right shoulder, my wingman was gone. "Red Two! Red Two, get back in formation!" I screamed over the radio.

No answer. I glanced around. He was nowhere in sight. A second or two later: "Get 'em off! Get 'em off my tail!" I recognized my wingman's voice. I rolled up on one wing and glanced down. Sure enough, there he was in a shallow dive, with two Zeros on his tail. He'd gone down after one, and two others had jumped him.

I whipped over into a diving turn and went after them. They were pouring a stream of fire into the P-38, and I knew they would get him before I got there. My only option was the one I'd used that day when the Zero had dived into the clouds: I raised the nose and fired a long burst. It was another of those miraculous shots: the tracers fell between my fleeing wingman and the pursuing Zeros, and they broke off immediately.

There was an ongoing controversy, among fighter pilots in World War II, about using tracers in aerial combat. Some of the top-scoring aces didn't use them, because they didn't want their prey to know they were shooting until it was too late. And that was a valid point, particularly when fighting the Zero, because if he saw tracers, he would snap into a steep turn or a split S and get away. But for most of us, who weren't very good shots, we needed to see where we were shooting. In any event I was glad I had tracers that day, and so was my wingman. Otherwise it would have been a good day for the crocs or the sharks.

"Now get your ass back in formation, Red two," I growled over the radio.

The words weren't out of my mouth when a stream of fireballs arched over my canopy, and I snapped into a split S almost as fast as a Zero could have. I never saw the one that had fired at me, but when I pulled out, there was another one directly ahead of me. All I had to do was squeeze the firing button.

I saw the flashes of my cannon exploding along his wing and tail, but I realized that because of my speed coming out of the dive, I was going to overrun him. I jerked back on the throttles and continued to fire. But now I was right on top of him and on a collision course. I swung over to the left and sort of slid right up beside him, just as his airplane burst into flames.

And there I was, wingtip to wingtip with the flaming Zero. I looked across and I could see the pilot plainly, sitting there in the cockpit, the sun flashing off his helmet goggles and the entire aircraft, from his engine cowling aft, a mass of flames.

Then he turned and glanced across at me, and for a bizarre, transfixing moment before the Zero exploded in a shower of flaming pieces, we looked at each other. It was an incredible experience that remains as vivid in my mind as it was the day it happened, more than a half century ago.

My gun camera didn't work that day either, but, unbeknownst to me, my squadron commander, Maj. Wally Jordan, saw it happen. So it was confirmed.

I was pleased to finally get a confirmed victory, of course, despite some deep, secret feelings that I have never discussed with anyone. And my folks and everybody back home were proud, of course, because it was in our hometown newspaper that 1st Lt. Richard Kirkland "Shot Down a Zero."

CHAPTER TWO

On the Wing of the Lone Eagle

The name of the place was Biak. It was one of those battered little islands in the Dutch East Indies that was pounded mercilessly by big Navy guns, even before the Army and the Marines landed. Then, of course, they pounded it some more.

My fighter squadron landed our P-38s there in the late spring of 1944, as an advance unit in Gen. Douglas MacArthur's historic return to the Philippines. Being an advance unit meant that we got the privilege of flying in and setting up fighter operations as soon as the landing troops had beaten back the Japanese and secured the airfield. It also meant that the place was still a smoldering mess, with the stench of death hanging in the air.

When I climbed out of the cockpit of my fighter that day, Army bulldozers were growling and snorting all around me, hurrying to build protective revetments for our aircraft. They didn't seem to pay any attention to the gunfire you could hear all around. Someone said the dozers made so much noise that the operators couldn't hear the shooting, so it didn't bother them. Maybe so.

We were used to this sort of thing, though, having moved several times into the mutilated remains of a Japanese installation during our trek through New Guinea to the East Indies. The only problem I had was losing my personal gear. You couldn't carry much in a P-38, and sometimes your gear went astray, when the transport ship got sunk or landed at the wrong island or something. But we were looking forward to our move to Biak Island, because it would get us out of the jungle for a while.

Our ground-support unit set up those moldy old pyramidal tents right along the coral reef, at the edge of the water. It was a welcome change to hear the waves on the coral at night, and it drowned out some of the gunfire.

Whereas my small problem was losing personal gear, Fifth Air Force Fighter Command had a bigger problem: the increasing range between the targets on MacArthur's agenda. You could look at the map and see the increased range between the various Japanese-held islands that would now be our targets. Our range problem would be even worse than it had been, and we were already at the limit of the P-38's range, often returning from fighter sweeps and bomber-escort missions with nothing but fumes in our gas tanks.

For about two weeks after our landing we flew patrol around the Biak area, waiting to see what the big brass at command was going to do. I guess the Japanese pilots were having the same problem, since none came to challenge us. Finally our squadron commander, Maj. Wally Jordan, called all the flight leaders to a meeting. After we had all crowded into his tent, Jordan announced: "Fighter command is planning on sending us on missions 1,000 miles out." Everyone laughed, and even the major grinned.

"Sure Major, and that little Aussie gal I fell in love with in Sydney is coming up on the next Bully Beefer to spend the weekend with me," joked one of the other flight leaders. Bully Beefer was the name given to C-47 transport aircraft that brought in personnel and supplies.

Everyone laughed again, including Jordan. But then he turned serious. "I'm not kidding fellows; I wish I were."

It was quiet for a moment, in the tent on Biak Island.

"Major, how are we going to fly out 1,000 miles?" asked our operations [OPS] officer. "Even with our largest drop tank, we don't have that kind of range."

Jordan nodded. "I know, Bill, but command has a solution."

We all looked at Jordan suspiciously. He shifted on the GI cot where he sat, pulled a cigarette out of a pack in his shirt pocket, and lit it with a beat-up Zippo lighter. After he'd taken a deep drag, he looked up and said, "Well, you're not going to believe this, but they have figured out that we can extend our range by reducing RPM."

"So what else is new. We already know that," scoffed the OPS officer.

Jordan took another puff of his cigarette. "Yeah. But they say we can pull our props back to 1,600 RPM."

If the major had dropped a bomb in the tent, it wouldn't have been more explosive. "Sixteen hundred RPM!" screeched someone.

"Wally, is this a joke?" asked a flight leader.

Jordan shook his head.

"I can tell you right now: if you pull the RPM back that low on those Allison engines, they'll blow sky-high," pronounced our engineering officer.

That was seconded by several voices, as more cigarettes were pulled out and fired up. I didn't know quite what to think. I had always been told never to reduce RPM on the P-38 below 2,000, because otherwise the fuel mixture would detonate prematurely and blow the cylinders. But since I was the youngest flight leader in the squadron, I thought it best to listen to what the old heads had to say.

"Whose crackpot idea did you say this was?" asked someone.

Jordan sort of rolled his eyes. "You're not going to believe this. The crackpot idea came from Charles Lindbergh."

It was deathly quiet for a moment. "Charles Lindbergh? Charles A. Lindbergh? The one who flew across the Atlantic?" our OPS officer asked, incredulous.

"Yeah. That Lindbergh," Jordan confirmed.

"Jesus. I didn't know he was still alive," someone said.

I was dumbfounded. I couldn't believe what I was hearing.

"I knew he was still alive, but I thought they were going to put him in jail for being a Nazi," said someone else.

"Yeah. That's what I thought too," agreed another.

I remembered hearing the same thing when I'd been in college. Something about his being an isolationist and not wanting to get into the war. He'd been accused of Nazi sympathies when he'd accepted a medal from Hermann Göring for his flight from New York to Paris. But I had refused to believe it. I couldn't imagine that Charles Lindbergh, the "Lone Eagle," the greatest hero of my time, could possibly have done anything wrong.

"Well, even if he's still alive, he'd be an old man, so what's he got to do with it?" one of the flight leaders asked.

"Apparently he's got a lot to do with it, because he's here," replied Jordan.

"You mean here in the islands?"

"Jesus. What's he going to do here?"

"He's going to show us how to do it."

Staring, disbelieving faces. "How is he going to do that?"

"He's going to fly with us."

"In a P-38?"

"This whole thing is crazy, Major. How can an old man like him fly with us in a P-38?"

Jordan shrugged. "I don't know. But that's the plan."

Like all squadrons, we had a scrounger. You had to have one to get stuff. Ours, a fast-talking Italian kid from New York, made a deal with the night-watch guy on a Liberty ship anchored in the harbor. For a bottle of Aussie schnapps, he threw a load of wood overboard after the captain had gone to bed. A bunch of us swam out, towed the wood to shore, and used it to build a small mess hall on the coral. It gave our island camp a little class. That's where I met Charles A. Lindbergh.

We were all sitting there on the wooden benches in our classy new mess hall, smoking and talking, when he came in with a colonel from group. I was shocked.

He was tall, all right, but instead of the curly-haired, bright-eyed young man I remembered from pictures, the man I shook hands with was old. He had crow's-feet at the corners of his eyes, and his hair was turning gray. And he wasn't thin anymore. I was terribly disappointed. I don't know what I expected. Of course, to a twenty-year-old, a forty-two-year-old is ancient.

But you couldn't help being impressed, because there he was: the man who'd flown the *Spirit of St. Louis* across the Atlantic Ocean. Probably the greatest aviation hero of all time. He didn't say much, just that he was looking forward to flying with us to demonstrate the new fuel-saving technique that he and Allison Engines had developed. Speaking in a low but confident voice, he assured us that the reduced-RPM procedure would not cause our engines to blow sky-high. But the pilots were skeptical. So was I.

A few days later, some of our pilots were scheduled to fly a mission with Lindbergh. It was a fighter sweep to Piroe Bay, which was a long enough flight to test the low-RPM procedure, but with a low probability of tangling with enemy fighters . . . or so intelligence said. We were told that Lindbergh had some kind of special permission, however, and could fly a P-38 with us on a combat mission even though he was a civilian.

I didn't know at first whether to be insulted or honored when I was scheduled to fly Lindbergh's wing. After all, I was a flight leader, not a wingman anymore. But when Major Jordan explained, I felt better: "Keep an eye on him, Kirk, just in case the Zeros that aren't supposed to be there show up. We don't want him to get shot down on our watch." I was convinced, then, that it was a pretty big deal for me to make sure that Charles A. Lindbergh didn't get shot down.

Maj. Tommy McGuire, CO of the 431st Squadron, led the mission, with Lindbergh leading an element and me on his wing. My first surprise, after we roared off Biak Island that day, was that I had no trouble staying on his wing. There is a skill to leading as well as flying wing, and he had it. Lindbergh was right on target for the join-up. He arched across McGuire's first circle and brought us sliding up into a perfect element formation without a bobble. I caught a glimpse of McGuire's face when he glanced back at us: he looked surprised.

I'm sure everyone in the flight was surprised, too: I knew they were all watching. I couldn't help wondering what was going on in their thoughts as they watched the "old man" handle the P-38 like he'd been born in it.

After we'd climbed up to our altitude and leveled off in loose formation, McGuire came on the horn and said: "This is Blue flight lead. Let's pull 'em back . . . now."

We had been briefed before takeoff on the procedure. But I'm sure everyone cringed, as I did, when I reached up and pulled the prop levers back until the tachometers showed the dreaded 1,600 RPM. The formation sort of wallowed around a bit as our airspeed dropped. And as the sound level also dropped, it seemed strangely quiet in that tiny cockpit.

Normally we'd have radio silence on a fighter sweep, but in this case we were allowed to communicate because of the fuel-test thing. But there wasn't much radio chatter. We all just sat there waiting for the first engine to blow.

Since we had two engines, we weren't overly concerned about one blowing. If it did, we could still get home on the other one. Actually the P-38 could outrun a Zero on one engine—as long as you didn't let him get right on your tail. As I already knew, if he did you were in big trouble, no matter how many engines were running.

Our course took us west over New Guinea and out into the Ceram Sea. It was dead-reckoning navigation, with no radio aids of any kind. That's the way we did it in that war. Just take up a mag heading (magnetic reading) on the compass and hope for the best. I never cease to wonder, today, with all the navigation aids and computers, how we managed to do that back in those days. None of our engines blew up; not one. It was almost a disappointment, because we were all so sure that they would. Our airspeed was a little less than normal, but pressures and temperatures all stayed in good range and we just purred along there, as slick as a whistle. We followed our standard procedure on the outbound leg, which was to burn fuel out of our drop tanks, in case we got in a fight and they had to be jettisoned. Because the drop tanks had no gauges, there was no way of telling how much fuel we were saving. We wouldn't know that until they ran dry.

When we finally switched to our main internal tanks, we had flown noticeably longer than usual. And by the time we got to the target area some two and a half hours later, we had quite a bit more fuel than we normally would have had, and not a single engine had blown.

As the target neared we armed and tested our guns, set the drop-tank switches, and tightened up the formation. I did my usual thing, shifting around to relax my cramped muscles—as much as the tiny cockpit would allow. Then I cinched the crash straps tight. After having bashed my head on the canopy numerous times before, I finally remembered to do that.

Glancing across at Lindbergh's P-38, I wondered how he was doing. All indications were that he was doing just fine. When Major McGuire gave the command to go to combat RPM, our speed picked up and the cockpit noise increased to its familiar level. I recognized how important this new fuel-saving technique was, but I remember feeling that old sense of security when the familiar sound of those big Allison engines returned to my ears.

McGuire led us on a couple of sweeps along the coastline, skirting the edge of some towering cumulus clouds. I was glad someone as good Tommy McGuire was leading, because he was one hell of a fighter pilot, so good that when the war ended, he was the number-two American ace of World War II. But my concern was that if Zeros jumped us out of the clouds, it would be my responsibility to keep Charles A. Lindbergh from getting shot down. As it happened, the flight went smoothly. Intelligence had called it right, and all that came up to challenge us was a little flak.

After a while we turned east and headed back across the Ceram Sea on a mag heading. We disarmed our guns, pulled our props back to 1,600 RPM again, and settled down in the cockpit for the long flight home.

There may have been some who were still waiting for an engine to blow. But I suspect that most of us had realized long before we landed back at Biak Island that the jury was in: nothing was going to happen, and Lindbergh had been right. The system worked, and it would indeed go a long way toward solving our range problem. I also suspect that most of the other pilots were experiencing something similar to my own feelings at about that time. It wasn't just that he'd been right about the procedure; all clouds of uncertainty and doubt about him just seemed to dissolve away.

But to me it was even more than that. It had been a humbling, unique experience. And I still remember vividly what went through my mind as I looked across the cowling of my left engine at the goggled cloth helmet in the P-38 cockpit a few yards off my wing. It was the helmet of Charles A. Lindbergh, the aviator, the legend. And in a transformation of time and space, I could see him sitting in that little Ryan monoplane, droning across the vastness of the Atlantic Ocean on his historic conquest, when I was four years old.

And in a sense, our flight across the vastness of the Southwest Pacific that day was another historic conquest. And what a profound impression it made on me, reaffirming what I had believed all those years: he was one of the great aviators of all time. Even now, a half century later, I still savor the experience of that day when I flew on the wing of the Lone Eagle.

Charles Lindbergh flew fifty combat missions in the South Pacific, demonstrating his fuel-saving technique. On 8 July 1944, he shot down a Mitsubishi Ki-51 fighter. He died in 1974 and, per his wish, was buried in a small graveyard overlooking the sea on Maui, Hawaii. On his gravestone is the simple inscription:

If I take the wings of the morning
And dwell in the uttermost parts of the sea.

CHAPTER THREE

Escape from the Stone Age

Lt. Richard Strommen made his decision: when the squadron leader initiated his final course correction to the target, he would make the radio call. He hated to do it, because he knew the major would be pissed. It always pissed the major off when someone aborted the mission, particularly when radio silence was broken this close to the target. But Strommen had no choice, and he'd been telling himself that for the last hour of flying: ever since the armament-firing solenoids had popped and would not reset.

He glanced out through the canopy at the formation of P-40 fighters ahead. It was an inspiring sight to see the morning sun glistening off the canopies of the graceful aircraft, as they gently bobbed and weaved through the cloud-studded sky. Richard was pleased to be a member of the 8th Fighter Squadron of the 49th Group, and he loved flying the "Warhawk," with its deadly firepower of six machine guns. Strangely, though, that was his problem on this beautiful day in the skies over New Guinea: his guns were inoperative.

When he saw the major bank his lead P-40 onto the target heading, Strommen reached across the tiny cockpit and made one last attempt to reset the solenoids. They immediately popped back out, indicating a serious malfunction in the armament system. The time had come. He put his thumb and forefinger to his throat mike and punched his transmit button. "Blue lead, this is Yellow Four; aborting for a mechanical."

Silence. Finally: "You need an escort?"

"No, sir."

"Go."

Oh, the squadron leader was irritated, all right. Strommen could tell by the sound of his voice. And there would be some explaining to do later. But it couldn't be helped, that was all.

Hearing the radio transmission, Yellow flight leader had turned his head and glanced at his wingman, across the short distance separating their aircraft. Strommen could see his face clearly framed in the goggled flight helmet. He gave him a little salute, then rolled his P-40 into a right bank and arched away from the formation.

As he brought the fighter around to reverse his course, Strommen saw a large thunderstorm directly in his path. After several turns and banks he skirted the billowing cloud, and when his bobbing mag compass finally settled down again, he put his fighter on the course back to base. It was a course that would take him over the jungle for a while, then out over the Bismarck Sea and down the coast to his home base on the northeast coast of New Guinea.

It would require a little more than an hour and thirty minutes, by his calculation. Although most of the flight would be over enemy territory, there was little danger of encountering Zeros in that sector. And even if he did, he could outrun them. That was why he had declined the major's offer of an escort. Strommen's only problem was that his guns were inoperative, and if he couldn't fight back his only option was to run. When he explained that later, the major would understand why he had aborted.

Strommen stretched his legs and relaxed as best he could. He wanted a cigarette badly, but that would require dropping down to lower altitudes to take off his oxygen mask, and he didn't want to do that. If he did by some chance encounter enemy aircraft, he wanted the advantage of altitude.

He gazed down at the New Guinean jungle far below. He could see the varying values and intensities of the mottled greens in the dense foliage. There was no worse jungle in the world than in New Guinea, and all you had to do was to look at it and you were convinced. The Aussie captain who had briefed the squadron on jungle survival had said that most of this northwest section of New Guinea was so primitive and impregnable that it had never been visited by a white man. He also said that the natives there lived in virtually a stone-age culture. And many of the tribes were cannibals who practiced head-hunting. It was a place to avoid at all costs. Fortunately, flying east, as he was, he would fly over only the eastern tip of that region, then out onto the coastal area where his home base was located.

Richard Strommen's first inkling that something was wrong came when he suddenly realized that all he could see ahead was endless jungle. He quickly rechecked his chart and his watch. It couldn't be! He should be over the Bismarck Sea by now, or at least he should be able to see it in the distance. But there was no sea in any direction. How could that be? He was heading east, and that had to take him out to the sea. It had to.

He glanced up at his mag compass and read it aloud: "Two hundred seventy degrees . . . right on the money . . . *two hundred seventy degrees!* . . ." Then the words froze in his throat, and a jab of fear struck him deep in the stomach. The compass read west. He had misread it and was flying in the wrong direction.

His first reaction was instinctive: he snapped the fighter into a steep bank and quickly reversed his course, so the compass now read what it should: east. Christ! How could he have made such a mistake? Probably he'd gotten disoriented when he'd dodged that thunderstorm. And he'd been upset about aborting anyway, so he had simply read east on a compass that was indicating west!

He grabbed his chart again and spread it on his lap. He'd been flying west for nearly an hour. He traced the route with his finger on the chart. His position would be . . . When the reality of his terrible mistake became clear, a chill ran up Richard Strommen's spine.

It was obvious that there was no way, now, that he could make it back to base. He would run out of fuel right in the middle of enemy territory if he continued flying east. He rolled the aircraft into a bank and headed back to the west. He'd long ago decided, from intelligence briefings, that he would never let the Japanese take him prisoner.

Glancing at his fuel gauges and computing his time, he studied his chart again. It might be possible, if the winds were favorable, to make it all the way across to the west coast. He'd heard there were Dutch settlements over there, and even though it was under Japanese control, the Dutch would be sympathetic and might hide him or help him escape. It was worth a try, and there was no other choice anyway. He quickly reached up and reduced power for long-range cruise. That would cost him airspeed, but it would also maximize range.

Now he wanted a cigarette desperately, but he had to maintain his altitude; it would take him farther. There was about forty minutes' fuel remaining in his tanks, maybe a little more. Could he make it? He looked at the chart again. He could only calculate roughly where he was, having not paid too much attention to his navigation. He'd expected to pinpoint his position easily after intersecting the east coast, where there were lots of recognizable landmarks.

But the New Guinean jungle below him now all looked exactly alike. And his calculations told him he was over that same section of jungle that the Aussie survival expert had said to avoid at all costs.

About twenty minutes later, when the fuel-warning light blinked, another of those cold, deathly chills ran up Richard Strommen's spine, while perspiration popped out on his forehead. He would not make it to the west coast. That was now overwhelmingly evident, since the jungle still stretched endlessly in all directions. And there was, at best, only twenty minutes' fuel remaining.

It was difficult to accept. There had to be an alternative . . . there had to be. Richard had always had that philosophy: there was always an alternative, no matter what the circumstances. Well, if there was one he'd better come up with it soon, because in a very few minutes those big Curtis Electric propellers that were pulling him through the sky were going to stop turning, and the cozy cockpit where he sat was going down, down into that hostile world below: a world that would be totally alien to anything he'd ever known.

There was no alternative. He must accept that now and prepare himself. Okay . . . okay, he'd have to bail out. Can't go down with the aircraft, into that maze of trees and foliage, it would be certain suicide. Not that bailing out was going to be much better . . . come on Richard, think positive. He'd been a Boy Scout and had won praise for his resourcefulness, hadn't he? Yes, and he had his .45 pistol and his survival kit, which were attached to his chute. God, when was the last time he'd checked his survival kit? He could only hope it was in good condition. He glanced down. The jungle was splotched with shadows of the usual thunderstorms scattered across the horizon, but no one spot in the jungle looked any better than another.

How should he bail out? There was a controversy among the squadron pilots over bailing out. The manual said to either roll out over the left wing or turn the aircraft upside down and drop out. He would do it that way, but he'd better do it before the engines quit . . .

Yeah, and since he was going down anyway, he'd nose it down a few minutes early and at least get in one last smoke. He leveled off at 10,000 feet, pulled off his oxygen mask, dug a cigarette out of his flight-suit pocket, and lit it with his Zippo lighter. The cigarette tasted wonderful and he smoked it greedily, knowing he was running out of time. All fuel tanks now showed empty. The time had come. Do it! he told himself. Roll it over and drop out! But his hands would not obey. He just sat there in the cockpit, frozen, unable to respond to his own command.

But with the first sputter of the engine a moment later, Richard Strommen quickly rolled the P-40 over on its back, pushed the canopy open, flipped his crash-straps release, and dropped out of the cockpit of his beautiful P-40 into the humid New Guinean air over the steaming New Guinean jungle.

After the initial shock of his parachute opening, the first thing Richard noticed was how surprisingly quiet it had suddenly become. He was still several thousand feet up, and, for a few minutes at least, he was safe and could enjoy the serenity. But as the jungle rose to meet him, he was reminded of Jules Verne's description of the yawning, green-black depths of those deep-sea waters in *Twenty Thousand Leagues Under the Sea*. And although there might not be a giant squid to greet him, there were sure going to be snakes and crocodiles and a lot of crawly things. Not to mention the headhunters.

As the jungle neared, Richard caught a peripheral glimpse of his beautiful Warhawk a short distance away, diving into the green sea and disappearing without out a trace. A few seconds later he braced himself and closed his eyes. Surprisingly, after a short jostling he came to a gentle stop and just hung there, swinging in his parachute.

It took a moment to orient himself, but then he realized that the soft landing had been a result of his chute hanging up on tree branches. He glanced up into a blanket of vines, leaves, and branches so thick that only a few cracks of sunlight shone through. The long nylon shroud lines that held him disappeared into the greenery above, where he could see only a portion of his tangled parachute.

Then he looked down and wished he hadn't. There it was, below his dangling feet: the jungle. The jungle of northwestern New Guinea that the Aussie captain had said to avoid at all costs. Strangely, in that traumatic moment, the words of one of his favorite squadron songs came to mind.

Beside a jungle waterfall, one bright and sunny day
Beside his battered Warhawk, the young pursuiter lay.
His parachute hung from a very high limb
He was not yet quite dead.
So listen to the very last words the young pursuiter said:
I'm goin' to a better land, a better land, I know
Where whiskey flows from coconut groves, play poker every night
We'll never have to work at all, just hang around and sing
We'll have a crew of women, O death where is thy sting?
O death where is thy sting
O death where is thy sting-a-ling-ling
O death where is thy sting?

In all the times he had sung that song with his buddies, after a couple of bottles of Aussie schnapps, it hadn't entered his mind that one day he might indeed be hanging in his parachute from a very high jungle limb. But here he was, and the only thing missing was the waterfall.

But hold on, he told himself: Richard Strommen was far from his "very last words." A long way. He was resourceful and he was determined. He would simply use his knowledge of the outdoors that he'd acquired as a Boy Scout. And with his long-held philosophy that there was always an alternative, another way to skin the cat, he would survive the jungle despite its worst adversities.

Okay. First things first. It was a good 20-foot drop into the jungle below, with or without his parachute. And since he needed it and the attached survival kit, he'd have to get it unhooked from the entanglement above. He braced himself for the fall and jerked on the shroud lines. Nothing happened, except for the loud screech from a bright-colored bird that came diving out of the branches. He jerked again, violently. Still nothing. Then, without warning, it came loose and down he plummeted with the collapsed parachute, into a tangled heap in a thicket below.

The thicket provided another relatively soft landing, and Richard was congratulating himself on his good fortune when he was suddenly and frightfully reminded of a jungle adversary that he had completely overlooked: mosquitoes. And they swarmed down on him in a black cloud.

As he struggled to free himself from his entanglement while swatting at the mosquitoes, he searched his memory for something the Aussie survival expert had said about combating one of the jungle's worst predators and its debilitating—if not deadly—bite of malaria, dengue fever, and other similar diseases. Mud. Yes, that was what the Aussie had said: "Plaster your face and hands with mud to protect yourself from the infectious mosquitoes."

When he finally pulled free of his entanglement, he quickly folded his parachute back into its harness as best he could, so he could carry it. He knew the chute and the attached kit would play a vital roll in his survival. But the paramount and most immediate requirement was to find mud—plain old mud. He scanned the area. Every direction looked the same: trees, foliage, vines, and thickets so dense he could see only a few feet. And there was no ground under his feet; it was like walking on a thick, wet sponge. There was no mud, only water, grass, and bushes. But he had to find mud, and find it quickly.

He picked a direction and sloshed off through the jungle, stumbling and clawing his way through the wet, slimy vegetation that was alive with swarms of mosquitoes and insects of every description. Within minutes he was soaked from the standing water and moisture on every leaf and vine, as well as his own perspiration from the steaming jungle heat.

After traveling only a short distance, Richard found himself inundated by another group of rain-forest inhabitants: leeches. At first he frantically tore the slimy creatures from his skin. But he soon discovered, to his horror, that for every one he tore off, another of the hideous things quickly attached itself.

After a while Richard gave up trying to pull off the leeches and swat the mosquitoes. He even ignored the slithering snakes, which seemed to be everywhere, as he struggled on through the endless vegetation, losing all track of time and direction.

It was late in the day when he finally stumbled through a thicket and onto a riverbank. He stood for a moment gasping for breath and stared at a group of crocodiles who suddenly scrambled off the bank and disappeared into the dark, muddy waters. The exhausted pilot stood as though hypnotized for a moment, then collapsed headlong into the river mud.

Richard lay there in the gooey, foul-smelling mud for some time, resting and trying to regain his composure. He knew that he must regain control of his runaway emotions, or he was doomed. Finally he pulled himself to a sitting position and began to pull the leeches off his face and body. He had just removed the last one when a sudden tropical rainstorm came down in a torrent. It was like a gift from heaven, and he stripped off his flight suit and just stood there naked, savoring the feel of the fresh rainwater on his raw skin, where he'd torn off the leeches.

The downpour stopped as suddenly as it had started, and the mosquitoes returned as quickly as they had departed. But the interlude and the fresh rainwater had cleared his besieged brain, and Richard set about doing what he knew had to be done. He put his flight suit back on, zipped it up tightly, and pulled his flight goggles over his eyes. Ignoring the awful stench, he scooped up the river mud and plastered it over his face and hands, so that there was no part of his skin exposed.

The mud was awful, but it did give him some protection from the leeches and mosquitoes. Now he must take stock and formulate a plan of action. Richard recognized that he had not done well in his first encounter with the jungle. He had not acted wisely, racing off without any real plan, thrashing through the jungle until panic had all but overcome him. He was just lucky to have stumbled onto the river. He promised himself that he would not let that happen again.

He sat down on a log next to the river and pulled out a pack of cigarettes. When he flipped his Zippo it flared to life, but the tobacco was so waterlogged that it would hardly burn, and the smoke tasted terrible. He dropped it into the mud and dug out another. It was worse than the first, and he angrily hurled the whole pack into the river. An instant later the water churned briefly and the cigarette package disappeared into the brownish, dirty water. He watched for a moment, horrified yet fascinated. Then a little smile broke across Richard Strommen's mud-plastered face. He wondered if the Aussie survival expert knew that crocodiles liked cigarettes.

Although it appeared the crocs were not going to bother him, he knew that they did attack humans, and he unsnapped his .45 pistol from his shoulder holster, slammed a cartridge into the firing chamber, and eased the hammer onto safety. If one of those monsters came out of the water, he'd be ready.

Pulling the parachute harness into his lap, he unfastened the tiny one-man rubber boat and the survival kit. He unzipped the kit and surveyed its contents. It looked intact, with the usual survival items that included two packets of K rations and two fruit bars. Hardly enough for an extended stay. He pulled out the waterproofed map of New Guinea to see if he could get some idea of just how long his stay might be. After studying it for a while, he could only confirm what he already knew: he was someplace in the middle of New Guinea's isolated northwest jungle, where the survival expert had said that no white man had ever been.

Yes, it would probably be an extended stay, all right. The only positive note to this dismal picture was his good fortune at having stumbled onto the river. He had no idea which river it was or where it went. But all rivers eventually lead to the sea, didn't they?

Yes, water ran downhill. And although there were dozens of rivers in New Guinea, he would simply get in his rubber boat and follow this one wherever it took him. Did crocodiles like rubber boats as well as cigarettes? He hoped not . . . and what about head-hunters? And the Japanese? Well, he wouldn't run into them until he got near the coast. As for the head-hunters and crocodiles, he had his .45.

Richard knew it was going to be the challenge of his life and would require all the resourcefulness that he possessed. But with a positive attitude and a little luck, he could do it. He had to. No other options were available, he told himself, as he folded the map and put it back in the kit. And he'd better start preparing for nightfall, which was only minutes away.

He made a hammock out of his parachute by tying it between two trees. This would allow him to sleep off the ground and thereby avoid most of the crawly things and the slithering things, many of which, he knew, carried deadly poison.

After his hammock had been prepared, he sat down on the log again and opened one of the K-ration packages. When he peeled the heavy protective wax paper away, there was a faded stamp on the side of the box. He could make out "U.S. Army" and a date that looked suspiciously like 1918. Couldn't be of course, but after he'd eaten a piece of the hardtack cracker he wasn't so sure. It was nourishing, however, and that was all that counted.

As he chewed on his K ration, his thoughts went to the major and his squadron mates. They would have returned from the mission by now and would know that he hadn't made it back. They would send out a flight of P-40s first thing in the morning to search for him, all right, but they wouldn't be looking in the right place, because he'd stupidly flown in exactly the opposite direction from the route he should have taken. But even if his buddies did fly over this area, how could they see him? They couldn't, of course. It would be impossible to see him from the air.

Eating with mud-plastered hands and face was a problem, but a minor one in the scheme of Richard's sustenance problems. The meager rations in his survival kit would last only a few days at best. He realized that his survival would depend on his ability to procure wild game and fish. And the survival expert had said that there were lots of berries, leaves, and other things in the jungle, if you knew which ones were eatable. In the morning he would read the survival manual. It would tell him.

After he'd finished eating the hardtack, he cut a small piece off the fruit bar with his sheath knife, to balance his ration and kill the taste of one of the quinine tablets. He knew the quinine would not keep him from coming down with malaria or dengue fever, but it could moderate the severity. The mosquitoes had bitten him hundreds of times earlier that day, so it was all but certain he'd been infected. He could only hope that the fever would not be severe enough to keep him from functioning.

When night came in Richard's jungle camp it was

pitch-black, since little starlight could sift through the canopy of thick foliage. He was tempted to build a campfire for psychological reasons, but certainly he didn't need the heat, and everything was so wet it probably wouldn't burn anyway. So he washed the mud off his hands and face with river water, hurriedly climbed into his improvised hammock, and covered himself with the nylon. It was hot and suffocating, but better than the mosquitoes and millions of other flying insects that came out after dark in such swarms that the sound of their wings echoing through the jungle was like the whine of many high-pitched motors.

Being exhausted from his ordeal, Richard slept reasonably well, despite the conditions and his anxieties. He was awakened the next morning by a woman's scream. Clawing his way out of the nylon hammock, he grabbed his .45 and listened. When the scream came again, he realized that it was some kind of jungle bird or animal. Looking up, he could see a few rays of bright sunlight sifting through the jungle canopy. He was thinking that it might just be an omen of good fortune, when reality returned abruptly with a swarm of mosquitoes that swooped down upon him. He swung out of the hammock and, holding his breath to avoid the smell, plastered himself with the awful mud.

His breakfast was another small piece of hardtack, a bite of the fruit bar, and another quinine tablet, washed down with a drink of water from his canteen. He made a mental note that when the next downpour came, he should remember to refill the canteen with rainwater.

After breakfast Richard sat down on the log with

his survival kit, to again take stock and map out his
strategy. He looked at each item and mentally re-
viewed its use. The safe-passage chit was supposed to
tell the natives they would be rewarded if they helped
him, but since no white man had ever been in this
area . . . think positive, Richard.

Compass: he should have used it yesterday, instead
of flailing through the jungle without direction. Well,
he'd keep track of his direction from now on. Signal
mirror: great for signaling aircraft, but would he ever
find a place where he could see the sky? Waterproofed matches: useful, if you could find something
to burn in a rain forest. A map of New Guinea: as
soon as he could identify a landmark, the map would
be valuable. A fishing kit: the survival expert had said
that all the rivers had lots of fish. Good. And he'd
seen worms for bait in the gooey mud. The one-man
boat: that little jewel was going to carry him out of
this place. And to think he'd almost removed it from
his survival kit because it made his parachute too
heavy.

Last, and very important: the survival manual. It
would give him rules to follow in the jungle and tell
him what things to eat and where he could find them.
He removed it from the water-protective bag and
read the title: *U.S. Army Aircrew Survival in the
Arctic.* At first Richard just looked at the manual in
disbelief. Then he thumbed through the pages: no
mistake. It told all about what to do and eat in the
Arctic. He stared at it for a moment, then burst out
laughing. Good ol' U.S. Army snafu. Well, at least he
hadn't lost his sense of humor.

Although Richard saw the humor, he knew that
not having the manual to guide him was a significant

setback. His morale got a boost, however, when he pulled the inflation lanyard on the little blue-and-yellow package labeled Boat: One Man. It popped open and quickly inflated, just as the instructions said it would.

After he had packed his parachute and other gear in the rubber boat, it occurred to Richard that the nomenclature should have been Boat: One Small Man. It was a tight squeeze to get his tall frame into the boat, and after he had crawled in and pushed off into the river, it also occurred to him that the only thing between his posterior and the crocodiles was a thin piece of rubber. He quickly pulled out his .45 and held it ready. But apparently the crocodiles didn't like rubber boats, because nothing happened, and after a while Richard put the .45 back in its holster.

He tried to keep track of his heading with the compass, but it was very difficult since the river meandered through the jungle in no apparent direction and was shrouded in a cocoon of heavy vegetation on all sides and overhead. He found it impossible to identify any landmarks for reference, and sometimes it appeared as though he was floating in a giant swamp of dark, stagnant water with no sides and no end. The current was slow, so slow that it often seemed his boat was not moving at all.

The mosquitoes were not as bad during the day, but they were there. At least the only leeches he had to cope with were a few that occasionally dropped from the foliage umbrella above.

The boat kit included a small rubber paddle, which he used to steer the boat and keep him away from the vegetation that hung down onto the water. He kept a sharp watch for crocodiles, but all he saw was an occasional water snake slithering its way across the river and paying him little attention. There were no human signs of any kind, but lots of colorful birds and some small animals that scurried through the tree branches. He thought at first they were monkeys, but when he got a closer look at one, it resembled a baby kangaroo.

After several hours of floating through the steamy vegetation and stifling heat and, seemingly, making little progress, Richard found himself fighting a growing feeling of suffocation. He decided to go ashore and get out of the cramped quarters of the small boat for a while. But to do that he had to find a place to go ashore. He'd noticed that for some time he had not seen the riverbank, or any other indication that he was following a river. All he could see was still, foul-smelling water and jungle foliage that hung so low over the water that it was becoming difficult to find a path through it.

Fighting to remain calm, he paddled the rubber boat for hours in whatever direction gave the least resistance, searching for some indication of solid ground. The shadows were darkening, signaling the approach of nightfall, when Richard finally spotted what appeared to be a riverbank. But as he approached, he saw that it was only a large growth of some form of slimy water plant. He stopped paddling and just sat there in the boat, dripping with perspiration while waves of depression swept through him and waves of aquatic insects swarmed over him.

He flinched when a loud thunderclap suddenly echoed through the jungle canopy, followed by a torrential downpour. The rainwater felt cool and soothing, and he pulled off his flight helmet and goggles and let the water cascade over his face, washing off the remainder of his antimosquito mud, most of which had already been removed by his own perspiration. But at this point, it didn't seem to matter. What difference did a few more mosquito bites make?

But it did matter, and Richard knew it. If he was going to let himself become despondent after only one day in the jungle, there was no way he would make it.

The rainstorm lasted only a few minutes, but it was a welcome relief from the flying predators and it cooled him and boosted his spirits. He wished he hadn't been so hasty in throwing his cigarettes away. God, he'd give anything to have one now, soggy or not. Never mind. Do what has to be done.

Darkness was closing in fast. He had no choice but to spend the night in the boat. That was going to be tough, real tough. His legs already felt paralyzed.

He quickly began to prepare. The boat was half full of rainwater, and the mosquitoes were back in full force. He put his helmet and goggles back on and began to bail out the water with his canteen cup. When he'd gotten most of it out, he tied the boat between two tree limbs to keep it from drifting into the foliage, which was alive with insects. Then he enclosed himself in a small tent fashioned with his parachute. It was suffocating and, since he was soaked, like a steam bath. But it kept out most of the crawly things and the flying intruders, who now sounded like an armada outside of the nylon canopy.

Richard Strommen's second night in the New Guinean jungle was an unimaginable ordeal. He slept little, and when dawn finally seeped into his tomb he was exhausted and every bone in his body seemed to ache. He forced himself to eat a piece of the hardtack and take one of the quinine tablets. Then he untied the boat and began to paddle, forging through the maze of vines, trees, and swamp vegetation, determined to find the river channel.

All that day he searched for the river, but when darkness settled on Richard that evening, his surroundings had changed little since morning. Again he tied his rubber boat between two tree limbs and spent another fitful, suffocating night.

The next morning Richard knew that the ache in his bones was not just from being cramped up in the boat. He knew because now he could feel the fever moving through his body. The mosquitoes had done their job: he was infected with one or more of the jungle fevers. He could only hope that it would not incapacitate him totally. If it did, he was doomed.

By midmorning he felt so weak and lightheaded that he could hardly paddle the boat. His forehead was so hot the mosquitoes wouldn't even land on it. He tried to reason about what to do, but it was difficult to even think, with the spinning images and disjointed thoughts that began to swirl through his aching head. He must paddle on . . . paddle on, don't stop. It was all he could focus on. Just keep paddling . . . keep paddling . . . eventually he would come to something . . . he had to.

Some time later, out of the spinning haze a vision came into focus: it was a riverbank of good old mud! There it was, directly in front of him. It looked almost exactly like the one he'd camped on two days earlier. Yes, even to the crocodiles lying there where they'd been before. He must get to that bank. He had to get there and out of the boat so he could rest. He paddled as fast as he could make his arms work.

As Richard neared the bank, the crocodiles spotted him and scurried off into the water in a rush. It occurred to him that he ought to get out his .45, but it seemed like such an effort that he didn't bother. Then one of the big crocodiles charged out into the deeper water and his huge, thrashing tail struck the rubber boat, turning it over and pitching Richard and all his gear into the water.

As he went down in the melee of churning water and scrambling crocodiles, a thought pierced Richard's spinning, aching head. It was something the Aussie survival expert had said: "If a big croc grabs you, he will take you down to the bottom and hold you till you drown. The best thing to do is jab your thumb in his eye and he will release you."

Certain that he would feel the croc's teeth any second, Richard told himself to be ready with his thumbs. Meanwhile he exerted every ounce of his remaining energy to fight his way to the surface of the dark water and head for shore. Surprisingly he made it and dragged himself onto the mud bank, where he lay gasping and coughing up river water that tasted worse than the mud. He was vaguely aware that the churning water in the river was the crocodiles having a picnic with all the intriguing things that had come out of his blue-and-yellow rubber boat. That was probably why they hadn't bothered with him.

When Richard Strommen finally pulled himself to a sitting position there in the mud on the riverbank it was nearly dark, and the raging fever within was clouding his vision with all sorts of fuzzy images. But he could clearly see, a short distance away, the same log he'd sat on three days earlier. A small piece of the waxed paper from the K rations still lay there in the mud. It was devastating to discover that for three terrible days he'd done nothing but mill around in circles, ending up right back where he'd started.

And with the realization that he'd lost all his survival gear in the river, total dejection swept through Richard. He closed his eyes and let his chin drop toward his chest. And there he sat for some time, watching all those crazy, disjointed images spin before his eyes, while the weird buzzing in his ears grew louder and louder with each rising degree of his fever, so loud that it even drowned out the whine of millions of mosquitoes and insects that were feasting on his skin. Finally, from somewhere deep down, that last vestige of instinct for survival surfaced and Richard pulled his head up, opened his eyes, and saw his deliverance.

Right there beside where he sat was a footprint: a bare, human footprint in the mud. It required all of his remaining strength to crawl over and pull himself up to a sitting position against the log. Then he opened his eyes and smiled. He'd done it after all, hadn't he? Yes. He'd found someone who would save him. Whoever had made the footprint would come for him. All he had to do was wait a little while, and they would come and save him. He was sure of it. But now it was time to sleep. Oh, God, he was so tired and sleepy . . . yes, now he could sleep.

When Richard Strommen next opened his eyes, the disjointed images were still spinning before him and the whining noises still echoed through his skull. He had no idea of how long he'd been unconscious, but he sensed that something was different. What? What was it? And where was he? He closed his eyes tightly and tried to make his fever-racked brain respond. What was it? Something different . . . was it the noise that was different? Yes, yes, that was it.

The high-pitched whine in his ears was now accompanied by a deep, booming base. It was a drumbeat! He could hear it clearly. He tried to pull himself up, but his head exploded and the images swirled violently. He aborted the attempt and lay back down. Then out of the swirl, a different image appeared before him. It was the weirdest of all: it was a tall black form, pierced with bizarre colored decorations. Richard looked at it intently, struggling to bring it into focus. Strange. It looked like . . . it was! It was a man.

Richard Strommen was aware that he lay on some sort of straw mat in a room with open sides and a thatched roof. Behind the human figure standing over him was a structural framework of hand-cut wooden beams adorned with numerous carved shapes.

Although it was semidark in the room and his vision was blurred by the spinning images, Richard could see that the figure was a tall black man. He was naked, except for a small piece of hide that covered his genitals. Much of his body was decorated with white and red paint and various tassels of bird feathers and straw, which were attached to his skin. His face was grotesquely disfigured with paint and various pieces of wood and bone that hung from his lips and his nose.

In Richard's delirium it was exceedingly difficult to think rationally, but he knew that this man, or one like him, had made the footprint in the mud and had saved him. He must speak to him and thank him. But when he tried, all that came out was a weak croak.

The black man stepped back quickly, raised the long spear he held, and let out a loud, guttural shout. Within seconds the drums stopped abruptly, and several similarly dressed men rushed into the room. They too held spears made of long, slender shafts of wood, painted and decorated with various tassels of feathers and grass. They looked at Richard curiously, grunting and jabbering to one another and holding their spears cautiously.

Suddenly they stopped and turned to one of their clan, who pushed forward to the front of the group. He was even more elaborately attired than his associates; his accessories included a headdress that jingled with an array of brightly colored bones and shells. Instead of a spear he held a decorated object, which Richard judged to be some form of scepter. It had a striking resemblance to a human skull.

Richard's weary mind struggled to comprehend what he was seeing. This must be their leader, he thought, or at least one of their higher-ups. They must be natives, primitive natives, and this was their village. Were they friendly? Was he a guest or a prisoner? He must speak . . . speak to this leader and tell them who he was, and that they would be rewarded if they helped him. He needed medical help urgently. Quinine—must get quinine soon, to blunt the fever.

When Richard managed to croak out a few words, all conversation in the room stopped and all eyes focused on him curiously. Then the one with the headdress held his scepter high and grunted a command. Everyone backed out of the room cautiously except for the original tall one, who backed up a safe distance but remained in the room, holding his spear on guard. Richard knew that they had not understood a word of his plea, and he closed his eyes and tried to think of some way that he could communicate.

But it all seemed so futile. He was so weak with the fever that he could hardly raise his head, let alone do anything else. Then he became aware that someone was near him. He opened his eyes and saw the most garishly painted and decorated of his visitors so far.

He was smaller than the chief, but he too carried some sort of scepter, and around his neck was a necklace that looked like a human jawbone. His eyes stared out from behind circles of thick white paint, and his nose and lips were painted a brilliant red, with a piece of white bone piercing his nostrils on both sides. A string of shells and pebbles hung from each ear, and another string encircled his straw hat, which also sprouted an array of brightly colored feathers. His naked body was painted with stripes of red and white paint, something on the order of a barber pole.

He squatted down beside Richard and poured some fluid from his scepter into a piece of coconut shell. Was it food? Poison? He grunted again and thrust the crude cup to Richard's lips. Richard sensed that it must be some kind of medicine: if they wanted him dead, all they had to do was bash his head in with one of their stone axes. And since he had little to lose anyway, he decided to drink whatever it was.

The fluid was bitter and tasted terrible, but Richard drank it each time the medicine man, or whatever he was, gave it to him over the next few days. Richard drank the fluid because he realized that it was indeed some kind of medicine made from jungle herbs that reduced the severity of his chills and fever attacks. His symptoms were typical of malaria, dengue fever, or both: burning up one minute and shaking violently from chills the next. After the chills, there would be a period when he could think and function to some degree, although he remained very weak and lay on the straw mat in a sort of semiconscious state most of the time.

During his rational periods, Richard determined that he was in a primitive native village, where the people were living in what the Aussie captain had described as a stone-age culture. He couldn't quite determine what his guest status was. A guard remained beside him constantly, yet they were treating him for his fever and brought him food. It was some kind of broth that tasted awful, but apparently it was nourishing, and he knew he must eat to regain his strength. At night they put a thatched cover over him that was held up by wooden braces. It was suffocating, with an awful stench. But it was that or be eaten alive by the mosquitoes and other insects that came in black clouds at sundown.

The chief and his entourage usually came to visit right after a big village meeting and a loud session of the drums, which occurred regularly over the next several days. Sometimes those visits came when Richard was in his rational phase, and he would pull himself to a sitting position for a few minutes and try to communicate. But it didn't appear that he was making much progress. All they seemed to understand was his basic need for fever medicine, food, and mosquito protection. It was evident that they had never seen a white man before, and Richard sensed that there was a good deal of disagreement over whether he was a god of some kind or just a special goody to eat.

Richard recognized that the chief's scepter was a human skull, all right, and he had seen others with skulls, jawbones, and decorated human heads. So there was little doubt that his hosts were headhunters . . . and cannibals. This was confirmed one day when he watched them drag a struggling captive into the village, hack him to death with stone clubs and spears, then divide him into portions, including his head, which they baked. They even ate the victim's brains, after shaking them out through a hole in his temple.

After observing this incident, Richard decided that he'd better do something to sway opinion toward his being a god. He knew they believed in magic, so he decided to play his trick at the chief's next visit. The only thing that he hadn't lost to the crocodiles was his Zippo, which had been zipped up in his flight-suit pocket. His decision was timely, since at that next visit a violent argument broke out between the elders, and spears and stone axes were brandished. Richard struggled to his feet and, holding the lighter up, let out a loud cry and flicked it to life.

The effect was just as he had hoped: the superstitious natives were astonished and drew back in fright. The trick worked, indeed, like magic for Richard. He was immediately transferred to the great-spirit house, where only gods, chiefs, and pigs were allowed. It was a large wooden structure, built on massive stilts of palm-tree logs. The main floor was at least 10 feet up from the jungle floor, and under it a number of dugout canoes were parked. The sides were a complex framework of beams under a thatched-grass roof, with a tall steeple at each end. Access was up a long ladder made of bamboo and lashed with vine. The entrance sprouted the figure of a female some 12 feet long, carved from wood and garishly painted a bright red orange.

Despite his weakness, Richard walked as godlike as he could to his new quarters and made it up the long ladder. The inside of the spirit house was decorated extensively with all types of figures and symbols carved from wood or made of stones, shells, and human bones, including scores of yawning human skulls.

Richard was given royal status in the great-spirit house, where no women or children were allowed. From that time on he was treated in a manner befitting his regal position. His trick with the lighter had apparently settled the question, and he was now officially a god. That day there was a great celebration with the drums, including 15-foot-long hardwood slit gongs that boomed out messages all through the jungle about the discovery of the new white god.

Although the stench was nauseating and the grotesque skulls distracting, it was a temporary sanctuary, and Richard's living conditions were much improved. He was now served prized pieces of pork, fish, sweet potatoes, and sago-palm starch. He was afforded great respect and presented with an array of valuable gifts, including several carved wooden figures, shell necklaces, bright feathers, and some poor soul's polished skull.

As a member of the great house he was given free rein in the village, which consisted of about two dozen homes, none quite as handsome as his. During the day the village was a beehive of activity, with the women doing most of the work, many carrying infants strapped to their backs. Older children played together on the jungle floor between the houses, which were all on stilts and built of palm, bamboo, and straw. Men and women alike went naked most of the time, having developed a form of immunity to the mosquitoes and the jungle fevers. At bedtime, however, they put the thatched covers over themselves, because that was when the insects came in swarms.

Within a couple of weeks, Richard had gained back enough strength to begin thinking about some plan of escape. But he faced a number of serious problems. He knew only that he was deep in a savage, hostile land and playing a dangerous game with superstitious, volatile savages. He still had made little progress in communicating and had no idea how far it was to civilization. Convincing his subjects that their new god must leave was not going to be easy. He knew, however, that he would need their help to have any chance of getting out of the jungle. And, although he had gained enough strength to function, he still suffered regular attacks of chills and fever that, when they came, disabled him for several days.

His problem was solved in a horrible but decisive way. The village was suddenly attacked, one morning, by headhunters from another village. They clubbed or speared to death most of the villagers, women and children included, then cut off their heads as prizes. A few were spared and dragged off into the jungle to be butchered later in grand style, at the home village. Richard was one of those spared. His captors, dressed and garishly painted similarly to those they had murdered, were cautiously curious about his fair features and white skin, and they appeared to recognize that he had some kind of special status. He was allowed to walk along the trail, but with guards on both sides. The other captives had their hands tied behind their backs and a rope around their necks, in chain fashion.

It was a long, exhausting trip through the rain forest, and Richard collapsed before they had gone halfway. They apparently wanted to keep him alive, as they slung him on a pole and made two of the women captives carry him. When one of his carriers later faltered, a captor ran his spear through her repeatedly, while the others laughed and shouted encouragement. Then he hacked her head off with a stone ax and hung it by the hair on a reed belt that he wore.

Fortunately, Richard spent most of the trip unconscious with a malaria attack. When he finally opened his eyes again, he was lying on a straw mat, in a typical native house. He could hear the loud beating of drums and the shouting of pitched, excited voices. It was dark, and the leaping flames of a huge fire reflected off the beams of the open-sided structure. He pulled himself up and looked out at a display of primitive, inhuman savagery.

The crazed natives, splattered with blood, were butchering the remaining captives. They were stabbing with spears, clubbing with stone axes, chopping off heads and swinging them around by the hair, as they laughed hysterically. It was a sickening, horrible sight, and Richard fell back on his straw pad in a state of total depression.

Each time he regained consciousness during the next several days, he expected to be dragged out and butchered like the others. But instead they gave him herbal medicine to combat the fever, and food similar to what he'd been given at the other village, only not as elaborate as when he had been in his god status.

The chief, the medicine man, and the elders all came to visit, as they too were awestruck over his white skin and uncertain about what to do with him.

When his malaria attack had subsided enough that he could stand, Richard decided that it might be good insurance to do his Zippo magic trick again. But this time, when he shouted and flicked the lighter, it wouldn't light. The chief liked the sparks the flint made, though, and took it for his own magic.

Richard's status remained in question until one day when the village was visited by a small group of travelers from a distant area. They were attired similarly, with wood, shell, and feather bangles and baubles, but these were huge, fierce-looking men with apelike arms and legs. When they saw Richard one of them started jabbering excitedly, making wild gestures with his arms. After a long, animated discussion, an agreement was reached and Richard found himself again on a trail through the jungle with the new group of strangers. He could only assume that he'd been sold or traded.

Again Richard collapsed after only a few hours on the trail. And again he was slung on a pole and carried between two natives. Fortunately, that part of the journey only lasted one day. The next day they came to a river, where they boarded a long, thin, dugout canoe and cast off into the murky waters. Richard was made to sit in the center of the narrow boat, while the tribesmen stood up and paddled with long-stemmed oars. Even in his delirious, exhausted state, Richard marveled at the incredible balance and control the oarsmen displayed as they propelled the highly unstable craft swiftly up the river.

The canoe trip took several long, grueling days.

Richard was astonished at the stamina and strength of the oarsmen, who paddled the canoe hour after hour without rest. On the last day, they were suddenly confronted by two war canoes, racing after them for the kill. But the big men outdistanced their pursuers easily, despite the deadweight they carried.

In the late afternoon of that day, they beached and hid their canoe in the brush. Then they trekked over a jungle trail that was mostly on solid earth and clear of wet, dripping foliage and the steaming humidity of the rain forest. Before nightfall, they arrived at a village that was built on solid ground. Richard guessed they were approaching the northern slopes of New Guinea's great Central Range, which included mountains with peaks more than 16,000 feet high.

The drums began pounding immediately upon their arrival, and the villagers rushed out to inspect Richard. It was evident that they too had never seen a white man, and they examined him in curious detail. These villagers were also tall and large-boned, but not as big as the giants who had brought Richard in the canoe. Then the chief and his entourage arrived, dressed in the usual bizarre, colorful attire. After their inspection, they engaged in a loud, animated discussion with the tribesmen who had brought Richard.

That evening he was given food, herbal medicine, and a straw bed with a mosquito cover. He had no idea what had transpired between his captors and the chiefs, but he was too exhausted to care and slept until he was awakened the next morning. Richard soon discovered that he had again been sold or traded to another group. When they came to examine him, this new group did not appear to be all that surprised to see a white man and apparently understood that he was worth a big reward, somewhere down the line. At least it was encouraging to know that he was more valuable as trade than as a headhunter's prize.

That morning, after another round of drums and fiery discussions, his new group of owners set off with Richard on a trail that soon became steep and difficult. He walked as far as he could, then collapsed. Again he was strung on a pole between two natives, but, thankfully, this time he was suspended in a reed net and carried up a steep mountain trail that soon began to wind through heavily wooded, mist-shrouded ridges and canyons that took several days to traverse.

The most severe malaria attack he'd endured since his first struck Richard that second day out, rendering him semiconscious for the remainder of the trip over the rugged mountains. He awakened once with a burning fever and was thankful for the cold mountain air. Then, a short time later, he awakened shaking so badly that his teeth were chattering, and he wished for the jungle heat.

Richard remembered little over the next few days, except an occasional vague image of that bouncing pole from which he hung. Once he awakened for a coherent moment and realized that he was very near death. In a passing thought, he wondered if the poor pole bearers would get their reward for carrying a corpse over mountains with 16,000-foot peaks.

It was days later before Richard became consciously aware of his surroundings again. He knew that he was no longer swinging in the reed net below the bearer pole. His first emotion was genuine surprise that he was still alive. He tried to focus on his strange surroundings and comprehend what he saw. There was some kind of greenish net all around him, and he was lying on something strangely soft, very soft. What? Where?

Richard closed his eyes again and reopened them as the green net parted, and a face looked down at him. A strange face . . . it had no grotesque red paint, or bones, or feathers . . . it was a white face!

"I say ol' chap, how do you feel?" the face asked.

It was a white face, and it spoke good old Australian English. Oh God, it was good to hear. Richard tried to speak, but nothing would come out.

The face smiled a good old Australian smile. "It's okay. Don't try to speak now. You've had quite a go. But you're in good hands now. I'm bloody curious to find out who you are and where in blazes you came from. But we'll do that when you're feeling better. I'd guess from that battered flight suit you're a Yank flier, righto?"

Richard managed the hint of a smile and a tiny nod. The Australian wore a handlebar mustache that turned up when he smiled. "You must have a whopping good story to tell, because no flier has ever come to this part of New Guinea before. In fact no white man has ever come from the north before. This is the northernmost outpost, and the only one for hundreds of miles. There are just a couple of us Australian Army blokes and a half dozen natives that run this radio reporting station.

"You see, my native boys heard a rumor through the jungle pipeline; they do that with drums, you know. Anyway, they heard that some group up north was holding a white man hostage. I was skeptical, because the Americans don't fly into that country. But I decided to have my boys check it out, and sure enough they found you, and just in time. I guess those sports up there were about to add your head to their bloody trophy collection."

Richard Strommen and I were in beds next to each other in the U.S. Army Field Hospital in Port Moresby in January 1944. As we both recovered from malaria and dengue fever, Richard told me the story of his incredible experience. From the isolated Australian radio outpost, he was taken to a secret location on the west coast and transported by an American submarine back to Port Moresby. Although he could recall some incidents of his bizarre journey, as related in this account, Richard had no way of recounting his actual route through the interior of New Guinea. It was as though he had gone through a time warp, in his escape from the Stone Age.

CHAPTER FOUR

Ace of Aces

When I sat down to write this chapter, I was searching for a way to begin the story when I happened to remember something that occurred just a couple of years ago.

It was late August 1995, and I was attending a seafood cookout in the beautiful tidelands of Virginia. One of the guests, recalling that August was the fiftieth anniversary of the end of World War II, turned to me and asked, "Weren't you in that war?"

I nodded, pleased that someone recognized there were still some of us around. One of the other guests looked at me suspiciously and said, "What did you do in World War II?"

"I was an Army Air Corps fighter pilot," I replied.

"You were a fighter pilot?" came the quick response from the young chef, tending a pot of clam chowder that was simmering on an outdoor broiler.

I nodded again.

"What did you fly?" he asked, his voice revealing a certain skepticism. But when I confessed I had flown the legendary Lockheed P-38 Lightning, his eyes widened.

"Wow!" he exclaimed, forgetting the clam chowder that he was stirring and giving me a look that said he was impressed. "I'm a warbird buff and I've read a lot about the top aces, like Maj. Richard Bong. He was a P-38 pilot too, you know. You ever happen to see him?"

"Yes, we flew in the same squadron together," I said.

"You're kidding!" he blurted.

I smiled. "No, I'm not kidding."

"Who was Maj. Richard Bong?" asked one of the other guests in the group gathered around the kettle of chowder, drinking beer and listening to the exchange.

"You don't know who he was?" said the chowder chef, a little indignantly.

The questioner looked sheepish and shook his head.

"He was America's top ace of all time," informed the chef.

"Oh, you mean like Tom Cruise in *Top Gun*?"

The chef sort of rolled his eyes and looked back to me. "I never met anyone who actually flew with Major Bong. Tell me, what was he really like and why was he so good?"

That young seafood chef had asked the same questions that I wanted to address in this chapter: What was Richard Bong really like, and why was he so good? I don't profess to know the absolute answer, of course. But I can relate what I remember about him, and, even after all this time, that memory still fascinates me.

He was an extraordinary young man in a unique period of aviation history. It was unique because, most aviation historians agree, it occurred at the apex of fighter-aircraft technology that relied primarily upon the individual skill of the pilot, rather than on the electronics and computers that are so integral to jet fighters today.

The fighter pilots of World War I were certainly as brave and skilled, but their warbirds were hardly more than motorized kites compared with the powerful, heavily armed, single-seat fighters of World War II. A duel to the death between opposing knights of the air required the same mental and physical resources in both wars, but the World War II duels were fought over great distances at three times the speed, and from the treetops to heights where never a Fokker or Spad ever flew.

And the greatest American fighter pilot of them all was Richard Ira Bong, a farm boy from Wisconsin. He was America's champion air knight, winning the contest forty times by destroying the enemy in aerial combat. He won more times than any other fighter pilot in U.S. military history.

Having flown combat missions with several World War II top aces, including Dick Bong, Tommy McGuire, Neel Kearby, and Gerald Johnson, I observed that they all had a couple of things in common: they were superior pilots who were as fearless as they were aggressive. Any one of them, if he hadn't been killed, might have been the top ace. But no fighter pilot ever topped Bong's record, nor will anyone, since man-to-man aerial combat as it was during that era will never occur again.

My part of the story of Richard Bong begins in the fall of 1943, when I reported to my new squadron, the 9th Fighter Squadron of the 49th Group, at Dobodura, New Guinea. Capt. Gerald Johnson, the Flying Knights' squadron commander, took me around the camp, which was a clump of moldy tents in the steaming jungle, to meet the other pilots. One of those introductions was to a sandy-haired, boyish-looking pilot: "Second Lt. Dick Kirkland, meet Capt. Dick Bong, the squadron's leading ace."

Bong was sitting on his mosquito-netted canvas cot, wearing a pair of crumpled khakis. We exchanged hellos, and he went back to whatever it was he was doing. I'd known he was a leading ace, and someone had told me he was in the 9th Squadron, so it was quite a thrill to meet him. But I remember thinking, afterward, that he seemed distracted and wasn't all that friendly. Later that day, I asked one of the other pilots if Captain Bong was sort of the moody type. He frowned at me and muttered something, which translated as brand-new second lieutenants should be seen and not heard until they know the score.

The squadron officers' club was built out of some scrap lumber and aluminum, a few discarded aircraft seats, some mosquito netting, and a couple of red-and-white parachutes hanging from the ceiling for decoration. It was crude, but it was a place to go in the evenings after the mission and relax, play cards, or just sit around smoking and talking. It was there, one evening after I'd been in the squadron a few days, that I discovered there was some controversy among the pilots over Capt. Dick Bong.

The conversation between a group of pilots playing cards at a homemade table covered with a GI blanket went something like this:

"It wasn't his fault George got shot down; he just couldn't stay on Bong's wing, that's all."

"I don't know about that. George was a damn good pilot. He could stay on anyone's wing."

"Well, obviously he couldn't stay on Bong's wing."

"Yeah, because Bong is a wild man and doesn't give a damn about his wingman. All he cares about is being a big ace and shooting down Nips."

"That's not true! And what the hell do you think we're over here for, to play tiddledywinks?"

"I know why I'm here, but we got to protect each other. That's as important as shooting down Nips."

"Yeah, but you know how it is in a fight. And the way Bong goes after those little bastards, it's almost impossible to stay with him. But what's he gonna do? Not attack because he's worried that his wingman might get shot down? After all the wingman's job is to cover his leader, you know."

"Yeah, that's true. And I know he feels real bad about losing George. He's been sitting over there in his tent, hardly speaking to anyone since George went down."

"Yeah, it really did upset him."

Hearing all this was particularly upsetting to me, since it was at this time that I was suffering my initial Zero shock, after two of my tent mates had been shot down the first day I joined the squadron. And since flying wing would be my job as a new pilot, all this wasn't very encouraging. But at least I was glad to know that Dick Bong had seemed unfriendly because he was upset and distracted over the loss of his wingman.

About that time, someone came in with a bottle of Aussie schnapps and passed it around the table. It was terrible stuff, but everyone drank it anyway and fired up fresh cigarettes, which added another layer of low-stratus clouds to our little club in the New Guinean jungle.

"I'd hate to be in Captain Johnson's shoes and have to make up the flight schedule. Who does he put on Bong's wing? It's the new guy's job to fly wing, and hell, not even the experienced pilots can stay with Bong," pronounced one of the pilots, prompting everybody to glance at me, and prompting me to take another drink of the Aussie schnapps.

"Well, if I were the captain, I'd make him fly alone," said one of the cardplayers.

"He can't do that; it's his own order that no one goes on a mission without a wingman."

"Yeah, and you know where we're going tomorrow?"

"Back to Rabaul!"

There was a unified groan around the makeshift table, and everyone took another shot of Aussie schnapps. Later that evening when all the schnapps was gone, they sang a song about Rabaul:

It's down to Sydney from Guinea I go
Down to Sydney from a place called Rabaul
When an ol' MP sergeant says pardon me please
There's blood on your tunic and mud on your knee.
I said listen here Sergeant, you bloody damn fool
I just came back from a place called Rabaul
Where shrapnel is flying and the comforts are few
And good men are dying for bastards like you.
Dinky dye, dinky dye, and good men are dying
For bastards like you.

Rabaul was the big Japanese base on New Britain that the Fifth Air Force attacked with B-24 and B-25 bombers, escorted by P-38s, numerous times in the fall of 1943. It was one of the hottest targets in the Southwest Pacific, and the Japanese defended it with a vengeance.

Since I was so new, Captain Johnson scheduled me on milk runs for my first few combat missions. It's a good thing he did, or I probably wouldn't be writing this now. We suffered some of our heaviest losses during that period. Those Rabaul missions were murder.

It appeared that Dick Bong's wingman problem was solved shortly after that, when he was sent home on leave. I guess he was long overdue for rotation anyway, but his leaving at that time did solve Captain Johnson's problem of whom to put on the ace's wing, at least for the time being.

Our squadron moved up the New Guinean coast a couple of times over the next few months, so I don't remember exactly when it was that Bong returned from the States, or where it was that we flew our first mission together. But I do recall the mission: we got in a heck of a fight with a flock of Zeros, and I had my first look at Dick Bong in action.

I saw for myself why it was so difficult to stay with him in an aerial dogfight. He was savagely aggressive and seemingly fearless as he pursued his prey, swooping down on the enemy aircraft to extremely close range. On this occasion, he closed to the point that when he fired his guns, the Zero exploded and he had to fly right through the disintegrating wreckage. Then wheeling away, he attacked another Japanese fighter bearing the rising sun on its wings. Again closing to point-blank range, he blasted that one out of the sky also.

It had taken all the skill I possessed, that day, just to keep from getting shot down myself, let alone having an extra minute or two to try to shoot down a Zero. But Bong had destroyed two enemy aircraft, and probably a third, in a matter of a few minutes. After we had landed back at our base, a couple of war correspondents came over to the squadron to interview him, and, as I listened to the exchange, I was astonished at the contrast between Dick Bong's two personalities. The conversation went something like this:

"How many did you get today, Ace?"

Bong, standing beside the operations tent in a soiled pair of sweat-soaked khakis with his .45 strapped under his shoulder, looked at the guy and sort of shrugged. "I think I got a couple," he said softly.

"Congratulations! Doesn't that make you our top ace?"

Bong shook his head. "I don't really know."

"According to my count it does," pronounced the war correspondent. "How does it feel to be America's ace of aces?"

Bong dropped his eyes and shrugged again.

"Tell us how you got 'em," persisted the correspondent.

"Uh . . . just lucky."

I could see that unlike the rest of us, who loved to tell of our triumphs, he wasn't eager to brag about his victories, and it was evident that he wasn't comfortable being interviewed. I'd heard some of the pilots who had known him for a while say that he was actually quite modest.

But it was hard for me to comprehend, after seeing

him in action that day. How could it be? How could this modest man talking to the correspondent be the same fearless tiger I had seen in a frenzied air duel a short time earlier? It was difficult to believe that it was the same person.

Not long after that incident, I went on rest-and-recreation [R and R] leave to Sydney, Australia, and it turned out that Bong was there too, and stayed at our squadron flat. We had a great place there called Buckingham Flats, not too far from Kings Cross, that we rented by the month. Since we were combat aircrew, they let us go down to Sydney for a week once every three or four months. It was heaven to sleep in a real bed, eat real food, and just get away from it all for a few days.

"Hey, my date tonight has a girlfriend; you want to double-date this evening?" I asked Bong one morning.

"No . . . no, I don't think so," he replied.

"She's real cute," I added.

He grinned. He was handsome, with a fresh face and a sort of pug nose that made him look like a little boy when he smiled. "Thanks, Kirk, but I'm going over to the RAAF [Royal Australian Air Force] base and they're going to let me fly a Boomerang." That was a single-engine Australian-built fighter.

I knew he had a girlfriend back home, so it didn't surprise me that he declined my invitation. But I couldn't believe that he was really going to go out and fly while on R and R. He did, though, while the rest of us chased Aussie girls and got somewhat disorderly on Aussie schnapps.

I finally had to conclude that Dick Bong was an enigma. A Dr. Jekyll and Mr. Hyde, so to speak. On the ground, away from a flying machine, he was indeed a modest person, with an almost shy personality. He never swore, hardly smoked, and never touched alcohol. But in the air he transformed into a fearless, wildly aggressive combatant, who pursued and attacked his opponent with all the skill and deadly force at his command. It was as though once he climbed into the cockpit of a P-38 fighter, he became another person, eager and determined to accomplish his mission of destroying the enemy. And, though he denied it, claiming that he lacked gunnery skills, he was a deadly shot. Usually he would close to very short range before firing. But I saw him flame a Zero one day with a deflection shot (described in Chapter 1, "To Shoot Down a Zero") from a good 500 yards.

Of course, one of the great advantages of the P-38 in aerial combat was that the guns were mounted in the forward section of the pilot's gondola instead of out in the wings, as they were in single-engine fighters. Because of that, it was as though you were looking right down the gun barrel and didn't have to worry about convergence. This feature provided better control for both long- and short-range shooting.

Dick Bong took full advantage of that awesome firepower in his P-38. He was a master at closing on his enemy and firing at the proper time. I overheard him once tell some visiting dignitary that he'd learned to shoot birds on the fly when he'd been a boy on the farm in Wisconsin. He said simply that he guessed that had helped.

After he'd got his twenty-seventh victory, breaking Eddie Rickenbacker's record in World War I, he was sent back to the States on a war-bond-selling tour and other public-relations duties for a while. But he didn't like that sort of thing and finally wangled his way back to the Pacific and the Fifth Air Force as a "non-combatant advanced gunnery instructor." That was kind of a joke, because in short order, he was back flying combat.

He would sneak over to our squadron and fly with us every once in a while, particularly when he knew we were going on a mission where there might be some action. Often he and Gerald Johnson, Tommy McGuire (both leading aces, with McGuire the second-highest-scoring American pilot of World War II), and one of the other aces would go out as a four-ship destruction team looking for a fight. It was a good way of solving the wingman problem, since they were very aggressive fighter pilots, but certainly worlds apart in their personalities.

Both McGuire and Johnson were pretty extroverted and wouldn't hesitate to talk about their victories with a war correspondent. Dick Bong, on the other hand, would disappear if he got the chance. I remember vividly being struck by the remarkable contrast between the three of them one day, when we were flying off Biak Island in late 1944. They were standing together talking in the revetment area after a mission. The official photographers and the correspondents were interviewing and taking pictures. Both Tommy and Gerald were fidgeting and scratching themselves and speaking in rapid, nervous voices, while Bong was leaning against the airplane as relaxed as if he had been on vacation, even though he'd just blasted another Zero out of the sky.

The last time I flew with the ace was during the Philippine campaign in late October 1944. We were the first Army Air Forces squadron to land fighters at Tacloban airstrip on Leyte, where Gen. Douglas MacArthur stepped ashore on his historic return to the Philippines. Dick Bong was with us there too.

We were tent mates there for a while, and I realized that despite all the glory and publicity, he had not changed a bit. He was still as modest and low key as before, yet as deadly in the air as always. As a "gunnery instructor," he added twelve more victories to his score. But when he hit forty on 17 December 1944, Gen. Henry "Hap" Arnold, chief of the Army Air Forces, grounded him and Gen. Douglas MacArthur presented him with the Congressional Medal of Honor.

I never saw him again after that. But I heard that he went home, married his sweetheart, Marge, and was killed a few months later, when the engine of a new P-80 jet fighter he was testing failed on takeoff. It was hard to believe that after 146 combat missions and more than 400 combat hours without a scratch (his P-38 did get shot up on occasion, however), he was killed right there in the States, with no one even shooting at him.

I told a modified version of this same story that day in 1995, at the seafood cookout in Virginia. After I'd finished, no one said anything for a moment. Then the young chef said, "That was a fascinating story, particularly when you stop to realize that kind of aerial combat will never occur again. But you know, I always thought those World War II fighter aces were pretty wild, heavy-drinking, extroverted guys."

"Yeah, me too, like in *Baa Baa Black Sheep*," added someone else.

"Well, a lot of them were," I admitted. "But I know one who wasn't: Richard Bong, America's ace of aces."

The Richard I. Bong World War II Heritage Center [www.bongheritagecenter.org] opened on 24 September 2002, at Superior, Wisconsin. The Heritage center honors all World War II participants in the name of Richard Bong, America's Ace of Aces and recipient of the Congressional Medal of Honor. The center houses World War II memorabilia, records, and a beautifully restored Lockheed P-38.

CHAPTER FIVE

R and R

Dressed in his U.S. Army Air Corps class-A uniform, with a swath of decorations and silver wings on his tunic, Capt. Gerald Johnson took a sip of his drink and frowned. "It's damn good scotch, but it needs ice."

"It's a hell of a lot better than that schnapps shit we're used to drinking, with or without ice," replied his companion, 1st Lt. John McLean, similarly dressed and standing next to the captain.

"That's the truth. And I ain't complaining. But it just seems criminal not to have ice with such good scotch."

"Somebody told me the Aussies like their drinks at room temperature," said McLean.

"Well, I'm not looking the gift horse in the mouth, there's a war going on you know," said Johnson with a grin.

"Yeah, that's what I hear," replied McLean, returning the smile.

Johnson took another drink and glanced around at the groups of people holding cocktail glasses and standing in clusters on a flower-shrouded patio. About half wore military uniforms of some type, and the other guests were well-dressed Australian civilians. Off one end of the patio was a sparkling swimming pool, with a beautifully manicured rose garden just beyond.

"From the looks of this place and the company, I'd say we're in top-drawer country here, John. How did you get us an invite?"

"Hey Captain, this is top drawer. The host is a big businessman here in Sydney, and he has only select guests at his parties."

"So what are we doing here?"

"A couple reasons," replied the lieutenant, as he surveyed the surroundings. "My Aussie friend that got us invited says these folks want to promote good Allied relations, and they like Americans. But what got my attention is that he tells me they always have good-looking, patriotic female guests."

Johnson glanced at his friend and smiled. "Patriotic female guests, huh?"

McLean bobbed his eyebrows and nodded. "Yeah, and I hope they have the same understanding of patriotism as I do, 'cause with only a week of R and R, I don't have time to indoctrinate 'em."

Johnson laughed. "Well, I'm happy just to be out of the friggin' jungle for a few days, wearing a clean uniform and drinking some good scotch, even without ice."

"Yeah, I hear you, but I . . . uh oh. Things just picked up. Look at those two lovelies that just walked in."

Johnson glanced in the direction McLean was looking and saw two young women emerge from the main house through French doors, then walk onto the patio. Both were attractive and wore bright spring dresses with matching wide-brimmed hats.

"Captain, I can sure see the shape of patriotism on that cute little blonde in the pink dress. Come on, let's go and give them an opportunity to be patriotic."

Johnson hesitated. "You go ahead, John. I'll just hang here and give you top cover."

"Aw, come on Captain, I need you on my wing for close cover. It won't do no harm to just talk to 'em; you know it's our duty also to improve Allied relations, right?"

Johnson grinned. "Yeah, I guess it is."

"Sure, come on," replied McLean, as he started across the patio on an intercept course with the girls, who had stopped at the hors d'oeuvres table.

When the two American pilots appeared beside the girls, the one in the pink dress smiled warmly. The one in the yellow dress gave them a look they could have used for ice in their room-temperature drinks. McLean turned on a big smile and said, "Good afternoon, ladies. In the interest of better Allied relations, may we introduce ourselves? I'm Lt. John McLean, and my fellow warrior is Capt. Gerald Johnson."

"I think Allied relations would be better served, Lieutenant, if you and the captain just buzz on off," snapped the girl in the yellow dress.

The smile on the girl in the pink dress faded, as she glanced nervously at her companion. The lieutenant held his smile. "Now that's not a very hospitable way to greet defenders of your sacred soil, is it?"

The girl's eyes narrowed for a moment, as she stared at the American pilot. "There are serious doubts in my mind if you Yanks are defending anything but your own selfish interests," she said in a low, cold voice.

"Uh, excuse me?" Johnson spoke up. "I can assure you, Miss, that my interest at this moment is being here and enjoying the hospitality of our host without having Japs trying to kill me, as they have in the stinking jungles of New Guinea for the past six months. Is that what you mean by selfish interests?"

The girl stood silent for a moment, staring at Johnson with a pair of the most beautiful blue eyes he had ever seen. She was petite and shapely, with light brown hair that fell in soft waves from under her yellow hat. Her lips were swollen red, and her nose turned up slightly, giving her a childlike, innocent look. But there were sparks in those blue eyes, and distrust on that innocent face.

Capt. Gerald Johnson was a handsome American. He was slender but well built, with fine facial features, brown eyes and hair, and a warm smile, which he suddenly switched on. "Tell you what: I think it's in all of our best interests right now to get acquainted, don't you, Miss . . ."

"Oh, I think that's a good idea!" blurted the girl in the pink dress. "I'm Pearl Ransome and this is Christine Manning."

All eyes turned to Pearl Ransome. She was taller than Christine, but also shapely, with blond hair and green eyes. She smiled brightly as McLean offered his hand, saying, "I think it's a great idea too. It's a pleasure to meet you, Pearl."

John McLean was taller than Gerald Johnson, but with the same dark brown eyes and hair, and an ingratiating smile that blossomed as he held Pearl's hand and said, "We're fighter pilots down here on R and R from New Guinea."

"Oh, you're fighter pilots?" echoed Pearl.

"Yeah. And Captain Johnson is an ace," informed John, peeking at Christine to see if she was impressed.

"He is? Gee, I've never met an ace before. That means you destroyed five enemy planes, doesn't it?" asked Pearl, also watching Christine.

"That's right. Captain Johnson is our squadron commander, and he's shot down nine planes," added McLean.

"Theirs or ours?" asked Christine Manning, sarcastically.

Shocked faces stared at Christine, including that of the ace. Gerald Johnson was the epitome of a classic World War II fighter ace. He was quick thinking, fearless, and highly aggressive, with an abundance of confidence in himself and his capabilities, and he rarely found himself flustered or confused. But suddenly he was, and a stricken look replaced the confident smile on his face.

The girl's implied accusation that he'd shot down "our" aircraft had touched a sensitive chord in the ace, a chord that revived a memory he preferred to forget. He had told himself that it was not a guilty conscience, because it hadn't been his fault that he'd shot down an Allied plane. It had been a mistake anyone could have made.

He'd been leading a flight of P-38 fighters that day on a routine fighter patrol between Lae and Finshafen, along the northeast coast of New Guinea. As he approached the area, he gave the usual hand signal to the other fighters to arm and test-fire their guns.

This also meant to sharpen their watch for enemy aircraft, since there had been reports of sightings in the area.

A few minutes later he spotted an unidentified aircraft in the distance. He watched it for a moment before determining from its silhouette that it was a single-engine aircraft of the Zero type, which meant it was Japanese. "All Captive flights, this is Captive leader, we have a bogey at twelve o'clock low," he advised. He turned on his gunsight and winged over in a diving attack on the lower-flying aircraft.

Johnson could tell that the enemy pilot did not see the P-38 diving on him. When the bogey filled his gunsight, he squeezed the firing button, and his four .50-caliber machine guns and a 20-mm cannon roared. The enemy aircraft lurched in a frantic attempt to escape, but the P-38's deadly fire had struck its mark. A stream of smoke erupted from within the body of the plane, as pieces of its structure spewed in all directions. Then, suddenly, the blue-and-white insignia of the Australian Air Force flashed clearly before Johnson's eyes as the stricken aircraft rolled over and began its death plunge into the New Guinean jungle, far below.

It had upset Gerald Johnson badly to have shot down a fellow Allied fighter pilot. But the Australian Whirraway reconnaissance aircraft not only looked like a Japanese Zero, it had been flying in an area where intelligence had reported only enemy aircraft. It was a mistake anyone could have made, anyone. So forget it, he'd told himself. Forget it and get on with what had to be done in a war: destroying the enemy.

But now, as he stared into the accusing eyes of the girl in the yellow hat, it all flashed back in a vivid picture. A picture he'd tried to forget, only to have it revived by this little snip of a girl, a girl who knew nothing. Nothing at all about what it was to lay your neck on the line day after day in deadly aerial combat.

As Christine Manning watched the smile on the American captain dissolve and a strange look cross his face, she realized that she had upset him. It was written on his face like a neon sign, and it pleased her. But it also surprised her. It was a reaction she hadn't expected. Obviously she had touched a sensitive nerve in the Yank. She wasn't sure why, but as long as it upset him, she liked it. She hated all Yanks intensely and would have nothing to do with any of them, particularly fighter pilots. But suddenly she was intrigued, and curious to know just what discord she had struck in this arrogant American.

"Well, Captain Johnson, has the cat got your tongue?" she asked disdainfully.

He looked at her intently for a moment. Finally, composing himself, he nodded and said, "Yeah, I guess you could say that. And what about you, Miss Manning? What is your problem?"

"Problem? I wasn't aware I had a problem, Captain."

"You do."

"Really?"

"Yeah, really," he said, taking a big gulp of his drink.

John and Pearl, who had been watching the exchange, glanced at each other and followed suit with their drinks.

Christine Manning held her cocktail glass up as though examining it in the sunlight and said, "Since you're so clairvoyant, Captain Johnson, why don't you enlighten me about my problem?"

"It would be my pleasure, but not in the best interest of Allied relations," he replied.

"Since this relationship is going nowhere in any event, Captain, be my guest."

"Uh . . . they have a beautiful rose garden here, why don't we all walk over and look at it," suggested Pearl Ransome nervously.

"Hey that's a great idea," agreed John.

The two couples exchanged glances.

"There's a beautiful rose right here, but it needs a little dethorning," said Johnson, as a smile eased its way back across his handsome face.

Christine glanced at Pearl and said, "I'm sure a walk in the rose garden would be more enjoyable than witnessing a messy dethorning process, so why don't you two go ahead?"

"Oh . . . uh, yeah. Okay," said John, quickly taking Pearl by the arm and leading her off toward the rose garden.

The captain and the girl in the yellow dress took sips of their drinks and eyed each other silently.

"Are you discriminating, Christine, or do you dislike all Americans?"

"No discrimination; I dislike all of you."

He shrugged. "Well, that's some consolation. Any particular reason?"

"Yes."

Hesitation.

"Care to discuss it?"

Another hesitation.

"No."

He set his cocktail glass on the hors d'oeuvres

table, dug a pack of cigarettes from his blouse pocket, and held it out to her. She shook her head. He lit one and put the pack back in his pocket.

"The condemned should at least know of what he is accused."

"I can't see that it would make any difference, in this case. Furthermore, it's a personal matter."

"Well, this has become a personal matter, hasn't it?"

She looked at him curiously. "There certainly isn't going to be anything personal between us, so why do you say that?"

He took a deep pull on his cigarette and let the smoke roll out slowly. "Because I'm personally offended by your ungrateful attitude and your unjust accusation that all Americans who are over here risking their lives to defend your country are doing so for selfish reasons."

"You can save that rhetoric for your exaggerated press releases. It doesn't cut any ice with me," she snapped.

He grinned and glanced at his drink. "Yes, well, speaking of ice, it's evident that among other things, we have a basic disagreement on what should be hot and what should be cold."

"Yes, and that is a perfect example of how you Yanks are: it has to be steaming hot or ice cold, no moderation in anything."

"Well, you're right about that. We do like our drinks cold and our women hot. Down here . . . uh, I guess I should say down under, it's hot drinks and cold women."

Her blue eyes narrowed. "The problem with you Americans is that you are all—"

"Oversexed, overpaid, and over here?" he interrupted.

"You said it, I didn't."

He laughed. She couldn't help a little grin and said, "You really are an overindulgent lot, you know."

He nodded. "I suppose from your standpoint, we appear that way. But I really don't think you should judge us all by the actions of a few, or one, or whatever it was that soured you on us."

"That may be, but so far I've not met an American who has changed my opinion one iota."

He watched her a moment and said, "As long as we're being brutally frank, and since you have decreed this relationship is destined for nowhere, why not get it off your chest?"

She looked up and their eyes met and held. "My brother was shot down and killed by an American fighter pilot."

Christine's words struck Gerald Johnson like an exploding bomb. He could feel the emotion race through his body and the flush burn his face as he stood staring at her incredulously. The only thought he could formulate was that it must be a mistake. Perhaps he'd misunderstood. Yes. It couldn't possibly be the same one, the same Australian pilot that . . . it couldn't be. He'd heard wrong, that was all. It had to be. "Your brother . . . was shot down by an American?"

"Yes."

God! It was! It was the same one! Of all the girls in the world, it would have to be her, the sister of the Australian pilot he'd shot down. Jesus! And as he stood staring at her, the banished image came crashing back for the second time in the few minutes he'd known her: the aircraft before his blazing guns, rolling over in its death plunge and branding the Australian insignia into his brain forever. He raised his glass of scotch and drank every last drop.

The girl in the yellow dress was surprised to see the same distressed reaction on the American pilot's face that she'd seen earlier, only now it was more acute. She was pleased at his discomfort, of course. Yet she couldn't suppress a touch of sympathy. Why she felt any sympathy for him was a mystery . . . or was it?

No, not really. It wasn't a mystery. Christine knew why. She'd known from the first moment she'd met him and her pulse had leaped. She could not deny to herself that she was emotionally attracted to the handsome Yank pilot. But she'd sworn she would hate Americans to her dying day for what they had done. She must remember that, and she must keep things in perspective, even if he did stir an excitement within that made it difficult. But she must not forget who he was: a typical arrogant American, using the war as a vehicle for personal glorification . . . wasn't he?

"I . . . I'm sorry . . . about your brother. Those things happen in a war," he finally muttered in a low, hoarse voice.

"Those were the same hollow words the American authorities used in explaining my brother's death."

"They may sound like hollow words, Christine, but it is one of the unfortunate realities of war. Sometimes the color of a man's uniform or the insignia on his fighting machine is lost in the killing process."

It was another typical Yank rationalization that initially offended her. But as his words settled in her brain, she was struck with a feeling of uncertainty.

For the first time since her brother's death, she wondered if there could be some truth in what the American pilot was saying. Probably not, though. Probably just more of the same. "Isn't that simply more standard rhetoric in the justification process, Captain?"

"No, I . . . I hope not."

"No? Is that based on your impression of these things, or do you have personal experience to call upon?"

"Yes."

Hesitation.

"Yes what?"

"Personal experience."

They stood staring at each other, both with burgeoning emotions racing through their minds and bodies. Christine raised her cocktail glass and took a drink. He did the same, but since it was already drained, he got only a drop. He set the glass down on the table and dug out another cigarette. She watched curiously as he fired the cigarette and exhaled a column of smoke.

"Are you going to tell me about it?" she finally asked, prompted by her own gnawing uncertainty as well as a strange curiosity.

"No, it won't solve or prove anything, so it's probably better left alone."

She hesitated. "I have no way of being sure, but I have the feeling that it might, indeed, prove something. At least for you, Captain. You may as well take your own advice and get it off your chest."

As the American fighter pilot stared at the pretty Australian girl, contemplating the terrible truth of what she'd asked him to explain, he was suddenly, agonizingly aware that an emotional attraction had exploded between him and Christine Manning. Despite the bristling conflict, there was electrified chemistry. But it was chemistry that could never be, because of the bizarre twist of fate that stood between them.

"I'm the American pilot who shot down your brother in New Guinea," said the captain hoarsely.

For a moment Christine stared at him in shock, her eyes huge and disbelieving. Then a strange, sad look crossed her face and she almost whispered, "I'm sorry, Gerald, terribly sorry. What a cruel trick fate has played on us."

Gerald Johnson looked at Christine Manning, also with wide, disbelieving eyes. Her reaction was so removed from what he had expected that he was speechless. "I . . . I don't understand, Christine."

"I know now with certainty that what you said earlier was true, Gerald. The horror of war and killing knows no bounds. I know also that you have suffered deeply over the tragedy of your accident, haven't you?"

All the ace fighter pilot could do was nod.

She reached across and took one of his hands in hers and held it tightly. "I'm sorry for all that I said. I . . . I simply didn't know or understand the truth, until now."

"But Christine, your brother . . ."

"He was killed by an American, all right, but it wasn't you, Gerald. My brother was in the Royal Air Force and was shot down in North Africa."

For a long moment they stared into each other's eyes. Then, as though it was the most natural thing in the world to do, they came into each other's arms.

And they stood there for long moments together, sharing their emotions and the tragedy of war.

John McLean and I were tent mates in New Guinea for a while, and one night he told me this story. Everyone in the squadron knew that Gerald Johnson had shot down the Australian Whirraway, but only John knew about his strange meeting with Christine. From what John told me, the tragedy between them was too deep, and they never saw each other again after that day in Sydney. Gerald went on to become one of the top aces of World War II, destroying twenty-two enemy aircraft. Both he and John McLean were subsequently killed. Ironically, the Australian pilot that Gerald shot down in New Guinea, Flight Officer R. M. Stewart, had actually survived.

CHAPTER SIX

Out of the Cockpit

That line in the Air Force song, "We live in fame or go down in flame," was more than pure romanticism for fighter pilots in combat during World War II. We got a lot of media attention all right, and the hot aces were hometown heroes and, in some cases, even national heroes. But we faced the enemy, in one form or another, every time we flew. My squadron lost nearly a quarter of our pilots in the Southwest Pacific, compared to the U.S armed forces, who lost only about 3 percent of their troops in all of World War II.

But just being there was almost as challenging as the actual combat flying. Everyone was affected by the separation from loved ones, the terrible living conditions, the stress, the climate. We all faced that test, no matter what our role in the war machine.

The general perception of the South Pacific is of aqua blue waters, gentle breezes, and swaying palm trees. There are islands out there like that. But not where MacArthur's Fifth Air Force trekked from one miserable jungle base to another, through New

Guinea and the East Indies. I think our military leaders did as well as they could to provide for our welfare, considering the obstacles and conditions. But it was indeed a struggle for all of us.

How the pilots of my fighter squadron behaved and survived out of the cockpit during that long trek involves some interesting and amusing stories that I think are worthy of telling for both posterity and reader enjoyment.

My squadron, the Flying Knights, was the top Army Air Force fighter squadron, with the top ace, Dick Bong, in the Pacific. But I doubt our behavior out of the cockpit was any different from any other squadron's. Of course, some of us did better than others, and those who applied a little imagination and Yankee ingenuity did the best.

I felt sorry for those who never quite got the picture. They suffered the most because they fought it every step of the way, and as a result for them the heat got hotter; the food got worse; the bugs, flies, mosquitoes, snakes, and disease got more unbearable; and the days got longer and longer.

The trick being that when you were out of the cockpit, you had to get your mind on some kind of other activity or interest. That muted the adversities, and made the time go faster.

For the most part it had to be an individual effort. But I will say the Army did a lot to help. They published a newspaper, brought in USO shows, and distributed movies to all the combat units, wherever they were. The screen was put up on a couple of poles right there in the camp and when it got dark the movie started. We would check around and see which outfit had the best movie or one we hadn't already seen, and go to it, either walking or by jeep. Sometimes the movie would be interrupted by an air raid, but when that was over, the show would be on again.

My favorite night at an outdoor movie occurred when we were on Biak Island in the Dutch East Indies. When our ground forces took the island some of the Japanese soldiers holed up in the caves above our camp. The brass decided it wasn't worth trying to get them out, so we just let them stay up there and starve. After a while they started sneaking out at night and stealing food.

Then one night the World War II movie *Objective, Burma!* with Errol Flynn, was shown. After the movie, one of the guys said, "Ya know, I'll swear there was a fuckin' Jap sitting beside me at the movie tonight."

"What makes you say that?" someone asked.

"Well, I couldn't see him there in the dark, but every time Flynn would shoot a Jap this guy would say, 'Sclew you, Ellor Frenn! Sclew you, Ellor Frenn!' "

We never actually caught any Japanese soldiers watching our movies at night, but I heard stories of such. It's funny to imagine a Japanese soldier sitting there in the dark watching our movies. I guess they, too, needed some outside activity after hiding in a cave all day.

The Army had a radio station that kept us up to date on the news and played music. They would also tune in Tokyo Rose every now and then, and we would lie in our sacks in the tent and listen to her program. She spoke perfect English and had a very pleasant voice. I know she was part of the Japanese psychological warfare effort, but I don't think the Japanese quite understood Americans because to us her broadcasts were funny. And our brass apparently figured it that way, too, or they wouldn't have played her program.

I guess the Japanese gurus thought she could really upset us when she turned on this sexy voice and told us that our girlfriends and wives were back home in bed with 4-Fs [men physically unfit for military duty], while we were out there dying for no reason. To us it was almost as funny as Jack Benny and Rochester. We would just howl.

But she did come up with some stuff on occasion that surprised us. Once her pitch went something like this: "I'm so sorry, Lieutenant Smith, that you received a Dear John letter from your fiancée, Jane. But that is to be expected when you go off and leave her to be exploited by USO commandos and 4-Fs."

We were surprised in this case because what she said was true. The pilot wasn't in our squadron but we'd heard about his Dear John. So even though we still thought she was a gas and knew that her pitch was bullshit, once in a while she came up with something unexpected.

What we liked best was her great music. She played all the latest Glenn Miller, Benny Goodman, and Tommy Dorsey music.

After the war, I found out that there were a number of English-speaking Japanese women who did Tokyo Rose broadcasts. The woman prosecuted by the U.S. Justice Department for treason was Iva Toguri D'Aquino. She was an American of Japanese descent who was in Japan on a visit when the war broke out. She was taken prisoner and apparently forced to make broadcasts. Historians now agree that her term of six years in prison was a miscarriage of justice. She was eventually exonerated and pardoned by President Gerald Ford in 1977.

In those days we got paid once a month in cash. Everybody lined up in front of the paymaster; he called out a name and counted out the cash. The big activities right after payday were poker and crap games. They generally lasted three or four days until one or two guys had won all the money. I never did very well, but it was always good for a couple days of diversion.

One miserably hot payday we carried our home-made table and chairs out onto the coral reef in front of our tent to play poker. Our camp was right in the landing pattern of the B-25 bombers and a group of them were coming in after a mission, so it was noisy.

Suddenly one of the planes made a strange sound. We glanced up. The B-25 was upside down within a stone's throw of our game. It happened so quickly that we had no opportunity to run. We watched, almost hypnotized, as a body came flying out of the waist window of the inverted bomber and bounced off one of our tents as if he were on a trampoline. An instant later the aircraft slammed into the coral and disintegrated in a huge ball of fire, spewing flaming pieces in all directions. One of the engines rolled up to within a few feet of where we sat.

We heard later that the crewman who bounced off the tent wasn't even scratched. The rest of the crew were killed.

After that, I gave up poker as a noncombat activity.

The army furnished the basics, but to get anything beyond that, you had to barter, and the medium of barter was booze. Liquor was like gold, primarily because the poor ground troops had no way to get it, so they would trade for whatever you wanted. Their advantage was that their supply sergeants had access to the incoming Liberty ships that brought all the supplies. Our advantage was that we went on R and R to Australia, where we could get booze.

The currency of barter in Australia was cigarettes, and we got all we wanted for free, so we traded cigarettes for booze. It might surprise you to hear that the U.S. government bought millions of cartons of cigarettes during World War II and gave them to the combat troops. I'm not criticizing, mind you. Everybody smoked. It was an important crutch in those days. And besides, that was before we knew that cigarettes are on a par with an overdose of radioactivity.

Anyway, it was a big game to get stuff to spruce up our camp and make our lives a little more tolerable. We even had an airplane in the squadron dedicated to "Fat Cat" runs. That meant going wherever we needed to go to get supplies, food, parts for our fighters, and booze.

Our Fat Cat was a Martin "Marauder" B-26 bomber. It landed at our fighter base one day badly shot up from a mission. The crew went off and left it, so we repaired the battle damage and, by the law of possession, claimed ownership. Fortunately one of our pilots had flown the B-26, so we made him our official Fat Cat pilot. I got to fly the Martin Marauder once. It was a hot airplane and fast enough to fly combat missions without fighter escort. It was also fast enough to make a Fat Cat run to Australia and back in nothing flat.

On Biak Island we built a squadron mess hall out on the coral reef with lumber we had traded for. We even built a little wooden bridge going out there, and it seemed to make the awful food taste a little better. The problem was they posted the flight schedule there at dinnertime for the following day's mission. That negated the effect of our beachfront ambiance.

I decided to counter that with something the pilots would enjoy, so I started drawing a comic strip and posted each day's episode beside the flight schedule. The guys loved it and wouldn't let me in the mess hall unless I had the next installment. It was called *Speed Flynn* and was about a hotshot fighter pilot who slew the Japs as well as the women. At the end of each episode he was always in deep trouble, of course, as he battled Zeros and a beautiful Japanese female pilot.

It was one of the things that helped in the battle for survival, and I kept myself occupied in creating and drawing the strip. I managed to save all the episodes and still have them in a special book in my den.

One of the pilots in my tent when we were on Biak Island was transferred out, and his replacement was 2nd Lieutenant Henry Frank. Hank, we called him, was from San Francisco and was a sailing enthusiast. He convinced me that we could build a sailboat and have a lot of fun sailing during our out-of-cockpit time.

It was a tall order, but we managed through some shrewd bartering to get what we needed to build the boat. After a couple of weeks of hard work, it was ready. We christened it *Lacka Nuki,* and the whole camp came out to see the launching. Admittedly, the boat was a bit crude, but the sail was made of a red-and-white parachute silk and really looked great as the wind caught it and carried us out on the blue waters of the Bismarck Archipelago.

Not being a sailor, I'm not sure exactly what happened then, but something went wrong. We floundered and went down like the *Titanic*. Fortunately we weren't in the North Atlantic and were able to swim ashore amid the laughter and razzing from our squadron buddies.

Hank wasn't discouraged and talked me into starting another boat. We got the framework for the *Lacka Nuki II* finished, but then Hank was shot down and killed. That took all the wind out of my sails.

After a while I bounced back with a new project. I bought a used phonograph at a secondhand store when I was on R and R in Sydney, Australia. It played those old Bakelite records and had to be wound up by hand. But it sounded great, and it was tabletop size so we could take it out into the slit trench with us during an air raid. Sometimes we would be there for hours, so we would sit and play records.

I was only able to buy a couple of records but I got my mother to send me more. Although some were broken in shipment, I finally had enough to last through most air raids. Then one night a bomb dropped close to us, and in the scramble most of the records were broken, as was the main spring of the Victrola. We tried but there was just no way to fix it.

I gave it to one of the pilots, and he learned to rotate the turntable with his finger at exactly the right speed to play a record. We had only salvaged two records: "Alloette and His Colored Baloo," and "The Boogie Woogie Bugle Boy of Company B." The words and melody of those two songs will be etched in my memory forever.

The Flying Knights squadron was an advance air unit. As soon as the infantry or the Marines captured another enemy base on MacArthur's agenda and the Corps of Engineers cleared the runways, we were the first fighters to land and set up combat operations to maintain air superiority. That meant that our campsite was usually in the stinking, smoldering remains of a Japanese camp. It also meant we didn't get to see many USO shows, though they did come to the Southwest Pacific area and did a great job entertaining the troops.

Our worst camp was in the jungle at Dobodura, New Guinea. It was so humid that your shoes turned green overnight and you had to kick the snakes out of your bed before you crawled in. But we did build an O Club there and it was screened-in, which kept out most of the mosquitoes and other flying predators that came out at night in armadas. We decorated the club with some parachutes and other stuff we bartered for. It was nice to have someplace to go other than your one-quarter share of a GI pyramidal tent.

Dobodura was the only place I got to see a USO show. After the show, the celebrities came to our little club to visit and say hello to Dick Bong, since he was America's leading ace. It was a really big deal for all of us, particularly for a country boy like me, to shake hands with Gary Cooper and Joe E. Brown.

New Guinea is almost 1,500 miles long and has 16,000-foot mountains in the interior. There are more than 600 different tribes of natives who live in separate villages and speak different dialects. It's a unique land with huge rain forests and some of the world's densest jungle. At the time of World War II it also had tribes of cannibals and headhunters.

When we moved from Dobodura into the Ramu

Valley in the interior of New Guinea, my buddy Lt. Bernie Krankowitz and I decided one day we would go on a sightseeing trip. We wanted to see the local landscape and maybe some of the native headhunter culture. We strapped on our .45s, took our cameras, and drove off down one of the dirt roads in a jeep.

The road meandered across the Ramu Valley, which lay between two mountain ranges. We kept looking for a native village so we could take some pictures but couldn't seem to find any. After a while the road ended and we were just following what was probably an animal trail. We stopped a few times and took pictures of some large birds and a small animal that looked like raccoon, but we didn't see any natives or native villages.

When the trail came to a river we did see some crocodiles that quickly jumped into the muddy river and disappeared before we could take a photograph.

We decided it was time to head back to camp, but as we drove back along the trail it didn't look familiar. Pretty soon the trail branched. We flipped a coin to determine which branch to take, but shortly we realized the branch we chose was going in the wrong direction.

That concerned us, but we still weren't too worried because all we had to do was find a path that led back across the valley where we could intersect the road to our camp. That didn't turn out to be as simple as it sounded. We couldn't seem to find any road that went in the direction we wanted to go. In fact, even the animal trail had now disappeared and we were driving through a sea of kuni grass.

I don't think kuni grass has any nutritional value, but the natives used it for everything else, particularly construction. It was extremely prolific and grew wild across the valleys of New Guinea. As we drove, the grass got higher and higher until it was taller than the top of the jeep. We couldn't see ahead and had no idea where we were. The sun had already dipped below the mountains so it would soon be dark.

About that time the jeep began to slowly lose speed, even though I had the accelerator on the floor.

"What's wrong?" Bernie asked as we ground to an abrupt halt and the engine stopped.

"I don't know," I replied, as I put the gearshift in neutral and hit the starter. The engine started back up and I breathed a sigh of relief. But when I put it back in gear and let the clutch out, it wouldn't budge and the engine quit again.

"I think we're in trouble," I said. I climbed out and looked under the jeep. The drive shaft was packed with kuni grass so tightly it couldn't turn.

We took turns crawling under the jeep and cutting the grass away with our sheath knives. By the time we finished it was nearly dark and the mosquitoes were beginning their attack.

"You got any idea which way to go?" I asked, wiping the perspiration out of my eyes and slapping mosquitoes.

"Not the slightest," he admitted.

"Jesus. We fly hundreds of miles on missions and find our way home. Here we are, only a few miles from home, and we're lost."

"Yeah, but there ain't no kuni grass up there."

Before we could get in the jeep, the kuni grass parted and there stood a group of New Guinea headhunters ready for the slaughter.

Instinctively we both grabbed our .45s.

The headhunters stood there eyeing us. They didn't look all that ferocious, but there was no question in our minds that they were dangerous savages.

"Don't shoot unless they attack," I warned Krankowitz, in the style of Frank Buck [famous big-game hunter of the time].

"If they make one false move I'm firing," he replied. Also in Frank Buck style.

Two of the headhunters suddenly started jabbering, probably discussing their attack plan.

"Somebody told me they like our cigarettes. Should we give them some?" asked Bernie, holding his .45 in firing position.

"Well, one spark in this grass and we all go up like the *Hindenburg*," I reasoned.

"Good point."

"Let's just get in the jeep and get the hell out of here," I suggested.

"Good idea."

"Move slowly, so we don't spook 'em," I cautioned.

The jabbering between the headhunters continued as they waved their arms and discussed their plan of attack.

I hit the starter and the jeep roared to life.

They stopped jabbering and looked at us.

I put the jeep in gear and we roared out through the kuni grass.

The headhunters watched with a look on their faces that said: Where do you suppose those dudes are going now?

We held on as the jeep bounced along, going as fast as it would go. I kept the accelerator on the floor for about ten minutes, until we suddenly popped out of the kuni grass and onto the main road. I slammed on the brakes and stopped. Bernie and I looked at each other and burst out laughing.

"Ya know what? We forgot to take pictures of the headhunters," I said.

"Yeah, and I hope I'm on the flight schedule tomorrow. I've had enough of this culture stuff."

We later found out that there were no headhunters in the Ramu Valley—or so the Aussies claimed. But there were plenty of them on up in the deep interior, as Dick Strommen related in his incredible story, "Escape from the Stone Age."

One of the major enemies we faced out of the cockpit was the mosquito, particularly in New Guinea, because they carried a number of dangerous diseases including malaria and dengue fever.

The Army lectured us on prevention, and gave us mosquito nets to sleep under and bug bombs to spray the insects. There were bowls of quinine and Atabrine [anti-fever pills] on the mess table to make sure we didn't forget to take them every day. The pills couldn't keep you from catching the fever, but they would blunt the effects if you got it.

I took my pills faithfully, tucked my mosquito net in every night, and sprayed with the bug bomb. But one night I was restless and must have slept with my arm against the mosquito net. The next morning it was covered in bites. The following day I felt lethargic, so I went to our shower hut, thinking a shower might give me a shot of energy. While I was showering everything faded to black.

When I awakened I was drenched in perspiration and burning up. My head was spinning; my vision was out of focus and laced with swarms of black spots. I didn't have a clue as to where I was, but I could tell I was on a litter in some kind of rack and that someone was taking my blood pressure.

I didn't know that I had been taken by GI ambulance to a field evacuation center in the Ramu Valley. They had a large tent set up beside an airstrip. Inside the tent were rows of metal racks; the medics collected patients and put them in the racks to await air evacuation. There was no field hospital in the Ramu Valley. The air evacuation planes arrived periodically, depending on weather and enemy action.

The person taking my blood pressure wasn't talking, and that was all right with me because I didn't feel like talking either. I drifted off into the sea of spinning black spots again. I don't know how long it was before I was awakened by voices.

"Okay, how many patients have you got for me?"

"How many can you take?"

"All ambulatory?"

"Yeah. All these are."

"I can handle about a dozen."

"All right, I'll tag the ones I want you to take."

"Okay."

Some shuffling and more talk and some more shuffling.

"That's it?"

"No. I can take one more. What about this lieutenant?"

I could sense that whoever asked the question was standing next to me.

"Naw, don't mess with him. He ain't gonna make it anyway."

Those words went through me like 10,000 volts of

electricity. My eyes popped open and I blurted, "Hold the damn phone!"

Or something like that. I can't honestly say those were the exact words. I also don't know if that medic was serious, but it sounded to me like he was. It sure got my attention.

The guy laughed and said, "Well, maybe he will make it. Hey, Mac you got any oxygen on that bird?"

"Yeah, we got some."

"Okay, he'll need it. Hustle him aboard."

I vaguely remember the flight over the very high and rugged Owen Stanley Mountains to Port Moresby. One of the medics gave me oxygen from a hand-carried bottle because the Gooney Bird [C-47] that took us over didn't have any.

I had both malaria and dengue fever and was in the field hospital at Port Moresby for some time. That's where I met Dick Strommen. He had them both, too. He'd caught it up in the mountains when he was with the real headhunters. But we both recovered enough to go back to our squadrons and complete our combat tour.

I had recurring malaria for a number of years after the war, but I finally took a special cure the Army had developed and haven't had an attack since.

We did live in fame or go down in flame. But sometimes it seemed that combat was the easy part.

CHAPTER SEVEN

Return to the Philippines

In my fighter squadron in the Southwest Pacific, we were in awe of the effort and formality that the ETO [European theater of operations] put into their combat mission briefings. You may have seen it in World War II movies. Over there they had giant enclosed briefing rooms, huge lighted maps, and even a stage for the briefers.

Our own mission briefings were informal. The flight schedule was usually posted on a pole in the mess tent the night before the mission. The next day our squadron leader would tell us what the mission was and our intelligence officer said something about the kind of enemy action we could expect. All this took place in the mess tent, in front of the OPS tent, or even standing around in the revetment area next to our P-38s just before takeoff.

One evening the OPS officer tacked up the next day's flight schedule, but it had a postscript saying those sixteen pilots would be required to attend a special mandatory briefing in the mess hall after dinner. That was so unusual that we knew something big was going down.

That evening the cigarette smoke was like heavy flak in the mess hall, where we gathered waiting anxiously to hear what the major had to say.

"That's what I like to see, lots of eager faces," Major Jordan, our CO, said when he walked in, grinning.

"These are more like the faces of curiosity, Major," said one of the flight leaders.

"Yeah, what are we gonna do, boss? Dive-bomb Tokyo?" someone else asked.

"Well, not quite," the CO replied, firing a cigarette and putting one foot up on a bench. "We're goin' back to the Philippines."

"Back to the Philippines?" someone blurted incredulously.

"That's correct. This is a top-priority mission ordered by none other than the man himself."

"You mean the 'I shall return' man himself?"

"That's exactly who I mean."

The Japanese attacked Pearl Harbor on 7 December and the Philippine Islands on 8 December 1941. At that time, General Douglas MacArthur was the commander of all U.S. Army forces in the Far East. His forces in the Philippines, however, were no match for the Japanese and were pushed back to the Bataan Peninsula, where they were shortly overwhelmed.

President Franklin Roosevelt ordered MacArthur to be evacuated, and he was taken out at night by PT boat, then to Australia by air. At his first press conference in Australia, and many times thereafter, he proclaimed emotionally, "I shall return."

It took nearly two years after that vow before he had the matériel and the manpower to reverse the Japanese juggernaut that had gobbled up most of the

South Pacific and threatened Australia. Finally, his forces were poised to fulfill the general's claim that he would return to the Philippines. The rumors had been flying around our camp with a lot of speculation as to when the invasion would come. The betting was sometime late that year of 1944.

"Is this gonna be the invasion?" I asked Jordan.

"No. That's coming, all right, but not quite yet. This is a special preinvasion mission our squadron's been picked to fly. Now, I don't think there's any Japs sneaking around our camp trying to get information, but I want you guys to keep this under your hat anyway, okay?"

We all nodded, impressed. It was beginning to sound like a top-priority mission. We didn't get many of those. For the most part, our missions were just dogfighting with Zeros, protecting our bombers, strafing Japanese ships, and dive-bombing their facilities. But this was something else.

"General MacArthur wants to show the colors, so to speak. He wants to tell the thousands of prisoners of war the Japanese are holding on the Island of Mindanao, and the Philippine people, that we are coming back. And I'm sure he figures it will shake up the Jap generals a bit. We'll be the first American fighters to fly over the Philippines since they took the islands in early 1942."

"Sounds good, Major, but it's a long haul to the Philippines," said the OPS officer.

Jordan nodded. "I know. It's nearly a thousand miles out and a thousand back. But we're gonna stage off an island out there somewhere. We will fly from here to the island, refuel and go on to Mindanao, do our thing, then reverse the procedure."

"Do we have an island out there, with a landing strip?" someone asked.

"Our HQ leaders tell me there is . . . or there will be."

"Where?"

"They haven't said yet. The mission will be laid on sometime in the next couple days, so in the meantime, the squadron will stand down to get ready. Our ground crews will install long-range fuel tanks on our birds, which, of course, will be dropped if we tangle with Zeros. But on this mission we're not looking for a fight. The object is to get there and fly low over the prison camps so they can see us. We'll keep one flight up for top cover and the other three will do the showing. If we get jumped by Zeros then we fight, naturally. But remember, if you drop your tanks, you've only got enough internal fuel to fight for a few minutes. Then you gotta head for the island."

"How far will the flight be from the Philippines back to the island?"

"Headquarters tells me that by using Lindbergh's low RPM technique, we'll have enough internal fuel to make it, but that's about all. We'll have a B-25 with a navigator aboard to lead us because it's gonna be a long drag over water, and since P-38 pilots aren't very good at celestial navigation, I recommend you keep that Billy Mitchell in sight."

"Amen," someone said.

My squadron flew a lot of long-range missions over New Guinea and the Dutch East Indies, but we weren't used to long overwater flights where we were totally out of sight of land. Our only navigational device on the P-38 was a magnetic compass, which wasn't accurate enough for pinpoint navigation—particularly when you were trying to find a tiny island in the middle of the ocean.

The mission was scheduled a few days later, and on 2 September 1944, we took off from Biak Island at dawn. There were four flights of four, our usual squadron complement. Major Jordan led the squadron; I led Blue Flight. Our course was west along the equator, which ran across the northwest tip of New Guinea and over the Moluccas Islands. That part was easy because there were islands all over the place to use for visual navigation. All you had to do was know how to read a map.

Somewhere over the Moluccas we met up with the B-25, and after following him for another hour we landed at the staging island for refueling. I don't think that I ever knew the island's name or where it was. You know how it is when you're following someone: he knows where he's going but you don't. I remember that the island was tiny and had a short coral runway. I assumed from the war wreckage lying along the beach that it was a Japanese base that had been recently captured—or one that had been captured just for this mission.

We stretched our legs while our birds were refueled, then took off for the next leg of our flight, over the Philippine Sea with nothing in sight but water and more water. I marvel at how our Navy pilots did that throughout the war: flying out over all that water, then having to find their carrier again after the mission. Tough duty.

Finally the tree-lined shores of Mindanao Island

formed on the horizon. I could see that Mindanao was covered with a layer of cumulus clouds, which was bad news. It wouldn't do much good to show the colors if no one could see them.

As we got closer it was evident we were gonna have to fly under the overcast if we were ever going to find the prison camps. Major Jordan had given us a briefing on what to look for, but that had been based on having enough altitude to see the landscape so we could identify landmarks.

"All Captive flights, this is Red leader," Jordan transmitted, breaking radio silence.

The three other flight leaders responded.

"The weather doesn't look good," Jordan said, "but we're gonna give it a try. Green and Blue Flight, follow me down; we'll go under the overcast. Yellow Flight, get on top of the overcast and if you spot bogeys sound off. . . . Escort One, you read?" [Escort One was the B-25 navigation ship.]

"Roger, Captive lead, this is Escort One."

"Escort One, and all Captive flights, stand by for a time hack. . . . 1330 . . . Five . . . four . . . three . . . two . . . one . . . hack!"

"Rendezvous at this location at 1430 hours for exit. . . . And if we get separated, don't be late, honeys, because the band starts playin' and there ain't no waiting. Everybody copy?"

The flight leaders responded, and Jordan nosed down with my flight and Green Flight in trail. Yellow Flight started their climb, and the B-25 entered an orbit over a prominent bend in the shoreline as a landmark for our return.

There was enough ceiling for flying beneath the overcast, but it was difficult to keep in formation because we had to constantly turn and bank to avoid the cloud formations and rainstorms. That made navigation difficult, but it also made trouble for anti-aircraft gunners. I don't recall that we took any flak on the flight into the area of the prison camps. Maybe the Japanese were so surprised to see us they didn't get a chance to shoot.

About the time it looked like we weren't going to find the camps, we skimmed over a hill and into a valley, and there they were: a huge compound of single-story wooden buildings. I'd seen Major Jordan find a mission target under adverse weather conditions many times before. He seemed to have an instinct for it.

"Okay, Captive—break into flights. Let's show the colors!" he transmitted.

Our three flights of P-38s buzzed the prison camp and nearby villages in fine style. We swooped down and roared over the buildings at treetop level so the star and bar markings on our wings left no question of whose aircraft it was.

Years later, I read some accounts by prisoners who saw us that day. They said it was a great boost to their morale and a real surprise to the Japanese. I haven't read anything about what the Japanese generals thought, but I'm sure it got their attention.

After we had buzzed the camp and the local villages several times, we headed back toward the rendezvous point but couldn't maintain formation due to the deteriorating weather. Then, just as we had to split up, somebody screeched, "Bogeys! Bogeys!"

"Where are they?"

"Three o'clock low!"

"Yellow lead, you got 'em spotted?"

"Negative. I don't see 'em."

"Who saw the bogeys?"

"I did."

"Where?"

"That big cloud off to the north!"

"Yellow lead, this is Captive leader. You got bogeys?"

"I don't see 'em, Major. Who says they saw bogeys?"

"Me. Yellow three. I saw 'em."

"Where are they now?"

"Well, I don't see 'em anymore. They disappeared behind a big rain cloud."

"Okay. This is Captive lead. All flights keep a sharp lookout for bogeys, but we don't have time to chase 'em. We gotta head back to the rendezvous point."

In dodging the clouds we became scattered, which added to our anxiety because of the possibility of a midair collision with our own guys—not to mention the enemy aircraft who were now apparently milling around in the clouds.

I took up an east heading and banked around a billowing cloud, only to confront another one that I couldn't avoid. I plunged into it. When I popped out the other side I saw an aircraft flying along the bottom of the adjacent cloud at my two o'clock low position. My first impression was that it was a Japanese fighter. But I wasn't sure. I watched for a second or two as it passed through the misty edge of the cloud, but I still couldn't get a clear look.

Was it a bogey, or wasn't it?

Since one of the other pilots in our group had declared he'd seen an enemy aircraft, it was a pretty good bet that what I had seen was another. I quickly armed my guns and nosed over into a shallow dive toward the cloud bank where I'd last seen it.

I leveled off over the cloud bank and watched the other side. Sure enough he popped out of the cloud but then went right back into another one. Was it a Zero? Had he seen me?

I flew along the top of the cloud bank for a few minutes, watching, but he didn't come out. I reversed course and flew back in the opposite direction for a while but still no sign of the bogey. I glanced at my watch and saw that it was nearly time for the B-25 to depart. I was still several minutes away from the rendezvous point.

I hated to give up, but I was out of time. Even now I was going to be late getting to the rendezvous. And Jordan had made it clear they would have to leave at the appointed time. No exceptions. Fuel was so critical that he couldn't endanger the whole flight waiting for one straggler.

"Red leader, this is Blue lead, over?" I transmitted. No answer.

I repeated the call. "Any Captive, any Captive. This is Blue leader. Hold the flight. I'm on my way. Do you read?"

Still no answer.

I reached up and pushed the throttles to full power and headed for the rendezvous point. I couldn't afford to have the formation leave without me; there was no way I could find that island alone.

I transmitted again with no results.

Maintaining full power, I called again a few minutes later. There was still no answer and, more ominously, no radio chatter, which I should be able to hear because the flights would be assembling over the rendezvous point for the return.

I knew now that my radio was dead. It was a stroke of bad luck because our radios were relatively dependable, considering their vintage. Generally, radio failures were caused by interference from lead—bullets made in Japan.

Jordan would take a head count, realize that I was missing and start calling me. But without an answer, he could only afford to wait for a few minutes. Then the formation would have to depart.

When I arrived at the rendezvous point there was no B-25 and no P-38s.

I will never forget the sinking feeling I got. I had an instant recollection of a mission when one of our pilots had tried to coax a battle-damaged P-38 home after a dogfight over New Britain. He finally had to bail out into the shark-infested waters of the Solomon Sea. He got down all right and into his little one-man rubber lifeboat. We circled him for a few minutes; then he waved as we flew off helplessly, leaving him bobbing there in the sea. That was the last time we ever saw him.

I could only blame myself. I had wasted precious time trying to find an elusive bogey and now I was in serious trouble. The radio failure was a bad break, but the real fault was mine, and there was nothing to do now but go it alone.

I reduced power and set RPM at 1600 for maximum range, just as Lindbergh, the Lone Eagle, himself had taught us. Then I got out my map and calculated the mag heading from where I was to where I guessed the island was—a precision navigation procedure. My old navigation instructor back in preflight training would turn purple.

The P-38 is the greatest fighter ever built in my opinion, but the cockpit was tiny and not very comfortable for a pilot more than five feet nine. I am six feet tall and had already been strapped in for nearly seven hours. But that was the least of my worries. To find that island my heading would have to be perfect, and that was assuming I had guessed right as to the island's location and assuming there were no crosswinds to blow me off course.

I didn't want to burn any more fuel than necessary, but I needed to get some altitude so I could see farther over the horizon and hopefully spot the island in time to make a correction if I was off course to one side or the other. I eased the bird up gradually to about ten thousand feet, leveled off, and settled in for the long haul.

As time went by and the fuel gauges inched toward empty, I strained to catch a glimpse of the island in the hazy distance. My thoughts went to Amelia Earhart and Fred Noonan when they were on their flight from New Guinea to tiny Howland Island back before the war. They must have been doing the same thing I was doing at this point: straining, perspiring, and hoping that an island would suddenly pop up on the distant horizon.

It hadn't for them . . . and it didn't seem likely for me.

As though to confirm that, the fuel warning lights suddenly glowed red on the instrument panel.

The manual said I had twenty minutes of flight remaining after the warning lights came on . . . and all I could see ahead was water and more water.

Five minutes later: still nothing but water.

Ten minutes later: just more water.

I wondered how the sharks were in the Philippine Sea. In ten minutes I would find out.

I had begun to prepare for bailout when directly over the nose of the P-38 I saw something—or thought I did.

Squinting, I watched, holding my breath so as not to disrupt the image of what I saw, which was a tiny dot on the horizon. By a fraction of a centimeter, the dot focused. It *was* something. . . . It was the island!

I let out a shout of victory there in the cockpit of my Lockheed Lightning. I had hit the island square on. I couldn't have done any better had I been an expert celestial navigator with the best sextant ever made!

But could I make it to that dot? It was still miles away, and I had at best ten minutes of fuel remaining.

The next ten minutes was like ten hours.

I pointed the nose slightly downhill and set the RPM so low that I could almost see the prop blades going around. That would conserve fuel and I could still keep up my speed since I was going downhill. The trick now was to make my downhill course intersect with the island. The only problem with that plan was that when I got below bailout altitude I was committed. What if the engines quit then?

As the island, now visible in my windshield, grew in size the fuel gauges stopped jiggling and became dead still. I was now flying on fumes.

I could see the war wreckage lying along the beach just off the end of the runway. My squadron's P-38s were parked along the edge of the runway being refueled. No doubt my squadron mates were standing there in a group smoking and talking. Probably just about now they would have spotted me coming and would be watching my approach.

Well, if I didn't make it, at least they would know what happened to me.

I willed those engines to keep running and they did. I swooped over the end of the coral runway and leveled off for touchdown, and both engines quit cold.

I landed dead stick, as they say in aviators' lingo, rolled down the runway for a bit, and came to a stop.

I had some close calls and many an anxious moment flying 103 combat missions in World War II, but I never flew another mission that I had to sweat out like I did that one. But it was worth the cliff-hanging suspense to have been a part of that first flight in America's return to the Philippines.

On 20 October 1944, the U.S. Sixth Army landed on Leyte in the Philippines. The landing touched off a bloody land and air battle, introduced the kamikaze, and brought about the largest naval battle in history: the Battle of Leyte Gulf. It was to the Pacific war what Normandy was to the European war. MacArthur's promise was fulfilled.

CHAPTER EIGHT

Mystery of the Magnificent Beast

It was a miserable Valentine's Day, 1950. I was sitting at the control-center desk staring out the window at the drizzling rain and fog and wondering how I was going to occupy myself for the next twelve hours, when the Teletype machine suddenly came alive, making noises that sounded like: *Jig-a-jig . . . junk . . . jig-a-jig . . .*

Hey, maybe it was some action, I thought, though I couldn't imagine what it could be. The weather was so rotten that not even the ducks were flying this day, so it didn't seem likely that there would be much demand for our services. I was the alert-duty officer at Flight C of the 8th Air Rescue Squadron, at McChord Air Force Base, Washington. Our rescue unit responded to all kinds of emergencies, but we primarily searched for and rescued military personnel involved in aircraft accidents.

Scooting my roller-legged chair across to the Teletype, I read the message as it came out of the machine: "A crash occurred this station at 0327 Zulu. On a heading of 180 degrees, subject flew into the control tower window while attempting a low visibility approach. Type: Canadian goose. Color: gray. Condition after crash: one bad goose headache and a few lost feathers. Survival probable. Cheers, JJ CG Sand Point."

I chuckled to myself. J. J. were the initials of the duty officer at the U.S. Coast Guard Station at Sand Point. We were on the same Teletype circuit and worked together on search-and-rescue missions. I knew he was bored too, but at least he'd gotten a little action. I flipped the send key and typed out: "Message received JJ. Will await progress report on goose crash. Suggest he take a course in GCA [ground-controlled approach] procedures. Cheers. RCK ARS McChord." In those days, GCA was voice-directed, used for low-visibility approaches.

It was against regulations to play on the Teletype, but what the heck, a little diversion helped break the monotony during those long, dull periods of waiting for a real call. But I was enjoying my duty in the rescue squadron, even if there were dull periods.

Of course, most anything would seem dull after 103 combat missions against the Japanese Zero. However, I was happy the war was over and I was back in the good ol' USA. I had come home and married the girl of my dreams whose name, Miss Jerry, and picture had been on the nose of my fighter plane all through World War II.

I hadn't planned on staying in the Army, since I wanted to be a writer. But I wanted to fly the new jet fighters, and I was enjoying the peacetime Air Force with my beautiful new bride, particularly since no one was shooting at me.

Back in those days you didn't always get your way, and I ended up being sent to helicopter school, then assigned to the air-rescue unit. I was upset at first, but after learning to fly the helicopter I loved it. I also enjoyed rescue work, which involved saving lives—the antithesis of what I'd done as a fighter pilot.

When I pushed my chair back to the desk, my peripheral vision picked up someone entering the alert room. I swung the chair around and found myself staring at a tall officer in class-A blues. He had a swath of ribbons on his tunic and big silver stars on his epaulets. I stared at him for a second, then leaped to my feet and froze at attention. I hadn't seen a general officer that close since the war.

I don't remember the exact sequence of events, of course, but essentially it went like this:

"I'm General Montgomery from SAC [Strategic Air Command] headquarters. Is your commanding officer available?"

"No sir. Everyone is off today, except the alert-duty officer, I'm him, I mean that's me, Lieutenant Kirkland, sir."

"Okay Lieutenant Kirkland, if you're the duty officer, alert your commander and call this rescue outfit to duty immediately."

"Yes sir . . . uh, you mean our standby alert crew?"

"No, Lieutenant, I mean your whole outfit: every single man you got, and do it quickly," he commanded.

"Yessir," I snapped, leaping across to the telephone on the alert desk and quickly dialing Maj. Bush Smith, our CO. He wasn't home, but I tracked him down at a Valentine's Day party, along with most of our other crew members.

When I had finally rounded up every pilot and crewman I could locate, we assembled in the briefing room, with our curiosity running at full speed. Standing before us at the podium, the general got right to the point. "Gentlemen, I am General Montgomery from Strategic Air Command headquarters. We have lost a B-36 on the Alkan Route."

Wow! It was something big, all right. That airplane was so big that in the air, it looked as if somebody had put wings on the *Queen Mary*. I had only seen the B-36 flying over, because it was too heavy to land at our base. We all knew they flew daily secret missions from their SAC bases to wherever. When one came our way, it was generally headed for Alaska, which was only a stone's throw from the USSR.

Their route up there was called the Alkan Route, and it was our responsibility to provide search-and-rescue coverage. They had never required our service before now, but that bird flew so high and had so many engines that we had never expected to get a call.

We all listened intently as the general continued: "The aircraft was en route from Eielson Air Force Base, Alaska, to Carswell Air Force Base, Texas. The last reported position was near Princess Royal Island, which is about 200 miles down the coast of Canada from Ketchikan, Alaska."

Montgomery pulled a telescopic pointer from the inside pocket of his ribbon-laced blouse, extended it, and tapped the big wall map that we used for crew briefings. "Captain Barry, the aircraft commander, gave his last position report at this point and advised that he couldn't maintain altitude because of extremely heavy icing conditions. He was down to 5,000 feet and headed for landfall so he could bail out his crew."

The general compressed the pointer and put it back in his pocket. "I'm here because your rescue unit will have primary responsibility for conducting the search-and-rescue mission and I want to emphasize the importance of locating this aircraft and its crew at the earliest possible moment. Major Smith?"

Our CO stood up from a front-row seat. "Yes sir."

"There is a squadron of SAC B-29s at Fairchild Air Force Base standing by to join your search aircraft as soon as the weather clears. I will establish a command post here at McChord."

Now, every man in that briefing room realized the serious implications of a crew bailing out into the wilds of Canada in the middle of winter. Searching for and rescuing downed airmen was our business. That was what we did in the new Air Force's Air Rescue Service. But having a general officer and a squadron of B-29s involved was highly unusual and suggested that there was more to this mission than a missing crew.

Sure enough, General Montgomery identified the missing element when he narrowed his eyes and added, "Gentlemen, there is classified equipment aboard the aircraft, and therefore this mission has the highest priority, right from the top."

Whammo! It was like a bomb going off. Then dead silence. You could have heard a pin drop in that briefing room. I'll never forget it. We all sat there staring at the general, wondering wildly if he was going to confirm what we all knew—the B-36 carried in its huge bomb bay the atomic bomb.

Although the USAF B-36 Strategic Air Command Intercontinental Bomber System was highly classified and its bases sealed off with armed guards, we all knew that the B-36 was the United States' primary nuclear deterrent, at that point in the Cold War.

The Peacemaker, as it was called, would be the Free World's big stick against armed aggression or nuclear attack for almost another decade, before other deterrent systems could be effectively put in place. How all that happened is a little-known, fascinating story that provides an excellent prologue for the incredible story of the missing bomber on that Valentine's Day in 1950.

The story actually begins on 1 September 1939, when German tanks rolled into Poland, and Britain and France declared war on Germany. Although this signaled the beginning of the shooting war in Europe, that part was over rather quickly. By the end of June, the Nazis had overrun France, along with most of Western Europe, and Britain stood alone.

Although the United States had declared its neutrality, our sympathies and interests were self-evident, and military strategists were faced with planning an offensive posture that would require a giant leap in aviation technology. If Hitler took the British Isles—which appeared likely, at that time—we would need a long-range bomber that could carry a load of bombs and enough fuel to cross the Atlantic without fighter escort, drop its bombs, and return.

At the urging of Gen. Hap Arnold, chief of Army Air Forces, a specification was issued to industry on 11 April 1941. It called for the development of a strategic bomber that could carry a 10,000-pound bomb load to a target 5,000 miles away and return to its base without refueling.

Boeing and Douglas had experimented with large aircraft in the mid-thirties: the Boeing XB-15 and the Douglas XB-19. But, other than building and flying prototypes, there had been no significant follow-on programs.

A number of companies grappled with the 10,000-mile-range requirement, and finally, in late 1941, Consolidated-Vultee Aircraft Co. [Convair] made a bid to develop the XB-36. It was an unparalleled, giant aircraft, with a 230-foot wingspan. It was 163 feet long and 46 feet high. Powered with six pusher-type R-4360-25 engines of 3500 hp each, it would have a gross weight of nearly 300,000 pounds.

Design proceeded on the project, but the initial priority was reduced a few months later, when the United States entered the war and it became evident that we would have bases in England for our B-17 and B-24 heavy bombers.

The B-36 went on the back burner until the summer of 1943, when it appeared that the big bomber might be our only means of striking at the Japanese homeland. The strategists then revived the priority, since there was nothing else in the inventory or under development at that time with the range needed. On 23 July 1943, the Army Air Forces ordered 100 production units of the B-36.

In late 1944 this all changed again after we'd taken the Mariana Islands, which gave us bases in B-29 striking range of Japan. Once again the priority changed, and the urgency of the B-36 program was downgraded. Then came the event that shook the world and the military strategists: on 6 August 1945, a single bomb dropped from a B-29 destroyed the city of Hiroshima, Japan. It was an atomic bomb. The second atomic bomb, dropped on Nagasaki on 9 August, ended the war and ushered in a new era in warfare and bombardment systems.

This new bomb underscored the need to develop a strategic striking force capable of long-range retaliation against an aggressor. The B-36 was the only system under development with that potential capability. The giant bomber was back on track with revitalized emphasis and, on 8 August 1946 it made its maiden flight of thirty-seven minutes at Fort Worth, Texas.

Now it seemed that the project would have clear sailing. The aircraft had flown, and there was both military and political support to continue development. But flight-testing on the monstrous aircraft met with unprecedented difficulties. It simply suffered from the problems of giantism. For example, the 100-inch-diameter wheels to support its nearly 300,000 pounds of gross weight limited it to only three airports in the United States. The 19-foot-diameter pusher-type propellers, powered by Pratt and Whitney R-4360 twenty-four-cylinder engines, created unacceptable vibrations. And the air inlets at the front of the 6-foot-thick wings were insufficient to cool the in-wing engines.

The project engineers at Convair struggled with these and many other seemingly unsolvable problems for three years, while critics labeled the program the "billion-dollar blunder." And technical problems were not the only dark clouds hanging over the B-36. The politically fired Army-Navy controversy of the late 1940s threatened to scuttle the program completely.

The crux of that controversy was a disagreement over tactical philosophy. Which could provide the most effective retaliatory force with the least vulnerability: long-range bombers or super–aircraft carriers? Both sides had good arguments.

Several factors helped the Air Force's position and saved the B-36. One of those factors was an event that occurred on 24 June 1948: the Soviets cut off all access to West Berlin, signaling the first crisis in the Cold War. Although that problem was solved by the famous Berlin Airlift and the genius of Air Force Gen. Curtis LeMay, it was a clear indication of the tension that lay ahead.

Ironically that was the same day, 24 June, that the Strategic Air Command took delivery of its first B-36A. Four days later the bomber took off, flew to a target, and dropped seventy-two bombs of 1,000 pounds each. That was a bigger bomb load than eleven World War II B-17s could carry.

The engineers at Convair had, indeed, solved their problems of giantism. Many of their solutions set future industry standards, such as the application of two four-wheel bogies on a single strut to solve the landing-weight problem, magnesium-alloy skin, aerodynamics boost, and innovative cooling techniques.

Performance-wise, they got a little help from one of their old competitors: Boeing, who came up with the idea of hanging jet pods from the wings of their new B-47. So in March of 1949, the Convair folks hung two J47-GE-19 jet pods from each wing of their "Magnificent Beast," as its crews called it affectionately.

Now, with "six turning and four burning," the B-36D could cruise at speeds of 435 mph at altitudes greater than 45,000 feet. This, theoretically, put it out of reach of fighter aircraft of that day. But just in case, it was armed with six retractable and remotely controlled turrets, mounting two 20-mm cannon each, and two more 20-mm guns each in nose and tail turrets. It was the most heavily armed aircraft ever built, and, with 21,116 gallons of fuel, it could stay airborne on a combat mission for more than fifty hours—and carry a bomb load of 10,000 pounds (the weight of early A-bombs) on a mission of 10,000 miles, without refueling.

Equipped with the revolutionary new K bombing-navigation system, the B-36 could navigate easily to any spot in the world and put its bomb on target from any altitude. That may not sound like a big deal by today's standards, but this was during the days when bombers were often lucky to find their targets, and even luckier to hit them.

The B-36 had finally achieved success, and in the nick of time. On 24 September 1949, President Harry Truman announced that Russia had detonated its first atomic bomb. Now there was no question about the validity of a long-range retaliatory striking force. The B-36 became the United States' primary nuclear retaliatory system, and the Strategic Air Command, under Gen. Curtis LeMay, established an unprecedented twenty-four-hour combat-readiness status. The B-36 crews flew round-the-clock global training missions and on-station airborne alerts, in full combat posture.

The big question on my mind, that Valentine's Day of 1950, was what effect an incident like this would have on the whole program. And what were the consequences of a lost atomic bomb? Was it armed? Could it go off? It all seemed too big and too frightening to comprehend.

General Montgomery stared back at us from the briefing-room podium for a long moment, before finally saying: "I cannot overemphasize the importance of locating this aircraft and its crew at the earliest possible moment."

He didn't say the aircraft had an atomic bomb aboard, and I realized that, of course, he couldn't. That was top-secret stuff. But he didn't have to say it. We all knew, and we all realized there was a lot at stake here. I raised my hand, and the general looked at me and sort of nodded. "Sir, although the weather is marginal, I believe I can fly the H-5."

The general looked surprised. "What's an H-5?"

For a second I thought he was kidding. I'd always thought generals knew everything. "Oh . . . uh, it's a Sikorsky helicopter, sir."

Montgomery glanced at Major Smith as though to verify my claim. "General, we do have a helicopter here, and it can fly in reduced ceiling and visibility because of its ability to vary forward speed," explained Smith, "but it's not suited to long-range search and—"

"I don't want to compromise safety, Major, but if the risk is within reason, then certainly the critical nature of this mission would dictate that we employ any means at our disposal. The weather forecast indicates that we won't be able to get aircraft into the search area for another forty-eight hours. The, uh, H-5, may be our best shot at this point. But I'm going to let you and the lieutenant make that judgment."

Major Smith looked at me and said, "Your call, Kirk. Do you feel it can be done?"

"I can always do a 180, Major. I'll give it a try," I heard myself reply.

Less than an hour later I was crawling into the cockpit of an H-5 to take off on what would certainly be on a par with the more exciting and perilous fighter missions I'd flown in World War II. The helicopter that I flew that day was primitive, by today's standards. It was an early Sikorsky H-5, with no flight instruments or night-flying equipment. But it performed reasonably well, had a couple hundred miles' range, and carried up to three passengers.

I took off in the midafternoon with one passenger, whom the general referred to as a security officer and who was also a B-36 pilot. The weather was below CFR minimums (visual flight rules were called contact flight rules in those days) and marginal even for a helicopter. The clouds were hanging so low that I was forced to skim along with my landing gear brushing through the top branches of the dripping evergreens. It occurred to me that I might have been a bit optimistic when I'd said I could fly in that soup. But I had convinced myself that what I was doing could be vitally important, and I guess that had got my adrenaline pumping.

I glanced back at my passenger, Captain White. He didn't look so good and was clutching the side of the helicopter with white knuckles. I could understand why he looked so wild-eyed: not only did it appear that we would crash into a tree any second, the chopper was shaking like a hound out of water. I knew what the problem was, but he didn't. You see, the rotor blades in those early choppers were made of wood and fabric and were subject to what we called blade set, particularly when it was damp. They would warp, and when you first took off they were out of track and would vibrate badly. But I figured that after a while, they would limber up and smooth out.

I punched the intercom switch and said, "One thing about the helicopter, Captain, I can land most anywhere anytime things get too bad. We don't need a landing field." I thought it might give him a little confidence. It didn't seem to. He gave me a sort of sickly nod, and I went back to my flying. I wasn't all that confident myself.

I headed north toward Seattle, flying just above the interstate highway, frightening motorists and dodging power lines. It was tough, and, despite the cold, my gloved throttle hand oozed perspiration. A voice inside said: "Hey, you're not back fighting Zeros. This is high-risk flying, and it's downright dangerous. Give it up and turn back." But the general's voice was ringing louder: "Critical . . . urgent . . . international repercussions . . . top, top priority."

Major Smith had advised the general correctly when he had said the helicopter could fly safely in reduced ceiling and visibility. But what I was doing was called scud running, and it wasn't all that safe. But at least the Sikorsky's rotor blades had smoothed out, so I managed to make it to Seattle, then up the coast to the outskirts of Vancouver, British Columbia.

When I called the control tower at the Royal Canadian Air Force Base, Sea Island, the operator advised me that the airport was below weather minimums and I couldn't land there. I told him I was a helicopter and flying clear of the clouds (sort of) and was low on fuel. After a pause, he asked me to repeat the type of aircraft. I could tell by the sound of his voice that he was incredulous and uncertain of what to tell me. By that time I was actually over the airport boundary, although he couldn't see me from the tower because of the low stratus.

So I landed there just short of the runway and asked him again to please let me land at his airport. He finally agreed, and I lifted up and hover-taxied down the runway to the parking ramp and landed in front of base OPS [operations].

I was glad to crawl out of the cockpit, as I was beat from the tension and anxiety that comes with that kind of flying. I guess my passenger was even more anxious to dismount the Sikorsky, because he was already standing there on the concrete ramp when I got out.

"I've had some hair-raising experiences, Lieutenant, but that flight tops them all," he muttered, looking pale and shaken.

I hated to do it, but I had to tell him, "I'm afraid there is more to come, Captain, we aren't even halfway to Princess Royal Island."

He didn't answer. He just turned and walked off through the mist toward base OPS. Squadron Leader Kip met us in the RCAF OPS office, and, after I'd introduced him to Captain White, we got ourselves a cup of hot coffee and sat down to discuss details of the mission. I had met Kip before, when we had worked together on a coordinated USAF-RCAF rescue plan for the Alkan Route. He was a super guy and, like most Canadians, had a great sense of humor. "I say Kirk, they tell me this is a top-priority mission, but the bloomin' ducks aren't even flyin' today. I don't know how you got that crazy windmill up here."

"It was duck soup," I replied, grinning.

Kip laughed and shook his head. "To be truthful, I don't understand how the bloody thing flies in the first place."

Like myself, Kip had been a fighter pilot in World War II. He could not understand why I had elected to switch to a "flying windmill."

Captain White cleared his throat and said, "Sir, have you spoken to our General Montgomery?"

Kip shook his head. "No. But I guess he has coordinated with Ottawa, because HQ [headquarters] called and said you were on your way in the helicopter, and we have already started the ball rolling for a maximum effort on our end. We've alerted all the agencies involved, and men and equipment are being readied as we speak. Our problem, of course, is the bloody foul weather. But we do have a crash rescue boat en route to Princess Royal Island that will have fuel aboard for the helicopter."

"That's good, Squadron Leader Kip, and we appreciate your help very much," said White. "It's critical that we locate this aircraft, and the crew, of course, at the earliest possible moment. . . . I mean, a night emergency bailout in this weather is bound to have caused injuries."

Kip took a sip of coffee, hesitated, then said, "I've been advised there is classified equipment aboard the aircraft. My question, Captain White, is this: Is there anything on board that aircraft that endangers the safety of personnel on this rescue mission, or of the indigenous who live in that area?"

After a pause, White said, "The . . . uh, classified equipment on board is safe. But we do want to prioritize security the moment we locate the aircraft."

Kip nodded. I had the feeling he was thinking the same things I was. But he said, "Righto Captain, I'll so advise our chaps. What say we pop over to the club now and have a belt before mess?"

White glanced at me uncertainly. "Well, sir, in view of the urgency of the mission, I . . . uh, guess we should move on toward our destination, don't you think, Lieutenant Kirkland?"

I could tell by the tone of White's voice that he was

torn between an obligation to proceed and the thought of getting back in the helicopter. I solved his dilemma: "It will be dark in thirty minutes, Captain, and the helicopter isn't equipped for night flying."

Spending an evening with Kip was always enjoyable, although I think we all felt guilty having dinner in a nice, warm place while the B-36 crew was out in that miserable weather. And when we stepped out of the barracks the next morning at dawn, not much had changed. It was still stinko, with the clouds hanging down on the treetops. But it wasn't any worse than the day before, so we cranked up the H-5 and, with Kip's help, convinced the control tower to let me take off.

It was more scud running, but I was able to follow the shoreline up the Strait of Georgia, and, a little over two hours later, we landed at the RCAF communications outpost at Port Hardy, on the northern tip of Vancouver Island. Our landing there created the usual commotion. But after their curiosity about the helicopter had been satisfied, the Canadians refueled our bird and we were ready for the next leg of our mission.

Although the missing B-36 had given its last position a couple hundred miles farther north, there were conflicting reports about which way it had been headed. So we started searching as soon as we departed Port Hardy and entered the Queen Charlotte Straits.

The coastline along that section of the straits is heavily wooded, with scores of inlets that meander back into the high mountains. I had to hug the shoreline because the mist was right down on the surface, which meant instant vertigo if I got out over the water. One bit of good fortune was that the tide was out, and there was an area between the water's edge and the tree line where I could hover along, dodging the boulders and tree stumps that loomed out of the mist. Those obstacles did help me with spatial orientation, but my concern was about the obstacle I wouldn't see until it came crashing through the windshield.

After something over an hour of this kind of tense flying, we hadn't spotted anything of the B-36 or its crew. I needed a rest, so I landed the H-5 and shut it down on a big, flat rock wedged in a conglomerate of smaller rocks and tidal debris. Captain White and I crawled out of the helicopter and stood there in the silent, dripping mist for a moment without speaking. The only sound we could hear was the muffled lapping of water against the rocks, somewhere off in the hovering fog.

"I sure hate to think of that crew being out in this stuff," I said.

"So do I," White replied, pulling out a pack of cigarettes and offering one to me. I took it, and he lit both of ours. "But our crews are well equipped and trained in survival techniques," he added, taking a puff of his cigarette.

"What's it like to fly an airplane that size?" I asked, genuinely curious.

He leaned back against the Sikorsky H-5. "Nothing like flying a helicopter," he said, grinning.

"I'm sure." I grinned back.

"Well, she's one big mamoo. Weighs more than six B-17s and has enough fuel to stay airborne for two days."

"Two days!"

"Yes. We fly with a complement of seventeen men that includes an on-duty and off-duty crew. The aircraft has two separate sections: the cockpit and the aft section. They are pressurized and connected by a tunnel. We got a little four-wheeled cart to pull ourselves back and forth. We even have a crew sleeping quarters and a kitchen in the aft section."

"Shades of the old Flying Clipper."

"And then some."

"You do have anti-icing, right?"

White smiled. "The B-36 anti-icing system can heat 120 five-room houses."

"Well then, how come Captain Barry had a problem? The general said he couldn't hold altitude because of ice."

"What the general didn't mention is that Captain Barry had lost two engines. And let me tell you, the icing conditions in the Alaskan area can be murder."

"You fly in that area a lot, huh?"

"Yeah, it's the shortest route to Rus— uh, yeah, we're there a lot."

He grinned, and I decided to go for it. "What's it like, Captain?"

"What do you mean?"

"Knowing what you got in the bomb bay."

His smile dissolved, and he took a puff of his cigarette. "You don't think about it," he finally said.

I nodded.

"It's tough on our crews and their families, because we're gone a lot and the demands are severe. But we all believe in what we are doing. The Magnificent Beast is a marvelous airplane, and I think we are doing an important job."

"I'm sure you are, Captain White," I replied sincerely.

A few minutes later I cranked the H-5 up, and we continued our course of following the shoreline hoping to spot something of the missing aircraft or its crew. I computed that I had enough fuel to reach Princess Royal Island, where we were to rendezvous with the Canadian crash rescue boat for refueling. But I hadn't allowed for winding around the inlets, so it was a close squeeze on fuel. But we made it, and I landed on a rickety pier at an old mine in Surf Inlet— with the fuel warning light glaring in my face.

The Canadian rescue boat was there, tied to the same pier and waiting for us with its deck full of 55-gallon fuel drums. The RCAF rescue boat carried a crew of seven, none of whom had ever seen a helicopter before. "I wouldn't have believed that thing could land on this bloody pier!" exclaimed the rescue-boat skipper.

"In another couple minutes we wouldn't have," I confessed, standing on the wet pier beside Captain White, who was hurriedly firing up a cigarette.

White looked at me and said, "Wasn't that cutting it a little close, even for a helicopter?"

"A little closer than I like," I agreed.

He smiled and turned to the Canadian skipper. "Any sightings or reports, Sergeant?"

"No sightings, sir. But the caretaker here told me he heard the bomber fly over, so I guess we're in the right area."

"There's a caretaker here?" asked White.

"Aye," said the sergeant, "that's him and his wife peeking around that toolshed at the other end of the pier. The heeleocopter gave 'em a fright."

We glanced down the pier and saw two sets of widened eyes peering at us as though we were creatures from outer space.

"This mine, Surf Mines it's called, was the biggest

thing in the territory back in the late 1800s," explained the Canadian skipper. "There were over 100 men worked here. They had a narrow-gauge railroad that brought the ore from the mines, which are all through the mountains behind us."

"And you say they heard the aircraft fly over yesterday?" asked White anxiously.

"Aye, they heard it a couple times. Woke 'em from a sound sleep."

"Okay. That's important," said White. "It coincides with our information that the aircraft was last reported heading for landfall over Princess Royal Island."

"Then the aircraft and the crew would be in the mountains behind the inlet," I reasoned.

"That's the way I see it," agreed White. "And that's where we need to start searching as soon as possible."

"Well, we got some ground-search teams coming up the inlet now in a motor launch, but it's slow going in this weather," informed the skipper.

Captain White nodded. "Yes, and when they get here, it will take time for them to make their way back into those mountains. But since there's no way to air-search in this weather, that's all we can do."

"You say there's a small railroad runs back into those mountains?" I asked.

"Aye. Look up the incline and you can just make out the old processing mill there in the mist. The railroad starts behind the mill and makes its way back into the mountains."

I glanced at White. He was looking at me curiously. "There is no way for me to search those mountains in this stuff, Captain," I said. "But I can shuttle ground-search personnel back there three at a time, by hovering up the old railroad bed."

White nodded. "If you can do that, it would save a lot of time."

We refueled the H-5, and as soon as the ground-search crew arrived in the motor launch, I ferried them back into the mountains. Again it was scud running and tough flying, but I managed to make several trips before darkness shut me down.

We spent the night there at Surf Mines, sleeping in one of the old dormitories. The next morning the weather was still lousy, but we did get reports from walkie-talkie radios that the ground teams had found some of the survivors. That was great news, and Captain White got on the Canadian rescue boat short-wave and notified the general.

Now we were certain that our search strategy was correct, and that the bomber and its classified cargo would be found momentarily. The search crews kept finding the scattered survivors one and two at a time, all that day and the next. But there was no report on the aircraft. The answer was always the same: no sight of the B-36. By late afternoon of the second day, all the crew was accounted for except two, and still no sight of the big bomber.

There were some injuries, but most of the crew had survived the bailout and their ordeal in the wilderness in pretty good shape. That was, no doubt, a result of their extensive survival training. The next morning it cleared, and the sky was filled with search aircraft. We were all sure that the B-36 would be found any moment.

But it wasn't.

The search intensified, but still no sign of the aircraft or the remaining crew members. How could that be? An airplane that big would clear out acres of forest when it crashed. And it would probably start one big fire, since it had thousands of gallons of JP-4 and high-octane aviation gas aboard, not to mention what else it carried that might blow up.

Then the mystery seemed solved, when it was learned from the survivors that after Captain Barry had bailed his crew out over land, he'd planned to put the autopilot on and head the plane out to sea, then quickly bail out himself. I had sort of guessed those had probably been his orders, considering what he had in the bomb bay. It seemed to all fit, now: the reason we couldn't find it was that it had gone out and crashed into the sea. That satisfied everyone, until Captain White talked to the Canadian radar operator at Port Hardy.

The operator confirmed that he'd had the bomber on radar and that it had gone back out to sea, all right, but then, he said, it had made a 180-degree turn and flown back to Princess Royal Island, where he had lost the blip in the ground clutter.

Search operations were back on again, in full force, with a massive air and ground search. For the next several weeks, we covered every square inch of that area for miles in every direction, without a trace of the aircraft. The B-36 and whatever was in its bomb bay had simply vanished. What had happened to it? Where had it gone? Was there some kind of secret Russian interference involved? Were the two missing crew members involved in some crazy conspiracy? To this day I don't know what the final SAC report said, because it was classified.

Our Air Rescue report simply stated that we hadn't

been able to find the aircraft and two of the crew members. We had no explanation for the mystery. The mountains were 10,000 to 12,000 feet high, and the crew had bailed out at 5,000 feet. The bomber had been going rapidly down, with tons of ice on its wings. It could only have crashed into the western slopes of those mountains. It was impossible not to have found it, but we didn't. End of report.

But the final bizarre twist to the mystery, at least for me, did not come until years later. I had been transferred out to the East Coast and was browsing through the newspaper one morning, when I found myself reading a short article about a Canadian prospector who had stumbled onto the wreckage of a giant B-36 bomber, deep in the interior wilderness of Canada's British Columbia. The article was sparse and said only that no bodies had been found, and the bomber had been identified as one that had disappeared on Valentine's Day of 1950 over Princess Royal Island!

I couldn't believe what I was reading. I was dumbfounded. I read the story over and over, trying to grasp some detail, some point that might provide answers to the swarm of questions that buzzed through my head. How in the world could it have flown that far when, at last report, it had been about to crash? How could that crippled monster climb over the Cascade Mountains without a crew? What had happened to the missing crewmen? And, most intriguing: what had happened to the 10,000-pound atomic bomb? The article made no mention of that.

The whole thing was unbelievable. It didn't make any sense. I was incredulous, and determined to find some answers. Over the next few days I made numerous phone calls, but I might as well have saved myself the time and trouble. I got little additional information. The newspaper didn't know any more than what had been printed, and the Air Force Information Office simply said: "Classified." I even called a couple of my old Air Rescue friends, but they didn't know anything about it either.

Strangely, to this day I have had little more success in trying to unravel the mystery. Most of the unanswered questions still remain classified, or else obscured by years of changes in records procedures. But, from my personal knowledge and some limited discovery, I have been able to piece together what I believe may have happened that Valentine's Day in 1950.

Captain Barry, the aircraft commander, brought the failing bomber over land, bailed out his crew, then headed it out to sea and jumped himself. The aircraft then entered a layer of lower, warm air (I verified that this existed, from old weather reports for that day). The ice melted off one wing first, and the big bird went into a bank. Then, as it completed its 180, the ice slid off the other wing, and it leveled.

Now, with tons of ice gone, the nose came up on that big monster, and it climbed up over the mountain range behind Princess Royal Island and flew, crewless, for hundreds of miles into the interior. It flew into an area we'd never dreamed of searching, because how could a faltering aircraft that was about to crash climb over 12,000-foot mountains?

Who knows if my theory is correct? And even if it is, there are still unanswered questions. What happened when they found the big bomber years later? Was the atomic bomb still in the bomb bay? What happened to the missing crewmen? If the bomb was still there, they would have to bring it out . . . wouldn't they? And, no doubt, in secret. What a gigantic operation would have been required, and the biggest helicopter we had in those days could not have budged it. The movie *Close Encounters of the Third Kind*, with its giant, secret operation at Devil's Tower, comes to mind when I think of what kind of a gargantuan effort must have been required for the recovery.

And so, nearly a half century later, it is still a fascinating mystery, involving one of the most significant military airplanes in history: the B-36. It was the airplane that may well have prevented a nuclear holocaust during those tense and volatile early years of the Cold War. It was the giant that would not die: the Magnificent Beast.

After reading the story of "Mystery of the Magnificent Beast," Mr. Tim Timmerman, of Arlington, Virginia, did extensive research under the Freedom of Information Act and verified that the B-36 did carry an atomic bomb. In accordance with their secret instructions for an imminent crash, the crew locked the bomb on safe mode and jettisoned it into the North Pacific off Princess Royal Island that night of Valentine's Day, 1950. The missing crew members were never found and presumed killed during the bailout.

CHAPTER NINE

The Ultimate Game

When the Korean War broke out, that summer of 1950, I was sure that the Air Force would transfer me back into fighters, since there was a sudden demand for fighter pilots. Sure enough, I got orders to report to Pope Air Force Base, North Carolina, for a special assignment. It appeared that I would soon be flying jets in aerial combat in Korea.

I had some mixed emotions about that. Whereas I still wanted to fly those new jet fighters, it occurred to me that after surviving 103 combat missions in one war, doing it all over again in another war might just be pressing my luck. And by this time I was really hooked on helicopters. My experience on the B-36 mission had convinced me that they would someday play a major role in future military aviation, as well as in the aviation world. Also to be considered, my bride and I now had two sons.

My dilemma was solved when I arrived at Pope Air Force Base and discovered that my assignment was not in jet fighters. It was to a secret helicopter project. In fact, it was so secret that it was designated only as Task Force 3.4.6.

After several weeks of impatient waiting, Capt. Albert Lovelady, who commanded our select little unit of four pilots, briefed us. "Men, we are going to be involved in some really exciting helicopter flying. We are going to test nuclear devices!"

Lt. Walter Hodgson and Lt. Pierce Myers, the other two pilots, and I looked at the captain incredulously. "Nuclear devices?" I croaked.

Lovelady, a tall, distinguished-looking officer and a dedicated helicopter enthusiast, nodded and said, "Yes, and it's top-priority stuff and top secret."

"Is that the same as atomic bombs?" asked Walter Hodgson, a handsome young pilot who also lived and breathed helicopters.

"I don't know," Lovelady replied. "All they told me was that it's nuclear-device testing and we'll be shipping out as soon as our security clearances are completed."

"Where we shipping to?" asked Pierce Myers, our fourth helicopter disciple.

"I guess we'll find out eventually," said Lovelady with a smile.

It struck me as somewhat ironic that I'd just had an experience with an atomic bomb on the B-36 rescue mission, and now I was apparently going to be involved in another. But then, was a nuclear device really an atomic bomb? And if it was, what could a helicopter do? We sure couldn't carry one of those things. And where in the world would they be testing something as devastating as that?

I found out where a couple of months later, when the four of us were shipped to a tiny hunk of coral in the Marshall Islands called Eniwetok atoll. "We're going to test nuclear devices on an island with two helicopters?" I asked Captain Lovelady, when he told us that our total complement of helicopters would be two Sikorsky H-5s.

Lovelady explained: "Not exactly. Eniwetok is only one of several islands in the Eniwetok atoll. The testing will be conducted on several of the outer islands. Our job will be to provide transportation between those sites for the nuclear scientists and key personnel. We will also be flying radiation-monitoring personnel during the tests."

So that was our job in this big deal: we weren't going to test anything, we were taxi drivers, plain and simple. And from a tiny island in the middle of the Pacific Ocean that you could throw a rock across. I was disappointed. Little did I realize that the next few months would be an even more fascinating, engraving experience than the B-36 mission.

We were quartered on the main island of Eniwetok, in a city of open-sided GI pyramidal tents. I figured it was back to those miserable hot, buggy New Guinean days. But it wasn't.

Although it was hot in the Marshall Islands, the trade winds blew at a constant rate, almost continuously. There were no bugs, and the temperature was quite pleasant. Our water was desalinated seawater and delicious. The official dress code permitted khaki shorts and short-sleeved shirts. And, best of all, they had a huge, spotless mess hall that served great chow. And the officers' club sold a mug of beer for ten cents and a double martini for twenty-five cents. I had the feeling that my old fighter-pilot buddies, who were now fighting the air war in Korea, wouldn't be enjoying such luxurious conditions.

Although we four helicopter pilots were taxi drivers, all right, we were rather exclusive taxi drivers. Only the scientists and top VIPs involved in the operation got to ride in the helicopter. They did have some small liaison aircraft that serviced three of the islands that were big enough to accommodate runways. Most of the personnel, however, were transported between islands by the Navy, in shuttle boats. Our helicopter taxi could service any of the islands in the sixty-mile circular atoll, and do it quickly. Needless to say, we were in high demand. And since we had received complete background investigations, we had top-security clearances and wore "Q" badges, which allowed us access to all the test sites and all scientific personnel.

My first taxi duty was to fly a couple of scientists around the perimeter of the atoll to look for a spot to set up some kind of monitor site. I was, naturally, curious, but when they showed up at the helicopter that morning in khaki shorts and shirts, wearing beanie caps with tiny counterrotating propellers on top, I had my first clue that these fellows were a breed all their own. But they seemed rational, and they listened intently as I gave them a briefing on safety procedures in the H-5 helicopter. Then I got them aboard and took off on the mission.

There are about thirty islands in the atoll, the largest being a couple of miles long and the smallest not much more than a sandspit. The whole island chain is actually the rim of a giant ancient volcano, rising from the Pacific Ocean floor to just a few feet above sea level. The lagoon in the center is the crater, filled with beautiful turquoise water and fascinating marine life.

Flying over the chain of islands that lay along the coral reef, some only yards apart and others several miles apart, provided a bird's-eye view of this island paradise. The contrast in color between the various shades of blue-green water against the sugar-white beach sand and the green palm trees was breathtaking.

It struck me as somewhat ironic that Operation Greenhouse, as the task force had been named, was here to test devices of mass destruction. But then I spotted the rusting hulk of some kind of war machinery lying on a reef, and I was reminded that bloody battles had been fought here when the Marines and the Army had recaptured this paradise from the Japanese in World War II.

I also began to realize, from the beehive of activity I saw on some of the islands, that Operation Greenhouse was a gargantuan undertaking. There was little remaining of the native culture; they had all been relocated to other islands in the Marshalls. What I saw now was all sorts of scientific and military equipment, and swarms of personnel involved in all types of construction, logistics, and transportation.

On one of the larger islands, I saw steelworkers, carpenters, plumbers, and bricklayers hard at work building an entire city, with streets and houses and large buildings. It was difficult to comprehend. I guessed that they planned to eliminate the tents and house everyone in the city. It made me wonder just how big this operation was going to get, and how long it would last. Just what were they going to test? And how were they going to do it?

As we passed over one of the small outer islands—West Spit Island, it was called—one of my passengers reached up and tapped me on the shoulder and pointed down. I nodded, banked the H-5 around, and landed on a glistening white sandbar at one end of the tiny deserted island. I cut the engine and, after the rotor blades had stopped turning, opened the side door. When the two scientists stepped out into the trade winds, the propellers on their beanies began to whirl again. They both grinned at me, and one of them said, "Our rotor blades may be smaller than yours, but they operate on the same aerodynamic principle."

"And they don't require fuel," I said, laughing.

"Right," he agreed. "We will just be a few minutes, Lieutenant."

I watched them walk off in the sand a short distance and stop under one of the rustling palm trees. They were middle-aged men, with thinning gray hair and thick glasses, but they jabbered between themselves like excited children. Since these fellows were top nuclear scientists and kept pointing at one of the islands in the distance, I assumed that they were discussing some complex geometry problem. I was mighty curious, and when they came back to the helicopter, I couldn't help asking, "Is this going to be one of the important test sites?"

"Very important," said the taller one solemnly.

The shorter one nodded in agreement. I flew back around the atoll and dropped them off at Parry Island, where all the scientific personnel were quartered.

"Thanks for the lift," the short one said. "After we make some preparations, we'll need to go back out there."

"Sure, just call the dispatcher when you're ready," I replied.

Later that afternoon I picked up my next passenger, with instructions to fly him on an inspection tour of several of the inner islands. He dressed and behaved similarly to the others I had flown earlier, and he also wore a beanie cap, but his only had a single propeller on top.

I had noticed during the morning flight that, among other things, on several of the islands they were constructing tall steel towers. I was asked to fly to each one and circle it for a few minutes, then land so my passenger could inspect it. The structures reminded me of fire-spotting towers in the forest back home. Even though I had a top-security clearance, I'd been briefed that I should not ask questions about what I saw during the course of my taxi duties. All information was on a need-to-know basis, and curiosity did not qualify. So I put the question this way: "For navigational purposes, can I mark these towers on my chart as permanent installations?"

My passenger turned his suntanned face to me. Of course we all got suntanned after being there a while, but he must have been there quite a while, because he was a dark copper color that made his teeth show white when he smiled and said, "You can mark this one as permanent, because it's a photo tower."

"A photo tower?" I persisted. "To take pictures?"

We were standing beside the helicopter, getting ready to board. He was looking at me, still smiling. "Yeah. With a picture-taking camera." He sort of hesitated, then added, "but a special one, a very fast one."

"You mean it takes a lot of pictures quickly?"

"Yeah, on the order of a million frames per second."

As I watched him crawl up into the backseat of the helicopter, I thought I must have misunderstood what he said. I had to find out. "A million frames per second?" I asked incredulously.

He nodded. "You ready to go, Lieutenant?"

After a couple of those twenty-five-cent martinis at the O [officers'] club that evening, I told my fellow helicopter drivers what the guy had said. Lts. Walter Hodgson and Pierce Myers were incredulous. Captain Lovelady, a conscientious, excellent commander, was concerned that I might have asked forbidden questions, but he'd had a couple of marts too and was just as curious as we were. "I can't imagine a camera that can take a million frames per second. And what are they going to take pictures of?" he wondered aloud.

"Well, the guy I flew today was some kind of supervisor on the construction of those towers, and he said those taller towers are where they are going to put it," offered Walter Hodgson.

"Put what?" asked Pierce Myers.

"I guess the nuclear device, whatever it is," replied Walter, twisting the Clark Gable mustache he'd decided to grow.

Lovelady pursed his lips and said, "Well men, I'm confident we'll be briefed on what's going to happen, sooner or later."

"I hope so. This whole thing makes me uneasy," admitted Pierce, running his hand through his close-cropped hair.

"What makes me nervous is these nuclear scientists. Boy, are they weird. I hope they know what they're doing," worried Walter, taking a big gulp of his martini.

"Aw, they're okay, just a little strange, that's all," I reasoned. "They know what they're doing . . . I hope."

A couple of days later, I picked up a scientist who was wearing the most unique beanie I'd seen so far. It had flashing red and green lights on top (remember, this was in the days before micro batteries and micro chips). I don't know how he'd done it. His name was Robert. He was very tall, with bushy eyebrows and intense dark eyes that seemed to look right through you one moment and dance with mischief the next.

"Neat hat," I said as he crawled into the helicopter.

"Yeah, it's my best effort so far," he replied, looking pleased.

I flew him to an island with one of the taller steel towers. It was apparently all finished, because there were no workers around. We landed and shut down, and then, surprisingly, he asked me if I wanted to go up with him. I glanced up at the tower. It was a couple hundred feet or more up to the top, accessed by a small steel ladder. Like most pilots, I am afraid of heights. But I had to see what was at the top of that thing, so I said, "Sure."

When I finally got to the top, I wondered how I would ever get back down, and, to make matters worse, there wasn't anything up there except some instruments and wires and stuff, in a small metal building. Since I'd risked death to get up there, I didn't hesitate to ask, "What are they going to put up here?"

"Oh, this is where a nuclear device will be placed, then detonated," he replied simply.

I decided to go for broke: "Is that the same as an atomic bomb?"

He nodded, his red and green beanie lights flashing. "Same thing, except we're not going to drop this little beauty. We're just going to put it up here and blow it up."

"What for?" I asked, seeing that I was on a roll.

"To measure the yield," he said rather absently, as he busied himself adjusting some of the instruments.

"You mean to find out how big the explosion is going to be?"

"Precisely."

That sounded kind of strange. I had dropped some bombs during the war, and you knew what was going to happen: big bombs blew up more than little bombs. "You don't know how big the explosion will be?"

"No, not really. We don't know just how far the chain reaction will go before it breaks down. That's the primary reason for these tests. This will be the first time we have ever taken pictures of the device as it explodes, and it should tell us a lot."

"You're going to take pictures of the bomb . . . uh, device, as it explodes?"

"That's right. Dr. Edgerton has developed a prism camera that will—"

"Take one million frames per second," I interrupted.

He glanced back at me and smiled. "You been talking to the good doctor?"

"I guess I have and didn't realize it."

"His camera is a remarkable innovation," he said, turning back to his instruments.

"Uh . . . if you don't know just how big an explosion you're going to get, won't that make it a bit risky to be around here when you set it off?"

"Oh, we know approximately what kind of yield we'll get."

"But not for sure?"

"No."

"Then it could be a lot bigger than you plan?"

"Yeah, it's possible."

"How big?"

He stood up from where he'd been kneeling over an instrument, turned, and looked at me with those intense eyes. "It could vaporize the atoll, but that's not probable with the device that we're going to detonate in this tower. Now, the final one is another story. Our last shot on this project will dwarf anything we've done so far. It's possible that baby could start a chain reaction that would blow up the whole world. I'm finished here; let's go."

When I told the guys about my experience that day with Robert, we all went to the club and each drank three of the twenty-five-cent martinis. After my experiences in World War II, I knew what it was to face danger. But somehow this was different. Just the idea that they were going to detonate a nuclear device, or bomb, or whatever it was, that might blow up the whole world was damn unnerving.

In a sense, it angered me. What kind of a game did these guys think they were playing, anyway? Messing around with something that could have such terrible consequences. I'll always remember how that incident affected me. Even after three marts, I tossed all night thinking about it.

A few days later, I picked up two passengers at Parry Island and was surprised to see that they were the two scientists with the counterrotating-propeller-powered beanie caps. "Hi, Lieutenant, think you can find our private little island again?" one of them asked, the props on his beanie spinning in the brisk trade wind.

"No problem," I assured him.

"Super. Mind if we take along a little baggage today?" the other asked, nodding at a couple of bulging duffel bags.

"Sure, Just stack 'em there in the seat beside you, and I'll adjust our weight and balance." I pulled the 25-pound lead brick from under the pilot's seat, walked back, and put it in a small compartment in the tail cone. That was how we adjusted our weight and balance, back in the days of that vintage helicopter. It worked well, as long as you didn't forget to transfer the brick back to the cockpit when you dropped off your passengers. I forgot once, the only time I ever looped a helicopter.

When I landed on West Spit Island, I could see that my two passengers were anxious to get started on whatever it was they were about. As soon as I opened the door, they jumped out quickly, gathered up their duffel bags, and hurried off across the sand. Almost as an afterthought, one turned and said, "We'll be a couple hours today. Will you wait or come back and get us?"

"I'm scheduled to wait, uh . . . you mind if I watch?"

"Be our guest," said the taller nuclear scientist.

I crawled out of the helicopter and followed them to a wide stretch of beach, where they stopped and eagerly removed the contents of their duffel bags. It was a strange assortment of items, and, even as I watched them assemble the things, I couldn't imagine what they were doing. But whatever it was, they were enjoying it: jabbering to each other about what part went where, as though they were two kids putting a jigsaw puzzle together.

Finally I couldn't stand it any longer. "Uh, could I ask what you're making there?"

The short scientist glanced up at me. "We're setting up a camera," he said, and turned back to what he was doing.

I hesitated. "A camera to take pictures?"

"Yeah."

I hesitated again. "What of?"

"The detonation."

"Of the nuclear device?"

"Yeah."

But they had already built gigantic steel towers to hold cameras that allegedly took a million frames per second. What were these guys doing? "Uh, what kind of a camera you going to use?"

"Oh, just a plain old Kodak Brownie: see?" the short one said, holding up what was, sure enough, a plain old box camera.

He saw me looking at him incredulously and smiled. "This is a little extracurricular project that Bill and I are doing on our own. Just in case Doc Edgerton's supercameras don't work out, we're installing a backup."

"It's not that Frank and I don't think Doc's camera will work, it's just that it could get vaporized," explained Bill. "But we figure that if the shot gets away from us, this island might survive and our camera will record what happened."

I stood there not knowing what to say, as they went back to work on their installation of the Kodak Brownie camera. I realized that these guys were in another world, but Jesus, did they have to be so nonchalant about vaporizing an atoll full of people . . . or maybe the whole world?

I'd smoked a half pack of cigarettes before they finally announced that they had done all they could, for now. "We have already made a reservation with the dispatcher for you to bring us out here the afternoon before the big shot, and we'll make the final adjustments and load the camera," Bill explained.

"When we come back to do that, we'll show you how it works, Lieutenant," promised Frank, no doubt in consideration of the look on my face.

I decided not to even tell the other pilots about this latest development, because it all sounded so bizarre that I began to wonder if maybe these guys weren't just doing a number on a naive helicopter jockey. Well, if they were, I'd soon find out, because the first detonation of a "device" was to be announced shortly. And, sure enough, a couple of days later the word came down that we were all to assemble at task-group headquarters there on Eniwetok Island, at 0400 the next morning, for a briefing and to observe the first shot of Operation Greenhouse.

It was pretty exciting, and you could feel the anxiety permeate the group that gathered there in the darkness before dawn to witness an atomic explosion. We had all seen pictures of the detonations over Japan. But no one seemed to know if this would be similar, or what. We were issued special dark glasses to wear and cautioned not to look at the explosion without them.

The four of us—Lovelady, Hodgson, Myers, and myself—were standing there in the coral sand among a crowd of others, waiting for the countdown to begin. Suddenly it occurred to me that the detonation was going to be in the same group of islands, at the far end of the atoll. And that was where the permanent city was being built. "The blast couldn't be very big, that close to the city," I commented.

Captain Lovelady agreed: "Yeah. They told me at Task Group HQ that this shot would be a small one."

"It would have to be pretty small if they're going to set it off that close to the city," agreed Hodgson.

"Well, if it's going to be that small, how come they evacuated all the personnel down to this end of the atoll?" asked Myers nervously, firing up a cigarette.

"Now hear this," the loudspeaker over our heads suddenly blared. "The countdown will begin in five minutes."

You could hear the sudden rise in the sound of anxious voices and shuffling feet. A couple of minutes later, the loudspeaker sounded again: "All personnel put on your dark glasses, now!"

I responded quickly, and, since it was still predawn, the dark glasses turned everything pitch-black. It became deathly quiet there in the sand on Eniwetok Island. A few seconds later there was a long single blast on the siren. Then, over the loudspeaker, the countdown began. From thirty seconds down to five, four, three, two, one. The blackness was suddenly transformed into a brilliant, searing white, and I was struck with a blast of heat as though a huge furnace door had swung open in my face.

It was a spectacular, awesome experience, beyond anything I could have possibly imagined. For a split second, the thought exploded in my brain that those crazy scientists had sure enough done it: they had blown up the world.

"Jesus Christ!" blurted someone. Then, an instant later, the brilliance and the heat began to subside, and I felt a surge of relief.

"Now hear this," the loudspeaker barked a few seconds later. "Stand by for the shock wave . . . five, four, three, two, one." *Wham!* I was nearly knocked off my feet by the force of the shock wave.

There were a few audible superlatives mixed with some nervous laughter, and someone said, "That was a small shot?"

"If it was, I don't want to be around here when they shoot a big one," said someone else.

"And we're nearly twenty miles away," muttered another.

When it turned black again, I pulled off the dark glasses and stood there silently for a moment, trying to collect myself as I watched the glowing, swirling mushroom cloud rising ominously into the dark sky. My brain was still spinning from the shock of believing—for a second or two, anyway—that I was witnessing the end of the world. Finally, I became aware that Captain Lovelady was speaking to me. "You better get going, Kirk, they said for you to report to the radiation-control area as soon as the shot was over."

"Oh . . . yeah, okay, Captain," I mumbled.

I was scheduled to fly a radiation monitor up to the blast site at zero plus two hours, which required some extensive preparation. They dressed me like a man from Mars, in a silver protective suit that was like a large pair of overalls. That and the stories I had heard about what radiation could do to you made me a bit uneasy. But that was offset by my curiosity to see what had happened at the explosion site.

At exactly zero plus two hours, I pulled pitch for takeoff (with the control stick used primarly for lift) on my Sikorsky H-5 helicopter, and, with the radiation monitor in the seat behind me holding a Geiger counter in his lap, we headed up the atoll toward the far side.

It was daylight now, so I could see where I was going, but flying in all that gear was not easy. The first thing I noticed, as I got nearer to where the detonation had occurred, were the disabled seagulls flailing around on the beaches. I could see that their wings had been burned by the heat of the blast, and they could no longer fly. Then, as we proceeded, I began to see palm trees with their leaves burned off, many of them still smoking. A little farther along, some of the trees were burning.

But the real shock came as I realized that ground zero was the island where they had built the city! And, a few minutes later, as I approached it, I could see that the city was no longer there. It was gone. Nothing was left but pieces of twisted, smoking rubble. I couldn't believe it: a whole city, gone. A city of houses, buildings, streets, trees, lampposts . . . all gone.

"Okay. So far so good," I heard the radiation monitor say to me over our special intercom hookup. "But approach slowly, and don't fly over it until I can get a reading."

"Roger wilco," I replied, slowing the helicopter to a hover taxi as we came in over the beach at the tip of the island.

We had the side door of the H-5 open, and he was holding the Geiger counter outside and watching it intently. "Hot! Hot!" he suddenly exclaimed. "Back off, back off!"

I kicked rudder, brought the H-5 around, and swung out over the lagoon and away from the destroyed city.

"Head for Eniwetok, quickly!" he shouted. Clearly he was upset. "The damn needle went off the fucking scale!"

"What does that mean?" I asked anxiously, as we headed back down the atoll at top speed.

"It means we probably got an overdose," he replied grimly.

"So what do we do about that?"

"Depends on how much we got. The damn scale monitor hung up on me, and when I got it to flip over it was too late, we'd already took a hit," he explained.

It was unnerving, but I remember being pretty philosophical about the whole thing: I sort of figured that an overdose of radiation was better than having the whole world blown up.

When I landed back at Eniwetok, they made me park the helicopter in an isolated area. The monitor and I were immediately taken to a decontamination building, and I found out what happens when you get an overdose of radiation: they nearly scrubbed all my skin off.

My Sikorsky H-5 got the same treatment, and then some. It had to cool down for several days, then they scrubbed it, too, before they finally said it was okay to fly again. The overdose apparently wasn't all that serious, because neither of us got radiation sickness or anything like that, and I was back flying in a couple of days. From that time on, however, we had to wear dosimeters that were monitored daily. This was a small cylindrical object, about the size of a fountain pen, that measured radiation. For years later I got letters from some government agency wanting to know if I'd grown two heads. But I never did.

We had all now seen and felt the awesome power of a "small" nuclear device. A device that had obliterated an entire city in an instant. It was sobering, and, in a sense, it exacerbated the concern on all our minds: if that was a small device, what would a big one be like? And, of course, we all knew there was a big one coming.

A couple of weeks later, they detonated another small device, and it went about the same as the first one. It was certainly as awesome as the first one, but a little less dramatic, since we had experienced one and knew pretty much what to expect. What made the second one interesting and unique was that the Air Force flew the world's first radio-controlled jet aircraft, along with a couple of World War II B-17s, through the mushroom cloud after the detonation, to take radiation samples at various altitude levels.

I wasn't directly involved in the second shot, but one of my most memorable experiences came shortly afterward, on a flight with Robert. I had flown him several times, and we'd struck up a friendship of sorts. He was, apparently, one of the top men in the scientific group, and one of the most colorful and distinctive. On this particular day, he showed up at the helicopter wearing his latest in the beanie fashion parade: a set of tiny brass chimes attached to the top of it.

"Good morning, Richard," he said pleasantly, his chimes tinkling as he climbed into the helicopter. "I need to go over to the command blockhouse for a few minutes this morning."

"Yes sir. Uh, I like your latest creation."

"Thank you. It should take my colleagues a while to top this one," he said, chuckling.

"It is one of your better creations," I admitted.

After a short flight, I landed the helicopter in the sand next to the blockhouse. After I'd shut down, Robert climbed out and said, "Would you like to go inside with me?"

"Yes, I sure would," I said, leaping out of the H-5. I'd never been invited into the blockhouse before and was something more than curious to see what was in there. After all, the top nuclear secrets in the world were inside that place.

It was low to the ground, built of concrete, and looked like a World War II pillbox. There were no regular windows, only a slit opening on one side. The single door had an MP [military policeman] guard and a big sign that read NO ADMISSION.

Robert told the guard that I was okay, but he still checked the picture on the Q badge that was clipped to my khaki shirt. We walked through the door and entered a large room that had rows of dials and instruments, several telephone terminals, and all kinds of strange-looking gadgets. This was the nerve center of the whole operation, and, even though I didn't have a clue what I was seeing, it was impressive.

After Robert had spoken to a couple of his associates, he led me into another room, where there was an inner door marked ABSOLUTELY NO ADMISSION. I'd heard rumors about this most secret room, where no one was allowed except a select group of scientists. He opened the door with a key and motioned me inside. Wow! I was going to see the ultimate in secrets, this day!

I stepped inside and looked around. I couldn't believe what I saw: there was nothing in the room but a long workbench and some miscellaneous hand tools. I glanced at Robert. He was grinning. "You see, Richard, we're not the mad scientists we sometimes appear to be. However, our work is extremely complex and requires intense concentration. So we must have a diversion, like anyone else. This is where we get it. We come here to relax and do simple things, like trying to outdo each other designing and building these crazy hats. Our little competitive games keep us sane while we struggle in the ultimate game of harnessing this awesome power we're dealing with."

In a sense, it was an enlightenment that gave me a different slant on what they were doing. Yet it didn't relieve my concern about what Robert had said could happen when they fired the big one.

A few days later, we were told that the last test of Operation Greenhouse would be conducted the following week. We were all happy to hear that, because it meant we would be going home shortly. We went to the club that night and had a batch of the twenty-five-cent martinis and celebrated. But no one mentioned what was on all our minds: the last one was the big one, the big shot, the one Robert had said could blow up the world.

I had forgotten all about Bill and Frank's camera project, until, the day before that last test, I was dispatched to Parry Island to pick them up. They climbed aboard the helicopter wearing their latest-design beanies: instead of the counterrotating propellers on a single shaft, they now had intermeshing props on separate shafts. Don't ask me how they'd done it. They greeted me warmly, and Bill, the tall one, said, "We need to go out to our little island and make final adjustments on our special project. Are you ready for the big one?"

"Yeah, I guess so," I muttered, as I got out of the helicopter and stowed the lead brick back in the tail cone.

On our way to the outer islands, we flew over the remains of the city that had been blown out of existence by a "small" atomic device. It struck me as an ominous omen. I landed the helicopter on the white, sandy beach of West Spit Island, right next to the thing, whatever it was, that they had constructed on their last trip out.

As soon as the rotor blades had stopped turning, they were out of the helicopter and hurrying to their creation like two eager children. "This won't take long, Lieutenant. All we have to do is set up the camera and load the film," said Frank.

I leaned against my 1940s-vintage helicopter, pulled out a cigarette, and fired it to life with my Zippo. It was a beautiful day in the Marshall Islands, as it usually was. The trade winds rustled the palm trees along the beach, and the lagoon water lapped gently over the sugarlike sand, reflecting shades of sparkling aqua.

My visit to the blockhouse and Robert's revelation had given me a different slant on these fellows, all right, but as I stood there watching them put the finishing touches on their creation, I still couldn't suppress a deep-down feeling that they were playing a very dangerous game, a game in which the destiny of all mankind was at stake.

"Okay, it's all ready. Come on over here, Lieutenant, and we'll show you how it works," said Bill. I ground my cigarette into the sand and walked over to where they stood, admiring their work. It was, basically, constructed of several lengths of perforated steel anchored into the sand. Several gadgets and things that I could not identify were attached, here and there.

"The heart of our program is this K4 timer," explained Bill, leaning down and touching one of the gadgets. "At exactly zero minus thirty seconds, it activates this lever, which opens the gate, and this steel ball will roll down the track . . . see it?"

"Uh-huh," I mumbled.

"Okay. The ball travels down the track at precisely 3.1 centimeters per second. It strikes this force plunger at zero minus twenty-three seconds. That opens this pressure valve and activates the swing arm, which strikes this sensor. It takes 2.5 seconds for the sensor to respond. The sensor activates the timer switch that controls the lever arm to the camera."

"Yeah," interrupted Frank, bending down beside Bill. "And you see, the lever arm rotates 203 degrees before it contacts the micro switch, which opens the outer door on the camera box. The door requires 4.3 seconds to fully open. When it's fully open, it strikes this micro switch at zero minus three seconds. It then trips the shutter at precisely zero hour, and the picture is taken at the exact instant the device is detonated."

They both looked up at me expectantly.

As incredulous as I was, the whole thing struck my funny bone and I burst out laughing. They sort of looked at me curiously. "Of all the crazy things I've seen you fellows do in the last three months, this takes the prize," I said.

They both smiled broadly. "You think it's our best, huh?" asked Frank, glowing with satisfaction.

"Yep, I'm sure of it," I said, grinning.

"Well, it's not only ingenious, it has a practical value," said Bill, feigning seriousness. "If Doc Edgerton's camera should get vaporized, this will provide a record for mankind of what happened on Eniwetok atoll."

There were an unusual number of patrons at the O club drinking twenty-five-cent martinis that final night before the big shot, myself and my fellow taxi drivers included. And, even though we all had to get up at three o'clock in the morning, everyone stayed late. Drink, laugh, and be merry, for tomorrow . . .

No one said anything about it, but everyone knew what was on all our minds. And, although I realized that Bill and Frank's little project on West Spit Island was just another of their games, I also realized that it contained an element of reality.

The routine for the final detonation of a nuclear device in Operation Greenhouse was about the same as it had been for the other tests—except at the briefing, we were warned that this one would be much larger than the others, and we were instructed not to take off our dark glasses until the explosion had completely died. We all assembled outside headquarters about an hour before zero hour and stood around nervously smoking and making small talk.

Finally the loudspeaker announced zero minus five

minutes, and you could feel the tension mounting, with nervous voices and shuffling feet. When the thirty-second countdown started, a pin drop could have been heard. I couldn't help thinking of the micro switches and sensors doing their thing across the lagoon on West Spit Island. I hoped they worked . . . just in case.

When the big one went off, I heard someone say, "Oh, my God!" And in that instant, I was confident that Robert and all the other scientists had lost their game and the end of planet Earth was at hand.

The difference between the "small" shots we had witnessed and this one was like that between a firecracker and a 1,000-pound bomb. It was as though the entire world was engulfed in a giant fireball that instantly seared my skin with a blast of fiery heat.

It was several seconds before I realized that the world was not ending and the fireball was rising upward. I stood there and watched in paralyzed horror as the gigantic mushroom cloud rose into the atmosphere, seeming to engulf both earth and sky in its monstrous assent.

I was so engrossed in the mushroom cloud that I was only vaguely aware of the loudspeaker countdown to the shock wave. And when it came, it was so powerful that I was knocked off my feet as though I'd been struck by a runaway truck. After the shock wave, it was like everyone there had received a last-minute death-sentence reprieve. Laughter bordering on the hysterical broke out, and everyone dug out a cigarette and lit it. Someone suggested that they should open the bar at the O club and we should all go get plastered.

Never, in all my experiences in World War II and

later in the Korean War, did a single event have the emotional and lasting effect on me that did that awesome explosion on Eniwetok atoll.

Robert gave me one of his little blinking lights that he'd used on his beanie. Although it quit blinking many years ago, whenever I look at it, I'm reminded of that morning as though it were yesterday. I didn't get a chance to find out how Bill and Frank's box camera worked out on West Spit Island, but I did get to talk to Robert one last time before I was sent home.

My question to him was: "Did you believe that you had destroyed the world when the big one went off?"

He smiled. "Yes. And so did a number of my colleagues. You see, Richard, that was the first of a new kind of hydrogen bomb, triggered by an atomic bomb. And for an instant or two, we thought it had gotten away from us."

"That's kind of scary, you know," I said.

He nodded and the smile dissolved. "I know. But there is no turning back now. We have no choice but to go forward. That device had many times the destructive power of the one that obliterated our test city. And from our test results, we will be able to make a bomb more powerful than the total of all the bombs dropped in World War II."

"Jesus."

"So powerful, Richard, that we dare not ever use it."

Over the years I have always remembered that statement that Robert left me with, and I guess he was right. He won the ultimate game. It hasn't been used . . . at least not yet.

CHAPTER TEN

Bluebird

Washington, D.C. 0903 hours. 15 March 1952.
When the buzzer sounded, John Mallory was so engrossed in the document he was reading, he reached across his desk without looking, picked up the phone, and put it to his ear. Before he could speak, the buzzer sounded again, this time piercing his concentration.

"Yeah?"

The buzzer rang again.

Mallory's eyes shot to the red phone on the table next to his desk. He dropped the white phone quickly and snatched up the red receiver.

"Mallory."

"Code red one!" snapped a voice.

"Red one?"

"Roger!"

"You're sure?"

"Confirmed! All stations alerted."

Mallory stabbed a switch on the red phone. After several rings a voice came on. "The chief is having a cup of coffee, John. This is the usual drill, right?"

"No! It's for real, go get him!"

"Are you serious?"

"Damn it, Mike. Yes, I'm serious! Get him and get him quick!"

"Okay, okay."

As Mallory waited for the White House chief of staff to come on the line, his thoughts spun. Could it actually be the real thing? It was hard to imagine that it was happening. Despite all the planning and testing, which they certainly had done in all seriousness, he hadn't really thought that a code red one—the signal that a nuclear attack on the United States was imminent—would ever actually come to pass. There had been lots of code red threes for practice, and even a couple of twos. But never a one.

"What is it, John?"

"Code red one!"

Hesitation. "A drill?"

"There is no drill on code red one, Bill."

"It's confirmed?"

"Yes. ADC [Air Defense Command] and SAC [Strategic Air Command] have been alerted. Notify the president!"

"He's on the *Sequoia*."

"Where are they?"

"They're down the river near Colonial Beach."

"Damn! Wouldn't you know this would happen when he's out of pocket."

"Do you think it's the real thing, John?"

"God, I don't know, Bill. Command says it is."

"Then we need the president back here quick."

"Yeah, you're right. I'll activate Bluebird."

Langley Air Force Base, Virginia. 0904 hours.

I was the alert-duty pilot, sitting in a little cubbyhole

in base operations, talking to one of the other pilots in our select group, Capt. Pierce Myers. Pierce was telling me a story about the elderly black maître d' at the Langley Officers' Club who had been there since the early days of the Army Air Corps. It seemed that Air Force Gen. Hap Arnold came into the club one day during World War II and the maître d' said, "Well, hello there Lieutenant Arnold, I haven't seen you around here for quite a spell."

"That's a great story," I said, laughing.

"Yeah. He knew all those early Air Corps pilots, including Billy Mitchell. One of the guys was telling me that he—"

The buzzer on my red phone shrieked.

Pierce and I looked at each other. I snatched it up and said, "Bluebird."

"Scramble Bluebird, code red one," instructed a voice.

"Red one?" It was an instinctive reaction, since I'd just assumed that I would never hear those words.

"Repeat: code red one!" snapped the voice on the line.

"Yes, sir!" I said and quickly punched the alert button, grabbed my "Mae West" [life vest], and headed for the front door of base operations.

The alert crew, responding to my signal, was already hurriedly removing the rotor blade tie-down ropes as I ran up to the Sikorsky H-5 helicopter parked out on the flight ramp. I quickly climbed into the cockpit, fastened my safety belt, and flipped on the master switch.

The alert-crew chief, standing beside the helicopter with a fire bottle, gave me a thumbs-up and a smile. I'm sure he assumed it was the usual practice drill.

When he saw the look on my face, however, his smile dissolved.

As required, the helicopter was already preflighted, full of fuel, and ready to go. I hit the starter and the Pratt & Whitney R-985 coughed, spit out a column of black smoke, and roared to life. As instruments stabilized and temperatures climbed, I punched the radio button and slipped on my headset.

"Langley tower, this is Bluebird," I transmitted excitedly. On routine flights we called the tower with our aircraft number. On an operational scramble, we were instructed to use Bluebird, which told the tower operator that we rated a priority over other traffic. This was my first such application.

There was no answer from the tower for a moment. I sensed the hesitation: "Was that Bluebird calling Langley tower?"

"Roger, Bluebird," I confirmed.

No hesitation now. "Roger, Bluebird, clear for immediate takeoff. All traffic at Langley Air Force Base, be advised we have a priority aircraft departing northbound."

"Roger, tower," I replied, then revved the Sikorsky up to takeoff RPM and pulled pitch.

There was a burgeoning excitement stirring inside me as I headed north on a special departure route. As soon as I'd cleared the air base I punched the button on my VHF radio that put me on a discreet frequency.

"Eagle Control, this is Bluebird," I transmitted.

"Roger, Bluebird, activate squawk now," came the quick reply.

"Roger, wilco," I replied, flipping the switch on another black box that had been installed next to my VHF radio.

After a few moments: "We got you, Bluebird. Take a heading of 340 degrees and climb to angels three" [an altitude of three thousand feet].

I repeated the instructions, took up the heading, and put the H-5 into a climb. I saw the York River below me now, and my peripheral vision picked up the Yorktown monument commemorating Washington's victory over Cornwallis, which had saved the republic. And then came a jolting thought: I had been scrambled on a code red one! Did that mean what I assumed it meant? An attack on the United States was imminent. I glanced down at the monument again, and suddenly I envisioned what I had seen on Eniwetok.

I'd been a helicopter pilot on Eniwetok atoll during "Operation Greenhouse" in 1951 and saw a nuclear bomb turn an entire city into a smoldering wasteland. As those images flashed through my memory now, a cold fear gripped me, and the terrible reality of the mission I was flying struck me like a sledgehammer.

When the atomic-bomb tests on Eniwetok atoll were completed in June 1951, I was reassigned to the 4415th Air Base Group at Pope Air Force Base, North Carolina. It was good to be home with my wife and two sons again after a year's separation. I was assigned as a helicopter instructor and was lucky enough to get on-base housing at nearby Fort Bragg. It was good duty, and I was enjoying the assignment, until one day a few months later when my commander called me in and said that I was being sent TDY [temporary duty] to Langley Air Force Base in Virginia.

I was not a happy camper because TDY meant another separation from my family. There were no provisions for dependent travel when the sponsor was sent on temporary duty. To make it worse, my commander said he didn't have a clue as to why I was being sent or how long I would be gone.

When I got to Langley, I reported to a major who had come down from the Pentagon to brief me. I can't remember his name, but the briefing went something like this:

"Captain Kirkland, you have been selected for this project because of your qualifications. You are an experienced helicopter pilot, correct?"

"Yes, sir."

"You have a top-secret clearance?"

"Yes, sir."

"And you participated in nuclear-weapons testing on Operation Greenhouse?"

"Yes, sir."

"Not a word of this briefing is to go out of this room. Do you understand?"

"Yes, sir."

The major nodded, dug a pack of cigarettes out of his blouse pocket, and offered me one. I accepted and we both lit up and blew clouds of smoke in the small office in one corner of Langley Base Operations. That was before we knew that cigarette smoke was almost as bad as radioactive fallout.

"This office is the duty station for the special unit to which you have been assigned. You and three other helicopter pilots will rotate on twenty-four-hour alert duty. You must be ready to pilot a helicopter as instructed by a controller on a discreet radio frequency. Your initial alert will come through this telephone," said the major, touching a red telephone on the desk.

I glanced at the phone. Since the Cold War started

I'd heard stories about red telephones associated with the SAC alert crews. But they were flying the giant B-36s with atomic bombs aboard to retaliate in the event of a nuclear attack. Why would the Air Force want helicopters on a red-phone alert?

The major took a puff of his cigarette and looked at me. "This is a very important mission, Captain. And I want you to recognize that."

"Yes, sir. What is it?"

"All information is top secret and on a need-to-know basis."

"I need to know what I'm supposed to do, sir."

"I'm coming to that."

"Yes, sir."

"Your function is to transport VIP in an emergency. When alerted, you will proceed as directed by an air controller to a specific destination, pick up a passenger or possibly two, and fly them to another destination as specified by the controller."

"Another taxi service, huh?"

The major frowned at me.

"Uh, that is what I was doing on Eniwetok: a helicopter taxi service for VIP."

"Captain, I can assure you this is more than a taxi service. The VIP you will be carrying is *the* VIP."

"What?"

"Never mind. Forget I said that. All you need to know is that you are to follow the instructions of the controller, understood?"

"Yes, sir. But what if I lose radio contact?"

"The helicopter has been equipped with redundant radio systems. Total failure is not likely. Any further questions?"

"Well, I'd like to know a little more of what I—"

"You have all the information you need, Captain."

"Yes, sir, but—"

"If you are incapacitated for any reason, you are to call me at this number on the regular telephone." The major scribbled a number on a notepad and handed it to me. "You are not to touch the red phone unless it rings."

We both looked at the red phone.

"You will receive periodic calls and be dispatched on missions classified as code two or three. You will not receive a code one unless it's the real thing, and it will be identified to you as 'code red one.'"

"The real thing?"

"An operational mission requiring you to transport a VIP."

I looked at the major questioningly.

". . . of the highest priority," he added.

I nodded.

The major glanced at his watch, ground out his cigarette, and got up from the chair. "Let's hope you never get a code red one, Captain," he said, and walked out of the room.

Command Center, Pentagon. 0915 hours. 15 March 1952.

Maj. Gen. Robert Moody, U.S. Air Force, stood watching the technicians hovering around a huge transparent map in the cavernous command control room, their headset cords trailing behind as they made notations with a grease pencil.

"Bob, where are we?" came the urgent voice of a four-star Air Force general who hurried into the glass-enclosed cubicle.

Moody turned and faced the four star. "All stations of Air Force, Navy, and Army deterrent systems are on red alert, as are all ADC and SAC aircraft."

"The president?"

"The White House has been notified. But we don't have confirmation."

"What?"

"They haven't confirmed contact with the president."

"What's holding them up?"

"I don't know."

"Did you contact Mallory?"

"Yes, sir. He says they're working on it."

"Jesus Christ! They're working on it? Don't they realize how serious this is?"

"I think they do, but the president is on the *Sequoia,* and I got a feeling they have some kind of communications problem."

The four star shook his head. "I was afraid of this. I told that fathead Mallory they should—"

A screeching buzzer interrupted the two generals, and Moody grabbed the red phone. "Moody," he barked. After listening a moment, he nodded and replaced the red receiver. "Bluebird has been activated."

"Bluebird?"

"You know, the helicopter."

"The helicopter?"

"Yes. It's supposed to pick up the president in an emergency and take him to the command center."

Presidential yacht *Sequoia.* Potomac River. 0919 hours.

Assistant to the president Col. William Scott hurried down the polished passageway, nodded to the

Secret Service agent on duty, and stepped out onto the aft deck of the *Sequoia*.

"Mr. President."

President Harry Truman looked up from where he sat in a deck chair reading. "Yes, what is it, Scotty?"

"Sorry to disturb you, sir, but we have a problem that I think you should be aware of."

"Well, you know my motto: 'The buck stops here,'" said the president, smiling.

Scott forced a little smile and nodded. "Yes, sir. The problem is that our entire communications system on *Sequoia* is inoperative, and we've lost contact with the command center."

"That doesn't surprise me. The trouble nowadays is that all this high-tech stuff is too complicated and when it goes ker-put you're up shit creek without a paddle."

"Yes, sir. The problem here is—"

"When I was in France in World War I, we got our info direct. None of this electronic stuff that's always shootin' craps for some damn reason or another."

"Yes, sir. I'm sure it's a temporary thing, and they'll have it fixed shortly, but meanwhile . . . if there should be an alert. . . ?"

Truman nodded. "Yep, you're right. I guess we better head for the barn."

"Yes, sir. I'll so advise the captain."

Near Tappahannock, Virginia. 0939 hours.

When I spotted the Potomac River over the nose of the helicopter, it was a lead-gray color reflected by the dull overcast that had gradually lowered on the horizon. Since the H-5 helicopter was not equipped for instrument flight, I'd been forced to lower my flight altitude to less than one thousand feet.

"Bluebird, this is Eagle Control. Are you receiving me?"

"Roger, Eagle, I read you," I replied.

"Bluebird, you're so low you're erratic on the scope, can't you get some more altitude?"

"Can't do it, Eagle. I'm already flying in scud along the bottom of the overcast."

Silence.

"Bluebird, turn left to a new heading of 270 degrees. That might get you into an area of a little higher ceiling."

"Roger, 270 degrees."

I banked the helicopter around, but within a few minutes I could tell the overcast was even lower to the west.

"Eagle, this is Bluebird. The weather is worse on this heading."

"Roger, Bluebird. Stand by."

Silence.

"Bluebird, turn right to a new heading of 090 degrees."

"Roger, Eagle, 090 degrees."

A few minutes later I spotted the Potomac River again in the distance, and, although there was a light mist hanging from the overcast, I was able to maintain enough altitude to stay out of the clouds.

"Bluebird, this is Eagle, we've lost you on the scope. Where are you?"

"Eagle, I'm coming up on the Potomac River."

"Bluebird, can you follow the river northwest?"

"I'm gonna give it a try, Eagle."

"Bluebird, be reminded this is a code red one, operational mission."

"I know, Eagle. I know."

I knew all right, and it had weighed heavily on my mind since hearing the words over the red phone. Could it actually be true? Was a nuclear attack really coming? I had never actually been told that a code red one meant that. But it was a logical assumption, since the major had left little doubt who my VIP passenger would be if it happened. And there was a lot of talk those days about the nuclear threat, because the war in Korea was going on with communist Russia and China supporting North Korea. But then, maybe I was overreacting. I hoped so.

Command Center, Pentagon. 0941 hours.

Maj. Gen. Robert Moody snatched the red phone as it screeched. "Yeah."

"General, we're at a point of no return. We've got to have a decision."

"Tell me about it. I don't have a decision. There is a communications breakdown, and we can't contact the president. It has paralyzed the whole damn system!"

"What are we gonna do?"

"There's nothing to do until we reestablish communications and get in contact with the president. He's the only one who can make the decision."

"Well, what are they doing about it?"

"They're working on it."

"Yeah."

"Meanwhile, Bluebird is en route."

"We really gonna do that?"

"That was the Bluebird plan, wasn't it?"

"Yes, sir. But as you know, that was just window dressing. Nobody really figured we'd ever actually do it."

"Well, it looks like our window dressing is gonna play center stage in this fiasco."

Near Colonial Beach, Virginia. 0945 hours.

The sky had turned a threatening shade of gray, the ceiling had lowered even more, and the mist streaked across my windshield. It seemed to mirror my feelings of pending doom. But I still had a three-hundred-foot ceiling and about a half mile visibility, which is enough for helicopter flying.

"Bluebird, this is Eagle, where are you?" cracked the controller's voice in my headset.

"I'm approaching Colonial Beach, Eagle."

"Stand by, Bluebird."

"Roger."

Thirty seconds later: "Bluebird from Eagle. Continue up the river. There is an installation at Dahlgren with a boat dock on the river. It will be your initial destination. Report when you have it in sight."

"Roger, Eagle."

Sequoia. Potomac River. 0946 hours.

Seaman First Class Daniel Martin hurried down the passageway and onto the Sequoia lounge where Colonel Scott and a couple of the president's guests were visiting and drinking coffee.

"Colonel Scott, sir, this message just came over our ship-to-shore radio. It's addressed to you, sir."

"Thank you," said the colonel. One glance told Scott it was coded. He excused himself, went to his cabin, and quickly decoded the message. Then he hurried down the passageway to the president's cabin, knocked, and was invited in.

"Sir, we just received a coded message on ship-to-shore radio recommending that, because of our communications breakdown with the command center, we dock at the Army installation at Dahlgren."

The president, sitting at a desk, hesitated. "We're still out of contact with the command center?"

"Yes, sir. I'm afraid so."

President Truman nodded. "Yep, the way things are right now with those sons of bitches over there, we better not take any chances."

"Yes, sir. I'll advise the captain. Oh, and the message also said that Bluebird has been activated."

"Bluebird?"

"Yes, sir. That's the helicopter to provide emergency transportation for you."

"Oh, sure. I remember now. Well, I think it's a good idea to go ahead and dock, just to be on the safe side, but I don't know that I need a helicopter."

"It was probably dispatched as a precautionary thing."

"Yeah, probably. You ever fly in one, Scotty?"

"No, sir."

The president leaned back in his chair. "You know, it would be kinda fun to take a spin around town in one of those things. And wouldn't Bess have a shit fit if I came flying in and landed on the front lawn of the White House in that contraption?" said the president, breaking into a grin.

Over Dahlgren, Virginia. 0947 hours.

Flying at about three hundred feet, I was following the shoreline of the Potomac River with both the weather and my anxiety getting worse by the minute, when I spotted the Dahlgren dock. As I approached, I eased off on the collective and started a gentle circle to scan the area for wires and obstacles.

It wouldn't be long now, and I would know who my VIP passenger was. Would it really be the president? Probably. That stirred the excitement—and the reality: if it were him, it would also mean that something bad was going on, like a nuclear attack.

"Bluebird, this is Eagle. Do you have your destination in sight?" cracked the voice in my headset.

"Roger, Eagle. I got it."

"Is it suitable for landing, Bluebird?"

"It is suitable."

"Good work, Bluebird. Stand by for instructions."

"Roger."

Sequoia. Potomac River. 0948 hours.

Michael Kelly, Secret Service agent in charge of the presidential security on the *Sequoia,* shook his head grimly. "I can't believe they're even considering this madness."

"You mean the helicopter, uh, Bluebird?" said agent Jeff Miller, the other Secret Service agent aboard the ship.

"That's exactly what I mean."

"Well, I'm sure it won't actually come to pass. It's just a precautionary exercise," said Miller, standing beside Kelly in the yacht's small control center.

"I know, but it makes me nervous. That program is only supposed to be activated in case of a code red one."

"Yes, but with command communications down, I guess they figure an alert could happen and the president would be out of touch. I think that's what they are concerned about."

"That's true. But from a security standpoint, putting the president of the United States in a single-engine aircraft to putsy out across the countryside is pure madness."

Miller nodded. "Yeah, I have to agree with that."

"After all there's no code red one in effect."

"Well, there could be."

Hesitation. "Yeah. That's true. In fact, when I stop to think about it, the chief wasn't all that thrilled about using a helicopter, so he sure wouldn't authorize Bluebird unless . . . Jesus! You don't suppose?"

Command Center, Pentagon. 0950 hours.

Lt. Col. Ray Benning pushed open the glass door of the general's cubicle without knocking and shouted breathlessly: "General Moody! Code red one is canceled!"

Moody looked at the officer incredulously. "What did you say?"

"It's canceled, sir. The signal just came in from ADC HQ Command."

"How . . . what?" The general grabbed the red phone on his console and punched the button. "ADC Commander," he growled.

After a moment. "What the hell is going on, Kevin?"

Another moment of listening. "Christ, Kevin, how could that be?"

More listening. "All right, all right. Get things shut down, and I'll talk to you later." The general set the red phone back in its cradle and looked at Benning. "Old Murphy's Law has really been in full swing today," he said, shaking his head, then added: "But thank God it was Murphy instead of the real thing." [Murphy's Law: If something can go wrong, it will.]

Approaching Dahlgren, Virginia. 0953 hours.

Col. William Scott stepped up to the polished wooden door of the presidential suite and knocked. "Come in," said the president.

Scott opened the door and stepped inside. "Mr. President, we'll be docking in a few minutes."

"Okay. I'm ready. Have the secretary and the others been advised?"

"Yes, sir. They are on deck and ready to debark."

"Okay, I'll go up and join them," said President Truman, getting up from the desk where he had been writing.

"You may want to slip on a jacket, Mr. President. It turned a bit nippy on deck."

A few minutes later, President Truman and Colonel Scott left the suite. "Doggone, the weather did turn a little sour on us didn't it?" said the president as they walked out under the canvas awning on the yacht's aft deck.

"Yes, sir, it sure did," said Scott.

"Sorry our cruise got interrupted, fellows," said President Truman, as he joined the secretary of state and a small group of his other guests. "We got a little problem with both the weather and our communications, so to make sure all the bases are covered we had to make a change in the schedule."

At the sudden sound of beating rotor blades overhead, everyone glanced up.

"By Jove, there he is, sure enough," said the president.

"What is it?" asked the secretary of state.

"Why that's Bluebird, my taxi service back to Washington," said President Truman, grinning broadly.

Secret Service agent Michael Kelly gasped and turned pale.

Over Dahlgren, Virginia. 0959 hours.

As I circled the Potomac River dock at Dahlgren, I was scanning my landing area so intently that I evidently flew right over the top of the *Sequoia* without seeing it. On the dock, there were armed weapons carriers, jeeps, and soldiers in full battle dress. It was the type of scene you would expect with a code red one in effect. And I knew with a sudden, terrible certainty who my passenger was.

"Bluebird, this is Eagle."

"Roger, Eagle. I'm preparing to land."

"Bluebird, this is Eagle. Code red one is canceled. Do not land. Your mission is terminated. Return to station."

"What?"

"I repeat, Bluebird. Do not land. Your mission is canceled. Take up a heading of 163 degrees."

I sat there in the cockpit of the Sikorsky helicopter for a couple of minutes. What in the world had happened? Was this all some kind of a joke? One minute a nuclear attack on the United States is imminent and I'm about to fly the president. The next moment a stoic voice says it's all canceled, go home.

"Bluebird, this is Eagle, acknowledge your new heading please."

"Uh, repeat, Eagle?"

"Your heading, Bluebird, is 163 degrees."

Silence.

"Eagle, this is Bluebird. What's going on here?" I transmitted. I shouldn't have, but I did.

Silence.

"Look at it this way, Bluebird: it's better than the alternative."

I thought about it for a moment and realized that, obviously, code red one had started out as the real thing, then someone, somewhere in all that complex structure of thousands of men and women involved in the defense of our country, discovered that it wasn't the real thing.

"Yeah, you're right, Eagle," I said.

Memory wouldn't provide me with some of the details involving call signs, timing, and such, so I improvised. But my role in the story is the way I remember it. The action at the command center, the White House, and on the *Sequoia* is how I envisioned it might have happened. As it turned out, a real code red one never came, fortunately, and President Truman never did get his spin around town in the helicopter. President Eisenhower was the first to fly in a helicopter on 13 July 1957. It was an Air Force Bell VH-13J. President Kennedy was the first president to use the helicopter regularly. Since then, it has been a common sight in Washington to see *Marine One,* a big twin-jet Sikorsky, coming and going from the White House lawn.

In front of my P-38 after a mission in New Guinea, late 1943. My squadron, the 9th Fighter Squadron of the 49th Fighter Group, Fifth Air Force, called itself the Flying Knights. The 9th flew P-40s, P-38s, P-47s, and P-51s in combat during World War II, from Darwin, Australia, in 1942, through the entire South Pacific war, to Japan in 1945. I was with the squadron from November 1943 to December 1944.

Beside a P-38 on Biak Island, Maj. Thomas McGuire confers with the Lone Eagle, Charles Lindbergh, July 1944. The great aviator himself taught us how to extend our range by reducing RPM. (Lindbergh House)

A gathering of aces, late 1944. Third from left, Gerald Johnson. From fifth from left: Wally Jordan, Richard Bong, Tommy McGuire, and Bob DeHaven. (49th Fighter Group Association)

Top guns of the 49th Fighter Group taken at Biak Island just prior to our return to the Philippines in the fall of 1944. Richard Bong stands directly under the nose of the aircraft with Gerald Johnson to his immediate left. The author is on the wing, second from the left. (49th Fighter Group Association)

Maj. Richard Bong, ace of aces, receives the Congressional Medal of Honor from Gen. Douglas MacArthur, late 1944. (49th Fighter Group Association)

Me on the right, with Lt. John McLean at our camp in New Guinea, 1943. John had just returned from his R and R in Sydney. He was killed shortly afterward.

The word *Greenhouse,* cut out of foil, was pasted on this piece of wood, nailed to a tree several miles from ground zero of an atomic explosion on Eniwetok atoll, early 1951. The blackened wood attests to the fiery heat of the blast. The "Q" identification badge shown here was mine, as was the small black cylinder, a dosimeter. We wore them to keep track of the amount of radioactivity we received.

Standing in front of our tent home on Ch'o Do Island, North Korea, that bitter cold Christmas of 1952. We were there to pick up jet pilots who'd been shot down over "MiG Alley." The sign over the door reads: You Ditch and Call. We Bitch and Haul. Behind the Lines, Anytime, Rain or Shine.

Me on the left, with Lt. Jerry Pouhlin at Seoul, Korea, winter of 1953. We were preparing to fly a Sikorsky H-19 helicopter up to Ch'o Do Island (150 miles into North Korea) to swap crews.

The village of Sosa Ri on Ch'o Do Island, late 1952. We called it So Sorry. It was just over the ridge from our camp and was the village where I Are Hongaree lived.

Painting at our camp in Korea, early summer, 1953. I sketched and painted all over Korea, as I rotated around to our many helicopter-rescue sites.

I took this photo in the operating room at the 8055 MASH in late 1952. The surgeons were working on a patient I had flown in from the battlefield.

One of the fine, brave young nurses at the 8055 MASH, winter of 1953, near the 38th parallel. She had just taken a shower after an all-night session in surgery.

My element commander, Capt. Charles Enderton, flying a Sikorsky H-5 helicopter, went down on a frontline mission near the 38th parallel in early 1953.

The Sikorsky model R-5A in which the author had his "First Flight" at McChord Field, Washington, summer 1947.

Photo taken shortly after their escape from North Korea on October 26, 1951. From left to right: Lt. Col. John Dean, 1st Lt. Charles DuPont, Cpl. Gerald Fryer, Capt. Robert Barnhill, and 1st Lt. Vernon Wright.

1st Lt. Richard Kirkland at Langley Air Force Base, Virginia, standing beside "Bluebird" Sikorsky H-5, March 1952.

Capt. Richard Kirkland and medic, with wounded GI in litter pod attached to Sikorsky H-5. We had just picked up the patient from the Korean battle-field and landed at 8055 MASH, winter 1952–53.

Dr. Sam Gilfand, alias "Hawkeye," at the 8055 MASH, Korea, winter 1953.

Author (left), copilot Lt. Bill Tuttle, and T.Sgt. R. T. Hanke shortly after arrival at the Sikorsky factory at the completion of a record-breaking flight in the Sikorsky H-19, December 1955.

Lt. John Harris beside his Boeing CH-46 helicopter, Vietnam, summer 1969. (Courtesy Lt. John Harris)

WO Bill Kirk (right) with Mark Babcock, his wing-man, in a UH-1, T-Bird 4 gunship at Soc Trang Army Airfield, Vietnam, spring 1968. (Courtesy Bill Kirk)

CHAPTER ELEVEN

Pedro One

After my assignment to the Bluebird Project at Langley Air Force Base, Virginia, I returned to Pope AFB, North Carolina. It was good to be back with my family again, but it didn't last long. A short time later I was sent to Korea as a helicopter pilot.

Well, I was pissed, and so were my wife and kids. But then, I had made my own bed, so to speak, so I would lie in it. It bothered me, however, that my combat experience was all in fighter aircraft, not helicopters. And I couldn't imagine what we could accomplish with slow-moving, unarmed helicopters in a combat zone. I found out.

The Third Air Rescue Group of the USAF Air Rescue Service was credited with saving the lives of nearly 10,000 United Nations personnel during the Korean War. And, I'm proud to say, I was a part of that great effort.

This chapter is an account of the action and emotion involved in one of the first lifesaving missions flown by a Sikorsky helicopter in the combat zone during the early days of the Korean War. I created the dialogue from one of my own experiences on a similar mission.

On 14 March 1951, Gen. Matthew Ridgeway's United States Eighth Army pushed the North Koreans out of Seoul, and the UN forces reoccupied the capital of South Korea for the second time since the Korean War had begun, in June 1950. A few days later, a lone U.S. Air Force helicopter from the Third Air Rescue Group appeared over the skeletons of burned-out buildings and smoldering remains of destroyed aircraft at Kimpo airfield. Eyes from every direction glanced up and watched curiously, as the alien machine settled to a landing in a small clearing within the devastation.

When the big windmill on top had stopped turning, the pilot, wearing a blue flight suit and a red baseball cap with a captain's bar pinned to the front of it, climbed out of the cockpit. The crew chief, in mechanic's fatigues with sergeant's stripes, crawled out of the rear seat. The two men stood beside the helicopter for a moment, silently surveying the scene.

It was a landscape filled with wreckage between islands of olive-drab tents, sandbagged bunkers, stacks of military equipment, and skyward-trained antiaircraft guns. Within the devastation, Army trucks, bulldozers, and men engaged in a beehive of activity swarmed over the remains of the air base.

Sgt. Ray Stevens, short and stocky, with a crop of auburn hair that he parted down the middle, squinted from behind a set of bushy eyebrows and said, "Those guys sure got their work cut out for them."

Capt. Rick Carpenter, tall and lanky, with intense green eyes and an unruly mop of sandy blond hair, nodded. "That they do, Ray. But they'll have that airstrip back in operation in no time. I've seen them, during the war, build an airstrip overnight while the fighting was going on all around them. Gotta give those Corps of Engineers guys a lot of credit."

"Yeah, sure do," agreed Stevens. The two men watched a bulldozer, with a white star painted on the hood, shoot out black smoke from its exhaust pipe as it dug into a pile of rubble.

Carpenter glanced around. "Some of our advance people are supposed to be around here somewhere, but good luck finding them."

"I got the feeling, Captain, that with all this confusion, we're going to have to fend for ourselves," said the sergeant.

"Yeah. I suspect our best bet is to utilize your special talents and scrounge ourselves some operating gear."

Stevens grinned. "We got a half dozen bottles of barter goods. I would've brought more, but . . . Hey, there goes an Army Quartermaster Corps truck now. Let's unload our goods, and I'll get to bartering."

True to his reputation, Sgt. Ray Stevens, "the scrounger," as he was known back in his squadron, managed to produce all the necessities for the two-man rescue unit to set up business: a pyramidal tent with wooden floor, two GI cots with mattresses, one potbellied stove with pipe, one field phone with wire, one large wooden crate for a table and two smaller ones for chairs, a two-burner Coleman lantern, and fourteen 55-gallon drums of 100-octane aviation gas, all delivered by Quartermaster Corps trucks to a choice location on the east side—considered the scenic side—of Kimpo airfield.

"I can't believe you got all this stuff for just six bottles of booze, Ray," marveled Carpenter the next evening, as they sat around their new potbellied stove in their new tent, eating C-ration dinners.

"Well, I could've done better, but that quartermaster outfit hasn't been over here long enough to really be hurting yet. I still got one bottle of Canadian Club left," replied the sergeant, spearing a miniature sausage with his sheath knife. "CC is premium goods, and I can use it to make a deal for us to take chow at that antiaircraft outfit as soon as they get their mess hall set up."

"That would be great, Ray, C rations get old pretty fast. I tracked down the group that's hooking up the field-phone lines, and they promised to get us connected with the air-controller folks as soon as they get set up. Then we can declare ourselves in business."

Stevens looked across the potbellied stove at Carpenter and asked, "Uh, Captain, would you tell me again just exactly what we are supposed to be doing?"

The captain hesitated. "Well, the colonel wasn't just sure how it's all going to work, because they're still sorting out details. But his plan is to set up a base for our helicopter-rescue operations here at Seoul. Now, that sort of depends on our troops keeping the Commies from overrunning us again. But it looks like General Ridgeway and his boys are going to be able to do that. Meanwhile, you and I are sort of an advance team to get things organized and provide rescue service until the rest of our unit gets here."

"Uh . . . who all do we rescue?"

"Well, whoever needs it. Wounded GIs on the battlefield, or pilots and aircrews that get shot down. The fighter-bomber guys are starting to really pound the Commies now, and there's bound to be losses."

"What if they get shot down behind the lines in North Korea?"

"We'll go get them wherever they are."

"Uh, Captain, isn't that going to be pretty risky, flying an unarmed helicopter into enemy territory?"

Carpenter thought for a moment. "Yeah. It's going to be high risk, all right, Ray, but that's what we're going to do. And if they go down out in the Yellow Sea, we'll go out there too and fish them out, and bring them back."

The sergeant speared another sausage from the C ration. "That Yellow Sea is awful cold this time of year."

"Yeah, I know. They say you lose consciousness after only a couple minutes in that water."

"Hey in there! Wake up!" shouted a voice at the entrance of the tent that housed the new helicopter-rescue unit, early the next morning.

Popping up from his sleeping bag, Rick Carpenter tried to focus on the round face that was peering through the tent door.

"Who gave you the authority to put up a tent here?" growled the face.

"What? Ah, what's the problem?" muttered Carpenter as he tried to fight his way out of a sleep fog.

"Who's in charge here?" demanded the face, as the rest of a short, rounded body came through the door.

"I guess I am," mumbled Carpenter. Then, noticing the silver eagle on the front of the fur cap, he added, "sir."

"And who are you? And what do you think you're doing, putting up a tent and parking that machine here, whatever the hell it is? You're right where a supply depot is going to be!"

"Well sir, uh . . ." Carpenter glanced across the tent to where Stevens was pulling himself up to a sitting position on his GI cot.

"The Corps of Engineers lieutenant said it was okay with him," explained the sergeant.

"He doesn't have the authority to approve that. I'm in command here. Now you guys get this tent and that machine, and the rest of your junk out of here, and you do it fast! Do you understand?"

"But Colonel," stuttered Carpenter. "We're setting up a rescue unit to respond to emergency calls, and—"

"I don't give a damn what you're setting up, it ain't gonna be here. Now get your asses out of those sacks and get this shit out of here, or I'll have it bulldozed and—"

"Excuse me! Excuse me!" interrupted an excited voice from the door, behind the colonel.

"What is this, Grand Central Station?" mumbled Stevens.

"Is this the new rescue unit?" asked the new voice.

"I don't know what it is, but I do know it ain't gonna be here much longer," growled the colonel.

"Oh, Colonel, sir, we got an emergency. An F-80 on an early morning strike is in trouble. He may have to eject. Could that heelocopter go help him?"

And so the newly arrived helicopter-rescue unit had its first official call of thousands to come over the next two and a half years of the Korean War.

"You got his coordinates and route?" Carpenter

asked quickly, as he and Stevens scrambled out of bed and began to hurriedly dress.

The lieutenant who had brought the request glanced from the colonel to Carpenter. "Well not exactly, but we're talking to his flight leader. I'm from K-16 control. We just set up operations on that ridge behind us. Our radar is working, but it's a little squirrelly."

"What are you talking to him on?"

"We got him on VHF [very high frequency] emergency."

"Go get the bird started, Ray, while I get the info."

"You got it, Captain," replied the sergeant, heading for the door of the tent while still pulling on his clothes.

"Hold on there!" barked the colonel. "I got my problems too. This place has got to be moved, now!"

The lieutenant again glanced from the colonel to the captain, not sure whom he should be addressing.

"You say you're talking to his flight leader?" asked Carpenter, ignoring the colonel.

"Yeah. Tiger Red lead. They're a flight of four. Tiger Red two is the one in trouble. They're out over the Yellow Sea, west of here. He took a hit up north and is trying to coax it to Inchon."

"If you don't get this goddamn tent out of here this morning, I'm gonna bulldoze it, you hear? I'm telling you, I—"

The crack of a Pratt and Whitney R-985 engine coming to life outside cut the colonel off in midsentence.

"What's your call sign at K-16 control?"

"We're Top Dog."

"Tell Top Dog, Pedro One is on his way. Sorry,

Colonel, this is an air-rescue emergency," said Rick Carpenter, grabbing his yellow Mae West [life vest] and running through the tent door.

A few seconds later, when he pulled pitch for take-off and the Sikorsky H-5 leaped into the air, he caught a glimpse of the colonel ducking his round head and running in full retreat from the swirling rotor wash. "Takes all kinds to make an Army," he muttered, as he increased the pitch even more, sending the H-5 skimming out over startled faces and the long black muzzles of an antiaircraft battery.

He watched the manifold-pressure gauge until it indicated maximum continuous power, then tightened the friction knob to hold that setting. "He's apparently out over the water east of Inchon and in trouble. We may have to use that new personnel hoist, Ray, so make sure it's working," he shouted over his shoulder to Ray Stevens in the backseat.

"I'll check 'er out, Captain," Stevens shouted back.

Switching on the VHF radio, Carpenter pulled on his headset, punched the emergency channel, and hit the transmit switch: "Top Dog, Top Dog, this is Pedro One, do you read, over?"

No response.

"Top Dog from Pedro One, Top Dog from Pedro One!"

Silence again. Then: "Pedro One, this is Longbow. I think they shot craps. I was talking to them a while ago, but they just went dead."

"Roger, Longbow. Are you in contact with Tiger Red lead?"

"Negative. I'm a ground mobile, Pedro One."

"Longbow, do you have any way of contacting Top Dog?"

"Negative, Pedro One."

"Pedro, this is Wild Card, do you read?" came another voice transmission on the VHF emergency frequency.

"Roger, Wild Card; I read you, go ahead," responded Carpenter.

"Pedro One, are you a rescue aircraft?"

"Roger, Wild Card: Pedro One is a rescue aircraft."

"Okay, Pedro. I'm a flight of four headed for the barn but I'm talking to Tiger Red lead, and he's got an emergency and he's lost contact with Top Dog. Can you respond?"

"Roger, roger, Wild Card lead; that's what I'm here for. Can you give me his location?"

"Stand by, Pedro One, where are you?"

"Pedro is westbound out of K-16."

"Roger."

"There's something wrong with this hoist switch, Captain, but I think I can fix it," said Stevens over the intercom.

"Pedro One, Pedro One, this is Top Dog, do you read me now?"

Surprised, Carpenter responded, "Roger, Top Dog. I hear you now, five square [okay]."

"Okay, Pedro One. We just got set up yesterday and we're having trouble with our transmitter. You the rescue aircraft?"

"Pedro One, this is Wild Card; Tiger Red estimates he's about 50 west of Inchon, but isn't sure."

"Wild Card, this is Top Dog. We're back on the air and we're trying to get a fix on Tiger Red's position now. Pedro One, stand by. Tiger Red lead, this is Top Dog. Do you read?"

No answer.

"Tiger Red lead, this is Top Dog, over?"

No answer.

"Top Dog, this is Wild Card, he's not reading you."

"Wild Card, from Top Dog, are you visual with Tiger Red flight?"

"Negative. We're in the Black Jack Sector" [the code name for the sector in which they flew].

"Okay, would you tell Tiger Red we're back in operation. We just picked him up again on the scope, and we'll keep trying to contact him on voice."

"Roger wilco."

"And tell him that the rescue aircraft Pedro One is en route."

"Roger wilco."

"Good morning, Top Dog, this is Fat Cat Zero Six. Could you tell me if K-16 tower is in operation yet?" interjected a new voice.

"Negative, Fat Cat, they're not in operation yet and get off this channel. We got an emergency in progress."

"Roger."

"Pedro One, Top Dog here: what's your position?"

"I'm about 10 [miles] west of K-16 heading for Inchon, Top Dog."

"Are you on the deck [flying low over the surface]?"

"Roger."

"Can you climb up a little so we can try to get a fix on you?"

"Pedro is starting to climb now on a 270-degree heading."

"Top Dog, this is Wild Card. Tiger Red lead wants to know Pedro's position and advises that his emergency chick [aircraft] is running out of altitude."

"Roger, Wild Card, tell him the rescue helicopter is 10 west on a 270-degree heading."

"What did you say was en route?"

"A helicopter."

Silence.

"Understand, Top Dog, you said a heelocopter is en route to Tiger Red?"

"Pedro One, from Top Dog. You are a helicopter? Is that affirmative?"

"This is Pedro One. That is affirmative, Top Dog. I am a helicopter."

Another silence. Then: "You just get here, heeleocopter?"

"Affirmative."

"Captain, I got the switch fixed and the personnel hoist seems to work okay," said Stevens.

"Top Dog, this is Fat Cat Zero Six. I got a load of priority cargo and I can't get anybody to talk to me."

"Fat Cat Zero Six, I told you to stay off the emergency channel!"

"Top Dog, this is Tiger Red lead, Top Dog from Tiger Red, come in please!" came another new voice on the emergency channel.

"Roger, roger, Tiger lead, we're receiving you now, loud and clear. We think we're painting you on radar about 60 west of Inchon."

"Roger, Top Dog; that's about our position. My hurt chick is losing about 500 feet a minute, but if everything holds he'll make it to Inchon. Where is the rescue aircraft now?"

"Tiger Red lead, he's en route, and we're in radio contact with him but haven't been able to get him on the scope; stand by . . . Pedro One, we still can't paint you, what's your position and altitude?"

"Tiger Red lead, this is Wild Card; got to leave you, we're getting low on go juice. Good luck!"

"Thanks for the assist, Wild Card."

"Top Dog, this is Pedro. I'm at 1,500 about 20 west of K-16."

"Pedro, that's probably why I can't paint you: you're still too low. Can't you get up higher?"

"Roger, Top Dog, I'll climb up some more."

"Pedro One, Pedro One, this is Tiger Red lead. I just picked up your transmission, do you read me?"

"Roger, Tiger Red lead. I'm reading you now; go ahead."

"Okay, Pedro. Understand you're a rescue helicopter, is that affirmative?"

"Roger, Tiger lead, Pedro One is a Sikorsky helicopter."

"How long will it take you to get that Sikorsky helicopter to Inchon, Pedro One?"

After a quick glance at his flight chart, Carpenter answered, "About ten minutes, Tiger Red lead."

"Okay, Pedro. Tiger Red Two has taken a hit and has a sick engine. His plan is to try to coax it in to the mudflats at Inchon and eject. We ought to arrive there about the same time you do. Your helicopter can pick him up out there, right?"

"Affirmative, Tiger Red lead. Pedro will get him."

"Great, Pedro! Frank, this is Steve. They got an air-rescue aircraft coming out to pick you up, ol' buddy. It's a helicopter, believe it or not! Yeah, a helicopter . . . beats me where they got it, but they got it. Just hang in there, man, and keep that baby perkin' just the way you're goin'. You still got partial power? . . . Great . . . Okay!"

"Pedro One, this is Top Dog. We still can't pick you up on the scope but we'll keep trying."

"Pedro One, Tiger Red lead here. At the present rate, I figure my chick will be down to angels five [5,000 feet] when we reach the mudflats, plenty of airspace for him to eject."

"Roger, Red lead."

"Tiger Red lead, this is Top Dog."

"Go, Top Dog."

"Red lead, be advised those mudflats will be covered with 20 feet of water if the tide is in."

"Oh, shit!"

Silence.

"Pedro, can you see the mudflats yet? I can see the coastline out in the distance, but I can't tell where the tide is."

Hesitation.

"Tiger Red, this is Pedro; hold on a second."

"Roger, Pedro, Tiger Red standing by."

"Tiger Red lead, this is Pedro One. I'm not quite there yet, but I can see that the tide is out, repeat, the tide is out!"

"Hot damn! Frank, you hear that? We're in luck, buddy, the tide is out . . . yeah . . . Those ol' mudflats are ready and waitin'. Won't be long now, you got it made!"

Minutes later, the Sikorsky H-5 passed over the unique textural patterns of the Inchon mudflats. A morning haze partially obscured the vast panorama, but Carpenter could see the tidal basin stretching for miles in all directions. He couldn't help but wonder, in a passing thought, how in the world the U.S. Seventh Army had managed to cross this during MacArthur's famous Inchon landing. No wonder it had been called one of the great feats in military history.

"Steve, she just quit dead on me," came the calm, clear voice in Rick Carpenter's headset, and he knew it was the voice of the pilot in distress: Tiger Red Two.

"Okay Frank, just keep her steady. Pedro One, Pedro One!"

"Roger Red lead, I heard his transmission. I'm going to try to talk to him direct. Tiger emergency, this is Pedro One, do you read me, over?"

"I can read you now, Pedro One. I've lost all power, but I still think I can make it to the mudflats. Can you pick me up out there?"

"Roger, Red two, we can pick you up, no sweat. I'm over the mudflats now. Let me know as soon as you spot me."

"Roger, Pedro One, I'm looking."

"Top Dog, this is Red lead, you painting the helicopter yet?"

"We still can't get him, Tiger Red."

"Frank, this is Steve. It doesn't look so good to me, ol' buddy. You're sinking too fast . . . I don't think you can stretch your glide to those mudflats, do you?"

"I got no choice, Steve. I got to try to make it. I'm not about to punch out into that ice water."

"But if you let 'er get too low, Frank . . ."

"I know, but I got to chance it, Steve, got to chance it."

As Rick Carpenter listened, his thoughts flashed back a lifetime, to recall almost the same conversation he'd had with one of his flight buddies over the waters off New Guinea in World War II. The terminology had been a little different. In those days it was: "bail out," not "punch out" or "eject." And the fear was not of ice water, it was of sharks in the warm South Pacific waters.

But his dilemma had been the same as that faced by Tiger Red Two: if he waited too long, there wouldn't be enough altitude for the parachute to work, and that meant staying with the aircraft for a water landing. Contrary to Hollywood's version, crash-landing a fighter plane in the water usually meant the fat lady would sing. Carpenter had managed to stretch his glide, that day, to a little island—and he survived a crash landing on a palm-studded beach.

But today, here in Korea, Tiger Red Two had a choice, didn't he? There had been no helicopter to pick up Rick Carpenter. But there was one to pick up Tiger Red Two. Yes, but could he be sure? Could he find a man in that vast water wilderness? And if he did, would it be in time? He knew that a man could only survive a few minutes in the Yellow Sea in winter. The water was that cold. And so what do you do now, Capt. Rick Carpenter?

"Frank! Listen buddy, you got to get out. You're not going to make it . . . Frank, punch out!"

"Tiger Red Two, this is Pedro. I can pick you up out of the water just as easy as I can pick you up out of the mudflats. I have a personnel-rescue hoist on the helicopter," transmitted Rick Carpenter.

"Can't do it, can't do it, can't go into that water. I'll make it . . . I can see the mudflats."

"Frank, you can't make it to the mudflats! You heard what that guy in the helicopter said? He can pick you up out of the water so get out, Frank. Get out! Please!"

"Pedro One, from Top Dog, I still can't paint the helicopter."

"Frank, for God's sake, punch out!"

"Can't do it, Steve."

"I got you, Tiger Red Two! Pedro's got you in sight!" shouted Carpenter over the radio.

"Jesus Christ, Frank, there he is! There's the helicopter! I can see him . . . you see him? See him down there! He's dead ahead . . . Frank! Get out, get out!"

"I guarantee I'll pick you up, Tiger Red Two, I guarantee it!"

Rick Carpenter, his eyes glued to the silver body of the jet fighter on its slanting course to the sea, watched with gripping fascination as, suddenly, two objects separated from the aircraft in a puff of gray smoke and arched away from its flight path. An instant later, a parachute popped open from the forked object while the other, the canopy, emitted glistening flashes as it tumbled through the morning sunlight. Another instant and the P-80 struck the Yellow Sea, disintegrating in a geyser of foam and flame, followed by a series of smaller geysers as pieces of the aircraft spewed out along its hurtling path. The forked object in the parachute made two oscillations and then also struck the water, with a smaller geyser.

"There he is, Captain! See him there in the water?"

"I see him, Ray . . . okay. I have hoist control and it's going down now. I'll come in to about a 6-foot hover over him. As soon as he's in the rescue collar, I'll winch him up and you pull him in."

"Okay Captain, I'm ready," replied Stevens.

The jet pilot's yellow Mae West and his floating red-and-white parachute were clearly visible against the dark blue water of the Yellow Sea, as Carpenter swung into the wind and brought the Sikorsky into a hover. Glancing down, he could see the rotor wash whip-

ping up a white-capped storm in the water around
the pilot, and for a brief instant he saw the pilot's
white face, stricken from the paralyzing effect of the
frigid water.

"Oh Jesus, Captain, the hoist cable has backlashed
and tangled on the drum!"

"What! Can you untangle it?"

"Pedro One, Pedro One, have you got him?"

"The fucking thing is jammed!"

"Try it from back there!"

"Won't do any good. It's completely jammed on
the cable drum!"

"Shit!"

"Pedro One! Pedro One! Answer me, goddamn it!
Have you got him?"

"I can't get it to budge, Captain!"

"Windmill, talk to me!"

"I'm going down, Ray. I'm going to hover down
low enough for you to reach out and grab him."

"I'll try Captain, I'll try. Don't get too low, you'll
draw water into the carburetor intake and kill the engine."

"I know! I know."

Down, lower and lower, Carpenter edged the H-5,
his peripheral vision watching the wheels submerge
into the whipped seawater. And then, for one agonizing second, his eyes met those of the jet pilot through
the canopy of the helicopter—only inches away, yet
so far—in the freezing hell below, his face framed by
the white crash helmet that had a small red tiger
painted on the front, his water-soaked eyes screaming: You promised! You promised!

"Right! Right a little!" shouted Stevens.

"Pedro One! Pedro One! Answer me!"

"Easy, Captain . . . hold it . . . back a little," instructed the sergeant, lying on the floor of the aft cabin and hanging halfway out of the helicopter, trying to grasp the downed pilot as Carpenter hovered so low the H-5 was immersed in a swirling cloud of sea spray.

"I got him! I got him!"

Oh God, he's got him!

"Hold, Captain! Hold 'er steady."

"Can you pull him in?"

"I'm trying! I'm trying! Hold on, fella! Hold on to me!

"Oh shit, he's still attached to his parachute! I've got ahold of him, but there's no way to get him in with a parachute full of seawater!"

"Hit the quick release on his chute, Ray!"

"Can't. Can't reach it!"

"What the fuck is goin' on, Pedro?"

"Pedro One, this is Top Dog, what's the status of Tiger Red Two, over."

"Is it off, Ray?"

No answer for an eternity. Finally: "I got it! I got it! I found the release, his parachute is off!"

"Can you pull him in now?"

After a few seconds: "Can't do it, Captain, he's too heavy, and he can't help himself, he's too far gone!"

"I swear to God, I'll shoot you down, Windmill, if you don't talk to me!"

"Attach the seat belt to him, Ray."

"The seat belt?"

"Yeah! Attach your seat belt to his harness and I'll lift him up that way."

"Jesus! You're gonna let him dangle?"

"We got no choice, Ray, do it! Hurry!"

"Okay, I'll try . . ."

No transmission for another eternity.

"Okay! I got it hooked. I don't know if it will hold him!"

"It's got to hold him, it's got to. Get yourself back inside, Ray, I'm going up!"

The Sikorsky helicopter lifted its wheels out of the rotor-whipped water and moved off over the swells of the Yellow Sea, with an inert figure dangling beneath its fuselage.

"You got him, Pedro? You got him?"

"We got him."

"He's got him. He's got Frank!"

"As soon as I get to the mudflats, Ray, we'll have to land and get him inside. It's only a few minutes' flying."

"Can you land in that mud?"

"I'll have to. He's probably already in shock, so we can't leave him hanging out there. He'll freeze solid."

"Pedro One, you got him hanging underneath that thing?"

"Affirmative."

"Jesus Christ, is he okay? Can't you pull him inside?"

"Negative."

"Pedro One, Top Dog. You have anything on Tiger Red Two?"

"Top Dog, this is Tiger Red lead, Pedro's down on the deck and can't read you. He's picked up the pilot, all right, but he's apparently got a problem and he ain't talkin'."

"I don't know how deep that mud is, Ray, but I'll ease her down to where you can get out and push him in. Okay?"

"I'll do my best, Captain."

"Pedro One, Tiger Red lead," came a calm voice. "We'd appreciate a word from you, man . . . please tell us something."

Carpenter glanced up at the three F-80s flying a weaving pattern above him. Their emotional calls about their buddy had registered in his brain, all right, but his concentration had centered on hovering the partially submerged helicopter. But he'd been in their shoes, and he knew how they felt. He pushed the transmit switch: "Roger Red lead. We've had some equipment problems and we're going to have to make a landing as soon as we reach the mudflats and get him inside the helicopter. Then we'll be off to the nearest MASH," he said, his voice calm despite the terrible uncertainty that raged inside.

"God, that's great, Pedro. Sorry for the . . . the . . . uh, other stuff . . . we got a little anxious up here."

Silence for a moment.

"I understand, Tiger Red flight, I understand," said the pilot of Pedro One.

The Inchon tidal basin, formed by the sediment carried out by the Han River for however many centuries, was a marine world marvel. It was also very deep and very gooey mud. Carpenter brought the H-5 to a hover, setting the dangling pilot down first and then moving sideways slightly and easing the Sikorsky's wheels slowly into the mud.

"Don't forget the tail rotor!" yelled Stevens, as he saw the main wheels disappear into the ooze.

"I'll have to hold her with power, Ray, otherwise she'll sink out of sight. I hope you can pull him in by yourself."

"I'll try, Captain. I'm going to jump out of the helicopter into the mud. Just hold her steady!"

As much as he wanted to look back to see how Stevens was doing, Carpenter knew he didn't dare. He was holding the H-5 in a hover, with the wheels and part of the belly buried in the soft mud. He knew the tail rotor was only inches from the mud: one bobble or tilt would spell disaster.

"Pedro One, how you doing down there. You got him in yet?"

"Tiger Red lead, this is Top Dog. On your request: the nearest MASH is about three miles down the river from K-16. It's just below the bombed-out railroad bridge. You copy?"

"Roger, Top Dog, I'll get that to Pedro. He's down on the mudflats and . . . hold on . . . he just lifted up and is taking off. All right! And he's got Frank inside the windmill! Pedro One, Pedro One, Tiger lead."

"Roger, this is Pedro One. I heard Top Dog's message on the MASH location, Tiger lead. We have your buddy aboard and we'll have him there in a few minutes."

"Thanks, Pedro One! Thanks a million! We got to cut; we're low on fuel. But we all owe you, man, we owe you and that windmill!"

During the early days of the war, the term *windmill* was commonly used. But after rescue helicopters had been in operation for a while, that changed to the revered term *chopper*. And every fighter and bomber outfit in Korea had a standing invitation out: free drinks for any chopper crew who came visiting.

CHAPTER TWELVE

Chopper Down

The tall, lanky pilot sitting on his GI cot in a GI pyramidal tent fished a cigarette out of his shirt pocket and stuck it between his lips. As he fired it with a Zippo lighter, a field phone hanging on one end of his cot screeched. He reached across his bed and pulled the phone from its canvas case.

"Panmunjom, Lieutenant DuPont," he said with puffs of smoke tumbling out.

"This is Captain Durbin at JOC [Joint Operations Control]. We got a pilot down, and we're trying to locate a chopper to go get him. You got one available?"

DuPont frowned. "This is special operations at Panmunjom, Captain. You need to call rescue control at K-16."

"I've already called them, and they don't have a chopper available that could get up there in time."

"Well, we got one. But as you know, it's on special duty for the VIPs at the peace talks in Kaesong."

"This is an operational emergency, Lieutenant. We got a pilot down in enemy territory, and that chopper is the only one that can possibly get to him before dark."

It was fall 1951, and the United Nations had been fighting a "police action" war in Korea since September 1950. Although peace talks were ongoing, little had changed in the vicious fighting. Lt. Charles J. DuPont, a U.S. Air Force helicopter pilot, stood mute for a moment, holding the phone in one hand and a burning cigarette in the other.

"Lieutenant?"

"Yeah. . . . Where is he, Capt'n?"

"He's down in sector 14 Zebra."

He knew where 14 Zebra was: not all that far in a fighter plane, but a long damn way into enemy territory for a slow-moving chopper. "Okay. Capt'n, we'll go get 'em."

"Great. Have the pilot call us on the emergency frequency as soon as he's airborne, and we'll give him details and CAP [combat air patrol] information."

DuPont nodded, dropped the phone back into its case, and took a last puff of his cigarette before grinding it out. He lifted his survival vest and .45 pistol belt from where they hung on a two-by-four tent railing and started out through the door when the field phone screeched again. He turned and picked it up. "DuPont here."

"Charlie, this is Bob. What's goin' on?"

Capt. Bob Barnhill was the operations officer of Detachment F of the 3rd Air Rescue Squadron at K-16, Seoul, Korea, to which DuPont was assigned.

"I just told JOC that we'd send our VIP chopper to pick up the downed pilot."

"Have you cleared it with the general?"

"No. He's not here."

Hesitation.

"Bob, this chopper has to go now if we're gonna pick up that pilot before dark."

"Yeah, you're right. Who's flying the mission?"

"Yours truly, and I gotta get going."

"What? You can't do that, Charlie. You're grounded from combat flying. Get somebody else to fly the mission."

"There ain't anybody else, Bob. I'm the only one here. The other pilots are up at Kaesong at the peace conference. Either I go pick up that pilot or he's in deep kimchee. As soon as it's dark his CAP will have to leave, and the commies will grab him . . . or kill him. One is as bad as the other."

"I know, but . . . Jesus, Charlie, you've flown your ninety missions and that's gonna be a rough one; 14 Zebra is in a heavy concentration of North Korean troops."

"Well, I sure as hell don't like hearing that, Bob. But it doesn't change anything. I gotta go try to get him. There isn't any other option, is there?"

Hesitation. "No . . . no, I guess not. We don't have another chopper available that could get up there in time . . . I guess you drew the short straw, ole friend."

"Yeah. So it goes, Bob."

Charlie had picked up the wounded off the battlefield and snatched downed air crew from the Yellow Sea and behind enemy lines ninety times in a slow, un-armed, and totally unprotected helicopter. The Ko-rean War chopper had not been designed for combat and was therefore highly vulnerable. But lifesaving on the battlefield had been Charlie's job, and he had done it. When he finished his missions, however, he knew that he had stretched his luck to the limit, and it was time to go home.

About that time, the North Koreans had agreed to hold peace talks (while the war continued to rage), and the colonel had talked him into extending his tour of duty because they needed chopper pilots to fly the United Nations delegates from Panmunjom, South Korea, to Kaesong, North Korea. Since ninety was the maximum missions a pilot was allowed to fly, he would no longer be flying combat missions, but would be performing a great service for his country and the United Nations—so the colonel said.

DuPont walked out of his tent across to the one next door and stuck his head in. "I need a volunteer for a pilot pickup in North Korea."

Medical technician Sgt. Joe Fryer, sitting on a wooden box sewing a hole in his sock, looked at DuPont, then glanced around the empty tent and grinned. "By process of elimination, I guess that means me, Lieutenant."

"You'll do. And hustle it up, Joe."

"How come you're flying a combat mission, Lieutenant DuPont? I thought you were grounded."

"Yeah, so did I."

A few minutes later, with Joe Fryer, his medical kit, and .30-caliber carbine in the rear seat of the Sikorsky H-5 helicopter, DuPont pulled pitch and headed toward Inchon, on the west coast of Korea.

"JOC, this is Pedro Zero Nine. I'm airborne," he transmitted on the emergency frequency radio.

"Roger, Pedro Zero Nine is airborne. We have confirmed that 14 Zebra is the grid location of the downed pilot. He is from the 51st Fighter Interceptor

Wing, and he's being CAP'ed by F-80s from his squadron, call sign 'Hammer.' The call sign of your CAP is 'Grenadier Love.' They're a South African flight of four F-51s, and they should be on the emergency radio frequency shortly."

"Roger, JOC."

That's one bit of good news, thought Charlie. He had been capped before by the South Africans and they were good, and the F-51 was an excellent CAP aircraft. It could get down where the jets couldn't.

"Pedro Zero Nine, for rendezvous with your CAP, what's gonna be your ingress position and altitude?"

"I'd like to rendezvous with Grenadier Love over Inchon at 5,000 feet, JOC."

"Okay, I'll so advise them."

Charlie would have preferred to go in on the treetops, because at 5,000 feet in a chopper you were a perfect target for antiaircraft fire. But then at low altitude you took small-arms fire—or so the rationale went that established the 5,000-foot policy.

To minimize exposure, his plan was to fly west until he was directly south of 14 Zebra, which was near Inchon, pick up his CAP, and then turn north. If the pilot's location was correct, he would have to fly about forty miles inside North Korea—a long time to be exposed to enemy fire. But the South Africans would be merciless toward whomever shot at him—and each fighter packed deadly firepower.

"Pedro Zero Nine, this is Grenadier Love, we have you in sight," came the radio call as DuPont approached Inchon.

"Roger, Grenadier Love, I have you in sight also, and I'm making my turn north," replied Charlie as he spotted the formation of four F-51s arching across the sky above him.

"Roger, ole chap, let us know if you take any fire."

"You'll hear me loud and clear, Grenadier Love. Request you send one of your birds on up to 14 Zebra and give me a report on conditions."

"Roger. Number Four, pop on up there and take a look."

"Righto, lead. Number Four breaking off."

Lieutenant DuPont watched one of the F-51s peel off and accelerate to the north as the remaining three circled above the slow-flying helicopter.

As he flew northward at 5,000 feet, DuPont could see the vast Inchon tidelands, dotted with islands, stretching westward to the Yellow Sea. To the north, an overcast blocked the late-afternoon sun and cast a dull gray over the mountainous area ahead, as though a harbinger of what lay ahead.

"Grenadier Love lead, this is Four; go to tach frequency."

"Negative! Negative!" barked Charlie on the radio. "I'm the one that's gotta go in there, so I want to hear what's going on!"

"Roger, ole chap, we'll stay on this frequency. What's the story, Four?"

"Not too good," replied the pilot of Grenadier Love Four. "The downed pilot is hiding in a graveyard. But the place is swarming with North Korean troops. They do have a CAP of eight F-80s up there, and they're tearing up the countryside, but there's troops all over the place."

"He's hiding in a graveyard?"

"Yeah, he's on a hill in the graveyard, and the gooks are all around it."

Damn! That meant ground fire when he went in to make the pickup. It was going to be a rough mission all right, Charlie said to himself.

"Pedro Zero Nine, did you receive that information?"

"Yeah. I'd rather not have, but I got it, Grenadier Love."

"More bad news, ole chap," transmitted Number Four. "There's weather moving in. You can see the storm front over the mountains to the north, and I'd guess it will be over that area within the next half hour or so."

"Super," DuPont grumbled. Checking his map against the landmarks below, it appeared he had about fifteen miles to go, which should put him there before the bad weather struck. But that was probably the least of his worries. The only good news so far was that he had taken no antiaircraft fire.

Turning around in his seat, he shouted, "Keep an eye out for antiaircraft fire, Joe!" Since this vintage chopper did not have an intercom, communications depended on good ole shouting.

The medic scooted forward in the backseat and shouted back, "Okay, Lieutenant! Is this gonna be a hot one?"

"I'm afraid it is, Joe!"

Fryer nodded and moved back into his seat. Charlie felt sympathy for the poor medic who could do nothing but sit back there and hope for the best. At least he, as the pilot, could feel that he had some control over his own destiny . . . or did he?

"Pedro Zero Nine, this is Hammer. You read?" came a new transmission in DuPont's earphones.

"Roger, Hammer, Pedro Zero Nine here."

"We're the CAP on station, Pedro, what's your ETA?"

"About ten minutes, Hammer. How does it look?"

"Our guy is okay for now, but you're gonna be just in time. The valley is swarming with troops. We've kept them off the mountain where he is, but a few may have slipped through, so we need to get him out of there—the sooner the better."

"Okay, Hammer, how is the weather?"

"Not good. It's moving in fast. But we'll be able to work the area over once more before you get here."

As he approached the area of 14 Zebra, about ten minutes later, Charlie could see mushrooming clouds of black smoke caused by the attacking flight of jets that were strafing and firing rockets into the North Korean troop installations. He could also see the dark weather clouds moving down from the north.

"Hammer, this is Pedro Zero Nine. I'm over the south end of the valley now with my CAP, Grenadier Love. I'll be in position in a couple minutes to go in for the pickup," transmitted DuPont.

"Roger, I got you spotted. Hammer flight from lead, break off. Repeat, break off, the chopper is here and starting his run. Pedro Zero Nine, you got the graveyard in sight?"

After a short eye search, Charlie spotted the mountaintop graveyard. "Okay, Hammer and Grenadier Love, I got the graveyard in sight, and I plan to make my approach to the north."

"Sound off if you take any fire, Pedro," responded the Grenadier Love leader.

"You'll be the first to hear about it, Grenadier Love."

"Joe, keep a sharp lookout for ground fire!"

DuPont shouted to his medic and lowered the collective, nosing the helicopter downward.

As he flew down over the valley, DuPont saw the mountain ahead with the graveyard on top, and suddenly he remembered that Koreans bury their dead sitting up. The graveyard was covered with mounds. He wouldn't be able to land, and the helicopter he was flying did not have a personnel hoist. What else could go wrong?

"Joe, we're going in for the pickup. Don't open the cabin door till I tell you!"

"Yes, sir! Are you gonna try to land?"

"Can't land because of the grave mounds! I'll come to a hover, and you signal the pilot to grab onto the helicopter, then try to pull him inside!"

"Okay, but I don't see him!"

"Neither do I!"

"Maybe the gooks got him!"

It would be a hell of a note if the pilot had been captured at this point, thought Charlie as he eased in aft cyclic and lowered pitch to set up his approach to the mountaintop.

"You getting any ground fire, Pedro Zero Nine?" asked Grenadier Love from the cockpit of his F-51, as the four South African fighters circled over the small valley.

"So far it's negative on ground fire, Grenadier Love. But I can't see the pilot. Where is he?"

"There he is, Lieutenant!" Fryer shouted suddenly, leaning forward from the backseat and pointing a finger.

Charlie saw a figure run out from behind a grave mound, waving his arms frantically. "I got him," he said, banking slightly and pulling pitch to establish a hover. But as the H-5 settled toward the graveyard, he realized that the swirling winds from the approaching storm had shifted, causing the helicopter to yaw and buck violently.

He pulled pitch, nosed off to one side, and kicked rudder pedal to bring the helicopter back around for another approach. He could see the pilot chasing after him through the grave mounds, apparently afraid they were leaving without him.

"Open the cabin door!" Charlie shouted. "When I come to a hover over the mounds, he's gonna have to grab on!"

"Lieutenant! There's soldiers with guns right below us!" yelled the medic.

Charlie saw the North Korean soldiers in his peripheral vision, but his concentration focused on bringing the helicopter into a hover that would allow the pilot to climb in. But if he went too low, the tail rotor would strike one of the burial mounds, and that would be all she wrote.

He glanced out and saw the pilot, who was racing toward the helicopter, suddenly stop, raise his arm, and fire his .45 at two soldiers who were chasing him. Then he turned and ran toward the helicopter that was yawing and pitching in the shifting winds.

The pilot ran up to the helicopter and made a desperate lunge for the open door. Joe Fryer, hanging out of the door, grabbed him and hung on. All DuPont could hope was that Fryer had a good grip on the pilot, because soldiers had suddenly appeared directly in front of the helicopter. It was either pull pitch now or take a head-on fusillade of North Korean lead.

Charlie cranked the throttle full open and pulled all the pitch he could get.

"Pedro Zero Nine from Hammer, did you get 'em?"

No answer.

"Hammer to Pedro Zero Nine! Did you get Vern?"

DuPont heard Hammer's plea of concern for their squadron mate, but his total concentration was on flying the helicopter as fast as it would go away from the ground fire that he knew was pouring into the H-5.

He glanced back. The pilot was still hanging onto the side of the helicopter, with Fryer struggling to pull him inside.

"Answer me, chopper!" came the angry voice of Hammer.

"I don't know yet," said Charlie.

"What?"

"I got 'im in, Lieutenant!" shouted Fryer from behind.

Charlie DuPont felt that sudden, acute feeling of relief that he had always felt after snatching someone from the enemy's grasp. "We got him, Hammer," he said calmly over the radio.

"Hey! That's great! Everybody hear that? The chopper got Vern!"

Cheers were heard on radio frequency 121.5 as the CAP pilots looked down and saw the flashing blades of the Sikorsky helicopter skimming out across the mountain ridges of North Korea.

In the cabin of the helicopter, Fryer leaned forward, tapped DuPont on the back, and shouted, "Lieutenant, the pilot says that when he jumped onto the chopper he saw oil streaming out of the engine! He's got it all over him!"

Lady luck giveth and she taketh away, thought Charlie DuPont as he glanced at the oil-pressure gauge and saw the needle pegged on zero.

"Grenadier Love, this is Pedro Zero Nine. I got trouble."

"What's the problem, Pedro Zero Nine?"

"I took ground fire, and I got no engine oil pressure."

Silence.

"What are your intentions, ole chap?"

Yeah, DuPont . . . what are you gonna do?

"Stand by, Grenadier Love."

"Roger."

You can't will that Pratt & Whitney to keep running without oil. How long will it run? Not long. . . . You're going to have to land down there, and it's too late in the day to get choppers up here to get the three of you out. . . . The commies will be coming when they see you go down. . . . And the CAP can't protect you at night—they will have to go on home. . . . You should have known your luck couldn't last forever. . . .

DuPont glanced down at the terrain below. The canyons were already turning a dark blue gray as nightfall approached and the storm clouds moved relentlessly over the ridges. Not many places down there to make an autorotation landing. . . . But that's what he had to do. The engine can't run without oil, and, barring divine intervention, the helicopter was going down when it quit. . . . Maybe he could make it to the coast before it quit? . . . It wasn't too far, was it?

"Grenadier Love, I'm gonna try to make it to the coast. Call JOC and have them launch an SA-16 [twin-engine amphibian aircraft]. If I can make it, they can pick us up over there."

"Roger, wilco."

"Pedro Zero Nine, this is Hammer. We're low on fuel, but we'll help cover you as long as we can."

"Roger, Hammer."

Charlie turned his head and shouted, "Joe, buckle yourselves in tight! We got a rough landing comin' up!"

When he turned back to the instrument panel, he saw the cylinder head temperature gauge had pegged in the red. The radio became silent now as the CAP of F-51 and F-80 fighters circled above the helicopter flying over the darkening mountains.

"Grenadier Love from Pedro Zero Nine. Can you see how far it is to the coast?"

"Yeah. I can see the coastline. It's not too far after you cross that next big ridge."

Directly ahead was a heavily wooded ridge. If the engine quit while flying over it he would have to autorotate into the trees—not good. Somebody would get hurt for sure. Directly ahead was a small plateau of rice paddies. He could land there all right, . . . but they were North Korean rice paddies. If he could just make it over that ridge. . . . Come on, baby, you can run just a little longer, can't you?

Oil pressure zero, cylinder-head temperature gauge pegged, and an engine making strange noises. It was decision time. Charlie eased off on the collective and back on the cyclic for an approach to the rice paddies directly ahead. "Grenadier Love, I'm gonna have to land in the rice paddies up ahead. Let me know if you see any activity."

"Pedro Zero Nine, you're not all that far from the

coast, and JOC has an SA-16 and a chopper en route to the area."

"I've got a feeling that I can't make it over that ridge, Grenadier Love."

Charlie had discovered in his first ninety combat missions that when he got that certain feeling, he should act on it. And it was well that he did. As he brought the helicopter up over the rice paddies, the engine gave out a groan and quit dead.

His instinct was correct, but he was just a few yards short of the rice paddy and had to make his landing on the lip of the paddy, which caused the H-5 to topple over on its side. The rotor blades struck the ground, and the helicopter thrashed around violently until the blades had beat themselves to death, hurling pieces all over the countryside.

When the thrashing subsided and all the pieces came to rest, the three men scrambled out of the wreckage, fortunately uninjured. They stood for a moment, staring at the twisted and broken helicopter. They had lost their means of escape, but somehow they knew the Sikorsky helicopter had given its all.

"She did pretty well, considering," muttered Charlie, noticing all the bullet holes in the engine compartment.

"Yeah, and it got me out of that graveyard," added Lt. Vernon Wright, the jet pilot.

DuPont glanced around the plateau of rice paddies. "I don't see any activity, but you fellows keep a sharp watch while I get out my URC-4" [utility radio communications].

"You got one of those?" asked Wright.

"Yeah, I'm lucky to have it. They're new and

there's precious few of them around. I just hope it works," said Charlie, fishing the small, handheld emergency radio out of his survival jacket. "Come on, baby, work," he mumbled, pulling up the antenna and switching it on. "Grenadier Love, this is Pedro ground, do you read?"

No answer. Then: "Who is calling Grenadier Love?"

"It's me! Pedro . . . I'm on the ground with a URC-4 radio."

"I say, ole chap, what a pleasant surprise, and I can read you five square," came the response.

DuPont knew at that instant the playing field had been leveled again. With ground-to-air communications, and a little luck, they could still get out of this alive. (This is believed to have been the first emergency use of the URC-4 radio in the Korean War. It subsequently became required survival equipment for air crews and was responsible for saving many a downed airman.)

"Pedro, are you okay down there? Your helicopter looks done in."

"Roger, Grenadier Love. But no one was hurt. What's the status of the rescue chopper?"

"JOC just called and said it had to turn back because of weather and darkness. I'm afraid you chaps are gonna have to spend the night there." That vintage helicopter had no lights or instruments for night flying.

The first report coming through the URC-4 was not good news for the stranded airmen. "That doesn't thrill us," groaned DuPont.

"But JOC is launching two choppers at dawn, weather permitting," added Grenadier Love.

"Yeah . . . weather permitting," Charlie muttered, as the cold wind of the season's first winter storm whipped his clothing.

"Okay. Do you see any military activity around us?"

"We can't see any activity in your immediate area. There is some kind of military installation a couple miles north of you, and we spotted what looked like troops moving out. You might want to get out of that area rather quickly."

"Okay. Grenadier Love, we're gonna do just that."

"Roger, Pedro. You can count on our being back up here at the crack of dawn . . . weather permitting."

"Thanks. Look for us south of here. When I see you overhead, I'll contact you on the URC-4. And, uh . . . Grenadier Love, if it doesn't work out, we want you to know we appreciate your efforts."

"Pedro, all the pilots and crews in Korea know the great work you chaps do, so you can count on us doing everything we can to get you out of there. Good luck, and we'll see you in the morning," said the Grenadier Love leader, who then winged over with his flight of F-51 fighters and swooped down over the three figures standing beside the wrecked helicopter. When the sound of the Rolls-Royce engines in the F-51s had faded, it was replaced by the howl of a winter wind sweeping across the hulk of the fallen chopper.

"We're in for a rough night, fellows, no matter what we do. But I think we better get on out of here before some of our North Korean friends show up," said Charlie, glancing up at the ridge. "I suggest we climb about halfway up the side of that ridge, then head south. I've got a magnetic compass with a luminous dial to keep our direction."

"Why halfway up, Lieutenant?" asked Fryer.

"Well, I'd bet that North Korean GIs are no different than any others, so they will do what is the easiest, which is to search the valleys and the tops of the ridges."

Vernon nodded. "Sounds reasonable to me. What's the plan if we do encounter soldiers?"

The three looked at one another. DuPont and Wright wore regulation .45-caliber service pistols. Fryer held a regulation .30-caliber carbine. "I suggest we let the decision to fight or surrender depend on the situation," offered Charlie. The others nodded.

The three men forged their way through the woods until they were about halfway up the side of the ridge. Then DuPont took a bearing with his magnetic compass, and they headed south.

Darkness had settled now, which made traversing the forest a stumbling, falling, cursing exercise, exacerbated by a howling wind and a brutal downpour of freezing rain. The winter storm had struck with a fury, and within a short time all three were soaked to the skin, and numbed by the freezing temperatures. They forged on, stopping occasionally to rest for only a few minutes.

"It's colder than a well digger's ass on the Klondike," groaned the medic as they halted for a rest after several hours of trudging doggedly through the freezing rain.

"I'm so cold I can't feel a thing," put in Wright. "You suppose we're freezing to death?"

"They taught us in medical training that just before you freeze to death, you feel warm and comfortable," said Fryer.

"Well, then I'm not freezing to death," growled DuPont. "Because I'm one cold, miserable, son of a bitch!"

That touch of humor spurred them on through the dark forest. They tried to move as quietly as possible, but it was difficult to suppress the noise of cracking brush and tree limbs, and an occasional outburst of cursing when someone fell or got a twig jabbed in his eye.

At one point Fryer stepped off a twenty-foot cliff and bruised his hip badly. "Maybe we should stop and try to find some kind of shelter," suggested Wright.

"The only shelter we're likely to find if we don't keep going is a North Korean prison," Charlie replied. "If Joe can walk, we've got to keep going."

"Yeah, I'll make it, Lieutenant. I'd rather freeze to death than end up in a gook prison camp."

The jet pilot, with freezing water dripping off his nose, nodded agreement, and they wordlessly moved out behind DuPont, who had assumed the role of leader.

Sometime in the early morning hours the temperature dropped well below freezing, but the wind and rain slacked off and occasionally the moon peeked through the clouds. The moonlight was a morale booster but made traveling more treacherous, since one moment they would be in bright moonlight and the next, pitch blackness.

At one point they stopped to rest and suddenly heard voices coming through the woods. They grabbed their firearms and dove for cover behind a clump of trees. They remained motionless, hardly daring to breathe for some time. Was it soldiers, or villagers? They never found out, since whoever it was went off in the opposite direction.

After that tense experience, they struggled on until shortly before dawn, when Fryer could not continue on his injured hip. Charlie had wanted to get to an open place in the forest, where the CAP could see them the next morning, but he realized that all three of them were exhausted and had gone as far as they could go. He would have to rely on the URC-4. If it worked as it had earlier, the CAP could find them, and the rescue choppers could be directed in to pick them up. If it didn't work . . . sayonara.

They didn't dare build a fire, so all they could do was huddle in the wet brush and count the minutes till dawn. Without movement, the terrible cold was now a real threat to their survival. Charlie recognized the dangers of stopping, and he had pushed them to the limit. But now there was nothing to do but hope the rescue aircraft would arrive early as promised.

When the first streaks of dawn broke across the North Korean ridges, Charlie checked off one of his worries. The storm had passed, and the sky was going to be clear. That meant the rescue aircraft would come. He reached into his survival vest for the radio, but his hands were so cold he couldn't grasp it. Then came a terrifying thought. Would the URC-4 even work in this bitter cold?

He climbed to his feet and began to beat his hands together to get some feeling. His cigarettes had turned to rain-soaked mush early in the night, but his old-fashioned Zippo lighter flamed when he flicked the little start wheel. He held his hand over the fire until he smelled flesh burning. Then he heard the distinct sound of an F-51.

"They're here! They're here!" he croaked.

As promised, a flight of four South African F-51s streaked across the early morning sky as DuPont frantically tried to get the antenna up and the radio turned on. It was difficult to tell if he had actually pushed the switch on with his frozen hands. He waited. The F-51s passed over and continued on. They would have gone by, of course, because they couldn't see him in the trees.

"Grenadier Love! Grenadier Love! You passed us!" he shouted into the mike on the URC-4.

The sound of the F-51s faded as they flew on north.

"Son of a bitch!" he groaned.

"Jesus, they flew right on by us," rasped Wright, who had struggled to his feet beside DuPont. "Is the radio working?"

"I don't know."

"Grenadier Love! This is Pedro! This is Pedro! Do you read?" DuPont repeated his frantic call several times, with no answer.

"Hey, I hear them coming back!" said Fryer, who had also stumbled to his feet.

"Pedro, this is Grenadier Love. Do you read me?" said a clear voice on the radio.

Charlie DuPont let out a shout: "Yahoo! You bet I do!"

"I say, ole chap, it's good to hear you."

"Times that by ten, and you'll know how good it is to hear you, Grenadier Love!" barked Charlie.

"Good show. Are you okay?"

"Other than frozen stiff, we're fine. Are the choppers coming?"

"Righto. They are en route. Where are you?"

"We're just south of your position. You're coming toward us now. We're in the trees on the ridge just to your right."

"Roger. Tell me when I'm directly over you."

DuPont could see the F-51s approaching. "Turn left a little . . . okay, that's good . . . keep coming . . . a little more left . . . hold . . . you're almost there . . . now! You just passed directly over us!"

"Okay Pedro, I got you spotted. There are two choppers coming, and they should be here within the next thirty minutes. We'll set up a CAP over you until they get here."

"Grenadier Love, I suggest you keep an eye on our location but orbit a bit north of us. That should mislead any of our North Korean neighbors who might be interested in what's going on over here."

"Good idea, Pedro, we'll move north a little."

"And Grenadier Love, we should destroy the chopper. I hate to do it, but I don't want the commies to get hold of it."

"Righto, we'll take care of it."

"Oh man, I think we're gonna make it," said Fryer, leaning against a tree.

"Sure, we're gonna make it. I never had any doubt," said Charlie with a grin.

"Me either. I knew you Pedro guys would come through," added Wright, also smiling.

"I hope they got a hoist on those choppers, 'cause there ain't no way they can get us without one," said Fryer, glancing up at the trees.

Wouldn't that be a bummer, thought Charlie. "Grenadier Love, this is Pedro, would you check with JOC and make sure those choppers have a personnel hoist?"

"Pedro, this is Col. John Dean in Pedro Zero Two. Are you reading me?"

Charlie was surprised to hear the voice of his commander on the URC-4. "Roger, Colonel, I read you."

"We've got a hoist, Charlie, and we'll be there in a few minutes to pick you up."

"That's great, Colonel. We're gonna have to be hoisted out. When I hear you coming, I'll talk you into our location."

"Okay. Bob Barnhill is flying Pedro Zero One. He'll come in and get the first two. Then I'll come in and get you, ole buddy."

DuPont grinned. His commander had never referred to him as his "ole buddy" before, but under these circumstances that was just fine.

A few minutes later, the two Sikorsky H-5 helicopters came into view, and DuPont directed them to his location. While the South African CAP watched over them, the first chopper came in and lowered the "horse collar" [a circular, collar device that went under the arms to lift the survivor] on the cable. Joe Fryer and Vernon Wright were winched up, one at a time, to the helicopter, which hovered above the trees. Then the colonel in Pedro Zero Two picked up DuPont. With Grenadier Love watching over them, the two choppers then flew out of North Korea and landed safely at K-16 in Seoul.

Korean War records indicate that this mission, flown on 25 and 26 October 1951, was the first successful rescue of a downed chopper crew in the Korean War. It was also one of thousands of rescue missions flown by U.S. Air Force helicopter crews in which pilots and aircrew, shot down in North Korea, were snatched from under the enemy's guns or from the waters of the Yellow Sea. The USAF Air Rescue Service was given credit for saving nearly 10,000 United Nations lives during the Korean War.

Lt. Charles DuPont was sent home after this mission, his ninety-first, and was recommended for the Distinguished Service Cross. I knew about Charlie's mission but needed some details to write the story. He gave me those details and a couple of additional anecdotes: He said the Grenadier Love leader told him afterward that they fired rockets and thousands of rounds of .50-caliber machine-gun fire into the fallen Sikorsky helicopter before they finally got it to burn. Charlie also admitted it took two days for him to thaw out, but that didn't bother him because that's how long he stayed inebriated.

CHAPTER THIRTEEN

Battlefield Taxi

Inside a "mummy" sleeping bag with all my clothes on except my boots, I was still cold. I'd heard someone the day before say that it was the coldest winter in Korea since 1840. I wasn't there in 1840, but I doubt it could have been any colder than it was that December 1952.

It was early morning, and four of us Air Force helicopter pilots were huddled in our sleeping bags in a pyramidal tent at the 8055 MASH [Mobile Army Surgical Hospital]. We were close enough to the 38th parallel, where the battle line ran, that we could hear artillery rumbling off in the distance. How those guys could get out of bed in that bitter cold and start shooting at each other was beyond my imagination.

Our field phone was in a canvas case hanging on a two-by-four that ran down the side of the tent. It didn't really ring, it sort of diddled. But it shattered the early morning tranquility of our canvas igloo, sounding like a four-alarm fire to me, because it meant I had to crawl out of my sack and try to coax a frozen helicopter into flying to a frozen Korean battlefield to pick up some poor soldier who now had bullet holes in him.

"You're next up, Kirkland," mumbled our element commander from inside his sleeping bag.

"Yeah, I'm going," I mumbled back, unzipping the sleeping bag and grabbing my boots.

"Turn up the fuel on the stove," grumbled one of the other pilots.

"It's already as high as it'll go," I replied, pulled on my heavy winter parka, and jerked the field phone from its case. "8055 chopper."

"Pick up a casualty at 23 Baker, 8055."

I pulled the gridded map out of my jacket pocket and quickly checked the designated pickup point. "Check, 23 Baker. Any change in the MLR [main line of resistance]?" I asked.

"No change in the past twenty-four hours."

It was critical for me to know if the MLR had changed during the night, since the only way I could get my battlefield taxi to the pickup point without getting shot down was to fly through the bottom of a canyon that was in friendly territory. Although the MLR never varied more than a few miles during the last two years of the Korean War, it did change often enough for historians to refer to that period of the war as the Battle of the Hills, because of the shifting ownership of such places as Old Baldy, Porkchop Hill, and Heartbreak Ridge.

Intelligence was supposed to keep us posted of changes, but that didn't always happen, and we would find ourselves flying over the guys in green uniforms who shot holes in our helicopters with lead balls made in North Korea, and the choppers of that day were totally unarmed and had no armor protection whatever.

"Okay, I'm on my way," I said, dropped the phone back in the canvas case, and headed out the door.

As I stepped out of the tent, I recognized the bundled-up figure coming across the compound. It was Hawkeye. "What are you doing up this early, Hawk?" I asked.

He pushed his parka hood up and peeked out at me. "Oh, I just love strolling in the early morning on such a beautiful day in breathtaking Korea," he chirped, his breath coming out in puffs of little white clouds.

I laughed, even though I wasn't in the mood. But that was the way Hawkeye was. No matter how bad things got, he never seemed to lose his sense of humor. I have always believed that his humor played a major role in the morale of the 8055 MASH. Often, when those fine doctors, nurses, and corpsmen worked around the clock saving the lives of wounded soldiers, Hawkeye's humor kept them going. Even when he himself was about to drop from exhaustion, he still cracked jokes. Hawk's real name, incidently, was Sam Gilfand. He was an outstanding surgeon from New York City, and a great guy. The folks who wrote the television series *M*A*S*H* did a pretty good job. Some of the characters were a bit Hollywoody, but a lot of it was pretty close to the way it was at the 8055 MASH.

"I suppose you're on your way to bring us some business this fine morning, huh, ace?" He always called me "ace," even though I wasn't. But he knew I'd been a fighter pilot and shot down a couple Zeros in World War II. He claimed I looked like an ace anyway.

"That's what I'm fixing to do, Hawk," I said over my shoulder as I hurried toward the helipad.

"Yes. Heavens to Betsy and four hands around, we wouldn't want this fine establishment to be without customers," he sort of said to no one in particular as he pulled his parka hood back down and walked off toward the OR, where he was probably on the early shift.

The crew chief on duty had managed to pry open the frozen helicopter door by the time I got out to the helipad, but that 1940s model Sikorsky H-5 was so cold it actually creaked and groaned when I climbed up into the pilot's seat. It was a good bird for its vintage. But it wasn't designed to operate in subzero weather.

"The battery won't last long this morning, Captain," advised the chief as he rolled a portable fire extinguisher beside the helicopter.

I nodded. I knew I'd only get one shot at starting the engine, but I must have had the magic touch that morning because after a couple of coughs, she spit out a column of black smoke and roared to life. The chief gave me a thumbs-up and backed off the helipad as my medic came running up, his medical kit slung over his shoulder. He had on so much bulky clothing he couldn't climb into the backseat, so the chief had to help him in.

It seemed to take forever before temperature and pressure gauges all showed green. Finally, I pulled pitch and nosed the H-5 north toward medical pickup spot 23 Baker on the Korean battlefield.

● ● ●

In World War II the Army Medical Corps practiced a battlefield system called triage, which was based on the brutally realistic fact that front-line surgeons could treat three or four walking wounded in the same amount of time required for one seriously wounded, so they were treated last. Then they had to endure a long, jarring ambulance ride to the field hospital. As a consequence, the mortality rate for the seriously wounded was high.

That all changed in the Korean War when the MASH was introduced. It consisted of a team of surgeons, anesthesiologists, nurses, and corpsmen, and the necessary equipment, that gave them the mobility to deploy and function on the fringe of the battlefield. The wounded were taxied by helicopter from the front-line aid stations directly to the hospital within minutes. Not only did the mortality rates drop dramatically, but military historians credit the helicopter-supported MASH with the greatest single boost to battlefield morale in modern warfare.

Although there were only a handful available, Korea was opening night for helicopters on the battlefield, and both the U.S. Air Force and Army deployed them for front-line MASH medevac [medical evacuation]. Army pilots flew the Bell H-13, and Air Force pilots flew the Sikorsky H-5 and H-19.

I was assigned to the 2157th Air Force, Air Rescue Squadron, at Kimpo Air Base [K-16] at Seoul. The squadron kept four helicopter pilots, four medics, a couple of mechanics, and two H-5s at the 8055 MASH full time. We lived with them in their tent city, and when they moved, we moved, helicopter and all.

The H-5 had three fabric-covered rotor blades

powered by a Pratt & Whitney 450-horsepower engine. The "chopper," as it was called in Korea, had two seats: a pilot's seat up front and a passenger's seat directly behind where the medic rode. The medic's job was to perform whatever emergency medical aid that was necessary to stabilize a patient, then load him into the personnel pod [an aluminum carrying case] attached to the side of the helicopter. Barring interference from the bad guys, we then flew him from the battlefield to the MASH, where he would be under the care of surgeons within minutes.

After takeoff, that brutally cold morning, I kept my eye on the instruments for a while even though the bird seemed to be functioning normally. The controls, although a bit stiff, were responding. So I set the friction on the throttle and the collective, to hold power, and pulled out my map. Identifying the correct canyon at the outset was the key to finding the pickup spot without running into the North Koreans.

In the subzero cockpit, it was difficult to even hold a map with gloved hands, and studying it with all the cumulus clouds my breath was creating added to the problem. I had the heater on full blast, but it wasn't doing much. On the plus side, it was a crystal-clear day, and I knew, at this point anyway, that I was in the right canyon to intersect the 38th parallel.

I had to fly below the top of the ridges to stay out of enemy gunsight while keeping a sharp watch for the branch canyon that would take me east to the aid station at 23 Baker. Although I had made several pickups at that spot, it wasn't easy to find. After two years of artillery fire, bombs, and mortars the ridges and canyons were so battle scarred they all looked alike.

"I think this is where we want to go," I said to my medic on the intercom, as I banked into a small canyon. He mumbled something in reply. Glancing back at him, all I could see was a bundle of clothing hunched down in the backseat.

I was reasonably confident I had turned into the right canyon until my medic suddenly came alive and began to screech over the intercom: "They're shooting at us Captain! They're shooting at us!"

I quickly looked out my side canopy window, and, sure enough, he was right: guys in green uniforms were shooting at us. I could even see the little white clouds their rifles made when they fired into the frigid air. So much for the twenty-four-hour intelligence report, I thought, as I slammed the chopper into a quick right bank and zipped over the ridge into the adjacent canyon. Later, intelligence told me that it was a North Korean patrol that had gotten themselves lost—they were the ones in the wrong canyon, not me.

After a short detour and some anxious moments, I got back into the right canyon again and landed a few minutes later at 23 Baker. Usually, I wouldn't shut the bird down at the pickup point. I would stay in the pilot's seat with the rotors turning and smoke a quick cigarette while the medics loaded the patient, then we'd be off. In this case I was concerned that some of those North Korean lead balls may have disturbed the integrity of my taxicab, so I kept the engine running but disengaged the rotor so I could get out and take a look.

The good news was that I couldn't find any damage to the bird. The bad news was that they had three seriously wounded patients at the aid station, and the H-5 could only carry two patients and a medic.

"All three are critical, and, with the temperature where it is, they won't last long," said a grim Army corpsman dressed in winter clothes and combat gear. Automatic weapons opened fire about that time in the near distance. I winced, but the corpsman seemed to not even notice.

"I'm sorry," I said, "I'll have to make another trip. I can't carry—"

"Are they conscious?" interrupted my medic.

The corpsman shook his head. "They're pretty much out of it."

"Okay. We can put one in the litter and give the other two stiff shots of morphine and strap them into the backseat," said my medic, glancing at me through the slit in his parka hood.

"And, what are you gonna do?" I asked.

"I'll stay here, and you can come back and get me."

I glanced at the Army medic.

He shrugged. The weariness in his parka-shrouded face was evident. "The gooks are on a roll, and they could overrun us," he said calmly.

I can't remember the name of my medic that day, but he was a brave young man. He said, "If it's okay with you, Captain, I'll stay."

I hesitated.

"It's worth the gamble to save a man's life," he added. And I knew he was sincere.

"Okay, let's get them loaded," I said, with a good deal of apprehension.

They gave the badly wounded patients heavy doses

of morphine, wrapped them in as many blankets as they could, put one in the external pod, and strapped the other two into the backseat of the helicopter.

"They'll be out for quite a while, Capt'n, so you shouldn't have any trouble," said the Army corpsman.

"Okay. I'll be back as soon as I can make it," I said to my medic.

"I'll be right here," he said with a grin.

"We'll try to keep him entertained," said the corpsman, and he managed a grin too.

I nodded, closed the door, and flipped the clutch-engagement lever. As soon as the rotor was up and turning at takeoff RPM, I pulled pitch and scooted down the canyon as fast as the bird would go.

There was just something about going off and leaving my medic that really upset me. I understood his reasoning. It was a brave thing for him to do, and his action could well save a man's life. But it could also cost the medic his life if 23 Baker was overrun by the North Koreans. So I wanted to deliver the patients to the MASH as fast as possible and get back to pick him up.

Everything went well for the first few minutes of the flight. I glanced back into the rear seat, and the patients were strapped in tight, and still unconscious. Then, just as I banked into the main canyon that would take me to the MASH, I heard a God-awful cry and something akin to a sledgehammer struck the back of my head. The force of the blow jammed my arm forward, which caused the cyclic stick to shoot forward, launching the helicopter into a nosedive. That somehow tore the fire extinguisher from its bracket, and, naturally, it also ricocheted off my head.

Now I was seeing stars, and the helicopter was diving toward the Korean landscape. I managed to pull out of the dive, but I did it so violently the bird shot straight up on its tail. There were all kinds of weird noises in my head, weird sights before my eyes, and even weirder sounds coming from the Sikorsky H-5. I managed to kick rudder pedal, causing the bird to swap ends, and now I was going straight down again.

I'm not sure how many oscillations I made, or how close I came to hitting the Korean earth, before I finally got the helicopter under control. But about that time I heard another one of those God-awful cries, and I instinctively ducked as another blow struck the back of the seat. I glanced back and saw that one of the patients had gained consciousness and was thrashing about, kicking wildly, and trying to pull himself loose from the seat straps.

I flipped open my safety belt and leaned as far forward as I could to keep away from his kicking feet, while trying to maintain some kind of control over the gyrating helicopter. The poor man's eyes were glazed and wild looking, and he was letting out one awful cry after another. He'd kicked off all the blankets and torn loose his bandages so that blood from his wounds was spewing in all directions as he thrashed around violently.

I knew I had to do something quick or we would all be in big trouble, because it was impossible to control the helicopter in the awkward position I had taken to avoid his vicious kicking. And I also realized that it was going to be impossible to land under these conditions without crashing. But I had no choice. I had to either pull out my .45 pistol and shoot the poor guy or try to land.

Since I couldn't shoot him, I lowered the collective and watched for the ground coming up from where I crouched between the seat and the instrument console. My head was still spinning, courtesy of the fire extinguisher, and my perspective was askew because of the position I was in. It would primarily be guesswork when to pull pitch. And that Korean landscape was frozen hard as a rock.

When I saw the ground coming up fast, I instinctively scrambled back into the pilot's seat, pulled pitch, and leveled the Sikorsky with cyclic. It was just something I did without thinking. My instincts would not allow the helicopter to crash. I cringed, anticipating the blow from the kicking feet. Then, after a second or two, I realized the kicking had stopped. I glanced back and saw that he was slumped over and unconscious.

I went down on the collective and back on the cyclic in one swift movement, executing a quick stop to a hover and then a landing. I chopped the throttle and just sat there a second or two, breathing a sigh of relief, thankful to be on the cold Korean earth in one piece and that was where I was going to stay. Then I looked out through the front canopy and saw a bunch of olive drab tents about a quarter mile down the canyon. One of them had a big red cross on the top—the 8055 MASH. I twisted on the throttle, eased up on the collective, and gently hover-taxied down the canyon to the helipad.

"Holy schmolly ace, I have the feeling you got a war story to tell," said Hawkeye as he and the corpsmen swung open the door and saw the patients in the blood-splattered backseat of the Sikorsky.

"You could say that, Hawk," I replied, swinging down from the pilot's seat and making a beeline for the male officers' quarters. When I opened the wooden door to my tent, the other three pilots were huddled around the stove in their winter clothes smoking cigarettes.

"Everything go okay?" asked my element commander, Capt. Charles Enderton.

"Not exactly," I said, grabbing the field phone and turning the crank. "I had to leave my medic and that sector is under attack."

"You went off and left the medic?" said Enderton incredulously.

"Yes, but . . . Get me G-2 quick!" I said to the field operator, then looked at Enderton. "It's a long story and . . ."

"It better damn well be a good one," he growled.

"G-2. Major Thompson," came the voice on the field phone.

"Sir, this is Captain Kirkland at the 8055 MASH. Can I get to 23 Baker?"

"23 Baker? Hold on."

I dug out a cigarette and fired it.

The loudspeaker outside in the compound started squealing as somebody tried to make an announcement.

Finally: "Uh, we're not sure. Our latest is that they are under fire, but we've had no recent reports."

"Then you don't know if they've been overrun?"

"No, we don't know. They call you for a pickup?"

"Yeah. I was just up there."

"Were they under fire?"

"Yeah."

"Well then you know as much as we do."

"Yeah. . . . Okay, thanks anyway," I said and dropped the phone back in the canvas case.

"What's going on?" asked Enderton.

I took a big drag of the cigarette and ground it out in a 90mm shell casing we used as an ashtray. "I'm going back to 23 Baker and pick up my medic," I said, zipped up my parka, and slammed out through the wooden front door.

When I got out to the heliport, the patients had been rushed into pre-op and the crew chief was there looking at the blood-splattered backseat.

"Jesus, Capt'n, what happened?" he asked.

"I'll tell ya later, Chief. I gotta go."

He nodded and looked at me strangely. "You know the fire extinguisher is lying in the backseat?"

I felt the knot on the back of my skull. "Yeah, I know, Chief. Would you put it back in the bracket while I get the bird started?"

I took off a couple minutes later and headed up the canyon with a vague idea of what I intended to do when I reached 23 Baker. As I skimmed along the bottom of the canyon, I tried to solidify a couple of alternative plans of action, but my still-aching head wasn't processing information well. Actually, I only had two options. If the North Koreans were there, they would shoot at me and I'd run. What else could I do? If they weren't there, I'd simply land and pick up my medic. It was that simple. But what if I couldn't tell, and, when I landed, they took me prisoner? I'd heard some spine-chilling stories of what a North Korean prison camp was like.

I detoured around the spot where I'd taken fire on the

last trip and found 23 Baker without a problem. As I approached, I slowed down to a hover-taxi and gradually edged up toward the spot. I couldn't see any smoke from artillery fire, and everywhere I looked appeared peaceful and quiet. The outside air-temperature gauge still showed below zero. Maybe everybody decided it was too cold to fight, and they were all in their bunkers having tea and smoking cigarettes.

As it turned out, that's exactly what they were doing. The North Koreans had backed off their assault, and the GIs were, indeed, in their bunkers thawing out. And when I landed, they talked me into shutting down the bird and coming into one of their bunkers for some hot tea. I'm glad I did, because it was a unique experience. The bunker was surprisingly comfortable, and warmer than I would have imagined. It was partially underground and crude, but it had a kind of homey touch with a little gasoline stove and even pictures of loved ones on the sandbagged walls. It was their place to escape, for a few minutes anyway, from the war that was going on outside.

The GIs were most appreciative that I had taken their wounded buddies to the MASH (I didn't mention the little problem I'd had). And, as we walked back out to the helicopter to leave, the sergeant in charge of the unit said, "You helicopter pilots and medics from the MASH are our heros, and frankly, if we didn't know you were there when we need you, I'm just not sure how many of us would be willing to do what we do."

I've always remembered what the sergeant said to me that day on a scarred Korean battlefield. It made me proud to be one of the "Battlefield

Taxi" drivers. The three wounded men all recovered, and I submitted a recommendation for a Medal of Valor for my medic. I'm also proud, on this fiftieth anniversary of the Korean War, to have been a part of that unprecedented lifesaving effort.

Upon my return home from Korea in late 1953, I was placed on special duty in Hollywood, California, to assist in the writing and production of a motion picture about the story of the helicopter pilots in the Korean War. The producers were Ivan Tors and Art Arthur. It was a gratifying assignment. We named the movie *Battle Taxi*.

CHAPTER FOURTEEN

Christmas at Ch'o Do

The Air Force had the same GI pyramidal tents in the Korean War as the Army had had in New Guinea during World War II. They were made of olive-drab canvas and held up by ropes staked into the ground. The big difference was that it had been warm in New Guinea. I nearly froze to death in Korea.

Fortunately we were able to scrounge up enough scrap lumber to build a floor and a door, in our little home away from home on Ch'o Do Island. One of the guys even built a heating stove. He took an empty 55-gallon fuel drum, filled the bottom with sand, and ran a line in from another drum of 100-octane aviation gas. He installed a valve so we could control the amount of fuel that flowed into the sand. Man, did that thing get hot. I don't know why it didn't blow us all up, but it didn't, and it kept us from freezing.

It was Christmas Eve, and I was trying to see through the faded Plexiglas window in our homemade door. But even with our blowtorch stove roaring, my breath made instant ice on the Plexiglas. There was nothing out there to see anyway, other than an austere

Korean hillside. But I rubbed the ice off and looked again, just in time to see the first snowflakes begin to fall. "Well it looks like we're going to have a white Christmas, all right. It's starting to snow," I announced.

"Big deal," growled one of the other pilots from across the tent, where he lay sprawled on a cot, wearing his heavy winter overalls and parka, as we all were.

Capt. Charles Enderton, our element commander, got up from the GI cot where he was reading, walked up beside me, and peeked out. "Yeah, so we are . . . not good, not good," he muttered and walked across to a small wooden table, also homemade, that held our plotting board and field phone. He lifted the receiver out of its canvas case and, after a couple of turns of the crank, said, "Kodak, this is Pedro. It's beginning to snow here. You got anything going?" Kodak was the radar-control site on top of the hill behind us.

The other two pilots sat up from their cots and listened anxiously. We all knew what the captain was concerned about. Our helicopters weren't equipped to fly instruments, so if one of our fighters or bombers went down out there now, a rescue attempt in a snowstorm over water would probably result in disaster. But if we didn't rescue him, he would be in what they used to call in Korea "deep kimchee." That water had ice cubes floating on it.

Ch'o Do was a North Korean island only 4 miles off the mainland, and nearly 150 miles into enemy territory. But it was controlled by the UN forces because of their naval superiority. It was used as a radar site and a base from which to launch rescue helicopters. It provided radar-tracking information on enemy aircraft and vessels, directed UN bombers and fighters, and guided helicopters to downed aircrews in the Yellow Sea.

The Third Air Rescue Group maintained a small unit on Ch'o Do, consisting of four pilots, a couple of medics, a mechanic, and two Sikorsky H-19 helicopters. We kept the choppers parked right out in front of our tents, so we could jump in and get going quickly when Kodak scrambled us. This time of year a downed airman could only last a few minutes in that frigid water, so we had to get him in a hurry. And because of that, we also flew in pairs to cover each other.

The island was inhabited by North Koreans. Although they didn't seem to be very partisan, our orders were to stay out of the villages and wear our sidearms at all times. They had a small garrison of South Korean Marines there on the island, to sort of protect us in case the locals decided to do us in. But I didn't see much of our protectors that winter; they were probably holed up somewhere trying to keep from freezing, too.

Normally we didn't worry too much about the North Korean military on the mainland, because if they tried to come across to the island, the radar folks would spot them and send out a Navy gunship or fighter aircraft to discourage them. Oh, once in a while they would fly over and drop a bomb or two at night, or lob a few rounds of artillery across, just to let us know they were there. But our camp was behind a hill, and they never hit us.

I could see Enderton grimace as he stood holding the field phone to his ear. "Okay. All we can do is wait and see how he makes out. Yeah . . . I know, I know. If it can be done, we'll do it."

He dropped the receiver back in its case, reached into his flight-suit pocket, and pulled out a cigarette. "They got a strike going on up north and one of the fighters took a hit," he said as he torched the cigarette.

"They're flying a strike on Christmas Eve?" croaked my copilot, Jeff Drake, a tall, gangly fellow with a head of unruly sandy hair.

"I guess they are."

"In this weather?"

"This storm is moving in from the northeast. I guess it's okay up in MiG Alley" [a corridor along the North Korea–China border where UN jets and MiGs often engaged in aerial combat].

"Well, are they gonna scramble us?"

Enderton blew out a cloud of smoke and shook his head. "Not yet. The hurt chick is going to try and coax it home, but they got us on standby."

"It looks to me like this storm is coming in pretty fast," I said, glancing out the Plexiglas window.

Enderton nodded. "Yeah it is, a lot faster than they had forecasted."

Enderton's copilot, Jim Belyea, a small, slender guy with large sleepy eyes, got up and came over beside me at the window. "Jesus, it's snowing bad. What are we going to do if they call?"

"It's a decision I'll have to make when the time comes," said our element commander.

As I stood there staring out into the sea of falling flakes, my thoughts spun back to that time in New Guinea when I had coaxed my P-38 back on one engine. I felt a pang of empathy for that fighter pilot out there somewhere. Then it occurred to me that at least he had a helicopter standing by to pick him up. But could we do it in this weather?

"Uh, Kirk, give me a hand, will ya? I want to make sure the birds are covered," said Enderton, pulling his parka hood up.

I could tell by the look he gave me that he wanted to talk to me in private. "Sure," I replied. I ground out my cigarette, pulled up my parka hood, and followed him out the door.

The mechanics had already put on the covers. They and the medics lived in the tent next to ours. The two tents and a pile of 55-gallon fuel drums were the extent of our little camp.

"You ever fly any instruments in a chopper?" asked Enderton, as we stepped up beside one of the Sikorskys and stood watching the snow spread a white blanket over it and the bare Korean landscape.

I shook my head.

"Neither have I, but we may have to."

I looked at him. "How are we going to do that, Charles? We haven't got any instruments."

"We got needle, ball, and airspeed."

I grinned. "That I can do. That's fighter-pilot stuff."

He chuckled. "These choppers ain't exactly fighters."

"I know. You think they're going to scramble us?"

"Are you game if they do?"

"I'll give it a shot."

"Okay, but we got another problem. The weather guys think this front is going to stagnate right over us. That means we could be without air cover for some time."

I nodded. "And the gooks from the mainland may come visiting."

He nodded.

"And they got big sharp knives to slit round eyes' throats."

He nodded again.

"Merry Christmas."

"Same to you."

"What's the plan?"

"Hopefully Kodak will give us a warning if they spot them coming."

"And?"

"We load everybody in the choppers and bug out south."

"Needle, ball, airspeed, and no nav aids?"

"You said that's fighter-pilot stuff."

I couldn't help but smile. "Yeah. But only to get through a cloud and shake a Zero off my ass. Not for no 150 miles in a snowstorm."

"No guts, no glory."

"Amen."

"Well, Kodak can give us radar steers, for a while."

"Until the sharp knives climb the hill and slit their throats."

"Yeah."

"We'll do what we got to, Chuck. I'm with you all the way."   •

Chuck Enderton was handsome and built like a prizefighter. He had grown a little mustache there on the island, and when he smiled, it sort of curled up. "Okay, partner. Let's keep this to ourselves until the time comes."

I nodded and we went back into the tent.

Since our facilities were primitive, our living conditions, particularly in the winter, were difficult at best. There was no way to take showers or wash clothes. All drinking water, which came from a shallow well nearby, had to be boiled for twenty minutes. And what you ate was what you fixed yourself. The Air Force furnished C rations that I suspect had been inherited from Army World War II leftovers. Needless to say, it was all but inedible. Many of us, myself included, survived on peanut butter and packaged crackers that we had brought ourselves. Helicopter-maintenance supplies, parts, and fuel were brought in periodically by boat or dropped by parachute.

But there was a plus side to all this, and that had to do with the satisfaction of saving lives. In unarmed helicopters, we picked up a lot of downed airmen from behind enemy lines, often under enemy fire. We also pulled a lot of them out of the Yellow Sea after they had been shot down over MiG Alley, including Capt. Joseph McConnell Jr., the top-scoring jet ace of the Korean War—a mission I personally flew.

The other two pilots watched Captain Enderton intently as he and I came back into the tent. He went over to the cherry-red fuel-drum stove, pulled off his gloves, and warmed his hands. "I guess we'd better put on our exposure suits, fellows."

"Are we really going to try to fly in this weather?" asked Jim.

"If they scramble us, we're going to give it a shot. If it's not flyable, we'll turn around and come back."

And so we all pulled on our rubberized exposure suits, which were very confining and uncomfortable, and tried to busy ourselves with some innocuous task, glancing often through the frozen Plexiglas window at the snow that was getting deeper and deeper.

When the field phone finally rang, it pierced the silence like a screeching banshee. We all leaped to our feet as Enderton snatched the receiver from its case. "Yeah," he snapped.

We watched his face as though it was a time bomb. He listened, expressionless, for what seemed an eternity.

"Okay . . . okay, Kodak," he finally said. Dropping the phone back in the case, he gave us a little grin. "The guy made it back to K-16."

We all let out a sigh of relief and began pulling off the exposure suits. "That's a Christmas present for all of us," pronounced Jeff Drake.

"Yea hoo!" put in Jim Belyea. "Let's pull out that bottle of Jack Daniel's and drink some right now!"

"Yeah, let's do it!" agreed Jeff.

Chuck glanced at me, and I could see his problem. There probably would be no more strikes scheduled for today because of the deteriorating weather. But what if we had to bug out? What if the North Koreans came across from the mainland and we had to try to fly out of there on instruments? Something none of us had ever done before. It would be risky enough sober. But if we'd been drinking?

"Uh, fellows, let's do what we planned and wait till Christmas. Don't you agree, Kirk?" said Charles, glancing at me.

"Yeah . . . yeah, let's wait till tomorrow, guys," I agreed.

We had planned a Christmas party for tomorrow that included fresh eggs for breakfast, an apple pie for dinner, and a bottle of real Stateside Jack Daniel's whiskey that we'd been saving. The Jack Daniel's would have to come after sundown: that was when we were off alert, since we couldn't fly at night.

You may wonder how we were going to eat fresh eggs and an apple pie for Christmas. Well, the day before, an Air Rescue Service twin-engine SA-16 aircraft had flown up from our home base and dropped us a whole crate of fresh eggs and a dozen real apples. Every once in a while, they would fly up to Ch'o Do and drop us some fresh eggs or fruit, or something like that. And when they did, it was like a mini Christmas. But there was one little hitch on this pre-Christmas drop, which wasn't funny at the time but lends flavor to the story now.

When they flew over our camp, we would always run out and contact them on a walkie-talkie radio. This day, they wished us Merry Christmas and said they were dropping fresh eggs and apples. We were ecstatic. On the first pass the apples came out, the parachute opened, and down they floated. On the next pass, out came the crate of eggs with the trajectory of a rock, striking the rough Korean terrain with a big, juicy splat.

"Sorry about that, fellows, we forgot to put the chute on the crate of eggs," said the guy in the SA-16, over the walkie-talkie.

What happened next is still classified: We all took out our .45 pistols and blazed away at the USAF SA-16 as it flew away. We didn't hit it, of course, but it soothed our fury. After that, we did manage to save enough of the mangled eggs for a batch of scrambled eggs for each of us. How we transformed the apples into an apple pie is another story, which comes a little later in the sequence of things.

Captain Enderton decided not to burden the other pilots, or the enlisted men, with our potentially serious security problem. But somehow they seemed to sense that something was wrong, and it was rather a solemn Christmas Eve. We all crawled into our sleeping bags early that night and wrestled with our own thoughts.

We did have some new Air Force sleeping bags, called mummy bags. One of the supply guys swore they really had been made in Egypt and sold at the Alli Ah Kahamani, the oldest-known continuously operating marketplace in Egypt. At any rate, if you got into the bag with all your clothes on, including your winter parka, and fired up a couple of those little Japanese pocket warmers, you could get through the night.

The next morning we got up to a white Christmas. The drab Korean countryside looked like a whole new world, with its glistening coat of white. But it was a dismal day, with low clouds spitting intermittent snow flurries. And it was brutally cold. I nearly froze doing the morning preflight on my chopper.

While I and the two copilots completed the preflight, Enderton called Kodak, and I could tell when I went back into the tent that it was not good news. "What's the word?" I asked, warming my hands over the stove.

"The good news is that there's no strikes scheduled. The bad news is that the weather picture is not good."

"I don't see that as bad news, chief," said Jim. "If there's no strike scheduled, we can hit that ol' Jack Daniel's anytime we're ready. And since it's Christmas, I say the sooner the better."

"Well . . . uh, they said we'd better stay on standby

anyway, just in case something comes up," said Enderton quickly.

"That's a bunch of bullshit," put in Jeff. "We can't fly in this weather."

Charles glanced at me. I was tempted to ask him to go ahead and tell them the serious reality of the situation: that we might have to fly out of there in a hurry, if the North Koreans from the mainland decided to come after us. But I said, "Aw, who knows what those guys down at command will do. If it clears, they might send out a strike. Let's wait for a while before we hit the whiskey. Besides, Jeff, you said you'd peel the apples if I make the apple pie. And Jim, you and Chuck agreed to make the oven. What do you say we get started?"

The enlisted guys had eaten their half of the precious apples straightaway, and they'd given us dubious looks when we'd told them we were going to bake a pie with ours. But we were determined, and the operation to convert apples to a pie began. It was good, in that it occupied our attention for the better part of the day.

Chuck and Jim made the oven out of a 5-gallon can, cutting the top off and hinging it for a door. Steel rods through the sides formed a rack to hold the pie while it baked. The plan was to put our homemade oven on top of the flamethrower stove and turn up the 100-octane gas flow to full power.

Meanwhile, Jeff peeled the apples. And I mean he peeled them with a razor blade, not wanting to waste any of the apple meat. I made the pie. After all, I'd seen my mom make pies. I knew about what went in them. We had a footlocker that had some basic food stuff in it, like flour, salt, sugar, baking powder, and some things like that. When I mixed it all up to make the piecrust, I couldn't remember just how much of each thing was supposed to go in there, so I just dumped in a bunch of each, added some water, and made up two piles of dough: one for the bottom crust and one for the top. We made a pie plate out of another 5-gallon can, and when I got the chopped-up apples in the crust and the top on, it looked great.

Finally we opened the door of our oven and slipped in the apple pie. Then we all sat back, fired up cigarettes, and waited anxiously.

"How long does an apple pie take to cook?" asked somebody.

"I guess about an hour," I replied.

"Oh, I think it takes longer than that," put in someone else.

"Well, we can take a peek after a while," I suggested.

"What's that!" said Chuck Enderton suddenly. "You hear anything?"

"I don't hear anything," I answered.

Enderton got to his feet and quickly moved across to the door. We all followed suit, crowding around the door, but Chuck was hogging the Plexiglas window, so none of us could see out. "Christ! Get your guns!" he barked, and we all raced for our .45s, hanging next to our cots.

"There's someone out there. I saw him hiding behind that rock next to my chopper."

We all slammed a cartridge into the barrel of our guns and crowded up to the window again.

"What do you see?" asked Jim anxiously.

"There's somebody hiding there, I can see part of him."

"Is it a gook?" asked Jeff.

"Maybe it's one of the guys," I suggested.

"No, it's not one of our guys . . . it's a gook!" snapped Enderton.

My thoughts raced: What we feared had happened! The North Koreans had come! And there was nothing we could do about it now, except to fight it out with our handguns and hope our South Korean protectors, wherever they were, would hear the shooting and come to our rescue.

"Down on the floor!" I yelled, and everyone hit the deck except Enderton, who suddenly got a strange look on his face.

"Holy shit," he said hoarsely. "It's a little kid!"

We looked at one another, lying there on the floor grasping our .45s. "It's what?" I asked incredulously, watching Charles.

"I can see him plain, now. It's nothin' but a little Korean kid," he replied, opening the door and walking out into the snow.

With our .45s in hand, we all cautiously closed in on the dirty-faced little kid who huddled behind the snow-covered rock. His clothes were in tatters, and he was barefoot. I couldn't believe it. His feet were blue and probably frostbitten. The boy couldn't have been more than seven or eight years old, and he was skin and bones. He looked up at us with huge dark eyes and said, "I are hongaree."

Chuck kneeled down beside him and asked, "Where is your home, little boy?"

He looked puzzled and repeated, "I are hongaree."

Enderton smiled and said, "Oh, your name is Hongaree?"

He still looked puzzled.

"Hey, I think the little kid is saying he's hungry," I said.

"Jesus, he looks hungry, and frozen," agreed Jeff.

"I think you're right. He's frozen and starved. Come on, I Are Hongaree, let's get you warmed up and something in your belly," said Charles, taking his hand.

We brought him in the tent, wrapped him in some GI blankets, and put him in front of the stove, where the apple pie baked inside our improvised oven.

"Where do you suppose he came from?" asked someone.

"Probably from So Sorry," said someone else.

So Sorry was what we called a poor, broken-down village just down the hill from our camp. Its real name was Sosa Ri.

"I suppose we're breaking regulations by having him here, since we're forbidden to fraternize with the natives," speculated Jim.

"Screw the regulations!" growled Chuck.

"I are hongaree," said the little Korean boy again.

"He's starved, let's get him something to eat," I said.

And we did. The poor little kid ate like there was no tomorrow, gobbling those C rations like they were the best thing he'd ever tasted. It was a heartwarming sight for all of us just to watch him. It sort of gave Christmas a special flavor, despite the lurking danger.

About that time we were all startled with a loud *bang!* We leaped to our feet, grabbed our guns, and stood looking at one another uncertainly. "What the hell was that!" barked Enderton.

"Aw, shit, look," I moaned, as I saw what had caused the noise. The door to our oven had blown off, and out of our makeshift oven oozed a huge glob of stuff that looked like nothing I'd ever seen before. It was our apple pie.

Well, you can imagine the rest. I really thought, for a moment, that they were going to bodily throw me out into the cold. I guess I must have put too much baking powder in the piecrust or something, because it sure exploded into an awful mess. Even little I Are Hongaree smiled at the sight of our apple-pie disaster.

But you know what? We scraped it out of the 5-gallon can, divided it into five portions, and ate it. I Are Hongaree ate his share eagerly and looked like he could have eaten more. We all agreed it was the best apple pie we'd ever tasted, and it sort of topped off a great Christmas.

After he'd eaten, the little boy dropped off to sleep, there on Chuck's cot, and didn't wake up till late afternoon.

"What are we going to do with him?" asked someone.

"Keep him right here," said Chuck.

"You can't do that, Charles," I said.

"Why the hell can't I?"

"What are you going to do with him when we rotate down to the MASH?" asked Jeff.

Because of the primitive and high-risk conditions at Ch'o Do, we rotated every few weeks with another crew. We would move down to where the infamous Battle of the Hills was going on, and there we'd fly medevac for a while with Hawkeye and the troops at the 8055 MASH. It was a welcome break for us.

"Why you can't keep him here, Chuck, is because

he's got a family down in So Sorry, or wherever, and they are going to be looking for him," I reasoned.

"Yeah, I know," muttered Enderton. "But they ought to take better care of him."

"How can they? They're probably frozen and starving to death too."

Charles just nodded silently. But when little I Are Hongaree—those were the only words in English he knew—arrived back at his home that day, I'm sure he brightened things up for a while. We sent him home with all the C rations and GI blankets he could carry. In fact it was a sight I'll never forget, seeing him drag that duffel bag full of stuff over the snow-covered hill. He stopped just before he went out of sight, turned, and waved at us. Then he went trudging off in a pair of Chuck's GI boots that were nine sizes too big for him and wearing one of Jim's parkas, also nine sizes too big, but the smallest one we had.

When he'd disappeared from sight, we went back in the tent and broke out that bottle of Jack Daniel's Kentucky whiskey.

"It ain't quite sundown yet," said somebody.

"Close enough," said Chuck, as he got out the four real glasses that we used on special occasions.

Then the field phone shrieked and we all froze.

Chuck set the glasses down carefully, picked up the receiver, and said, "Pedro."

We watched him silently. He stood listening, expressionless. Then he nodded, and a smile broke across his handsome face. "Okay, weather breaking, clear skies tomorrow. That's good news . . . same to you. Yeah, we had a great Christmas, Kodak, just great," he said, grinning across the tent at us. We all gave him a thumbs-up.

As it often happens as time goes by, I lost track of Charles Enderton many years ago. But I know that he did see little I Are Hongaree several times that winter, and met his family. I also heard that he was instrumental in getting them evacuated to South Korea.

CHAPTER FIFTEEN

Geisha

The "schoshi" cab passed through the bright lights of downtown Tokyo and made its way into the outskirts of the city, where smaller two- and three-story wooden structures dominated the narrow streets. The driver finally nosed the small car up beside a masonry wall, leaped out, pushed open a wooden gate, and gestured for his two passengers to follow.

"What about our bags?" asked one of the passengers, a tall, lanky American wearing silver pilot's wings and first lieutenant's bars on the blue uniform of the U.S. Air Force.

"Don't worry about a thing from here on, Kris," assured his companion, who was wearing an identical uniform but was as short and stocky as his squadron mate was tall and thin.

Lt. Kristian O'Donnell glanced around skeptically. "You sure you know where we're going, Ray?"

"You bet," replied Lt. Ray Carter. "Trust me, ol' buddy."

O'Donnell hesitated. "Well, I still say we ought to go on over to the BOQ [bachelor officers' quarters].

But as long as I can get a hot bath and a good meal, I'll be satisfied."

"Oh, you'll get that, all right, believe me," said Carter, laughing, as the two fell in behind the gesturing taxi driver.

The driver escorted them down a stone walk that wound through a garden, where Japanese lanterns reflected multicolored lights over a variety of trees, shrubs, and flowers. The pathway crossed over a meandering fishpond and terminated at a large, ornately carved wooden door, which swung open as they approached. A Japanese woman dressed in a brightly colored kimono bowed and said in English, "Welcome back, Lieutenant Carter. It good to see you again."

Carter returned the bow. "Thank you, Mama-san. Good to be here again."

Once inside, two similarly dressed young Japanese girls appeared and moved silently up beside the men. "They want your shoes," advised Carter, smiling.

"They want what?" asked O'Donnell.

"This his first time, Mama-san," Carter explained to the older woman, as he slipped his shoes off and handed them to one of the girls.

"Ah so," she replied, with a gold-laced smile.

"It's their custom, Kris. They don't wear shoes indoors," Carter explained.

O'Donnell hesitated, then, nodding, said, "I guess I do remember hearing something about that."

After the two men had put on cloth slippers, they were led down a spotless corridor to a room that they entered through a wood-and-paper sliding door. Inside, the room was decorated simply, with Oriental murals on the walls, an ornately carved dividing screen, and a low, polished wooden table on a woven-fabric floor mat.

Again out of nowhere, it seemed, the two girls who had taken their shoes reappeared. Standing before the men, they each held colorful embroidered silk kimonos in their hands.

"Now they are going to trade you a clean, sweet-smelling kimono for that stinky old uniform you're wearing," informed Carter.

O'Donnell looked at his friend suspiciously. "I don't remember hearing anything about trading clothes in a Japanese hotel . . . uh, just what kind of place is this, Ray?"

"It's a first-class operation, believe me. And when you get that uniform back, it will be all freshly cleaned and pressed."

"You're kidding."

"Nope, I'm not. Come on, let's get out of these monkey suits; they're full of Korean dirt and stink of kimchee."

"But Ray—"

"That's the way they do it here. It's just part of their custom. You know, when in Rome?"

"But—"

"They ain't looking at you. See, their eyes are turned down," Carter coaxed.

Kristian O'Donnell peeked at the Japanese girls, and, as his buddy claimed, their heads were bowed, revealing the festooned decorations in their glistening black hair. He also couldn't help but notice that they were very pretty girls, with shapely figures and creamy, flawless skin.

After the exchange had been made and the men had put on their bright kimonos, the girls disap-

peared with the uniforms. "You look great in that kimono, Kris," complimented Carter, grinning.

"I sure feel strange," muttered O'Donnell. "It's like
I'm wearing a dress or something. Ray, is this what's
called a geisha house?"

"You got it, ol' buddy, and I can assure you it's
going to be an experience you'll never forget."

O'Donnell looked at his squadron mate skeptically.
"And just what all do you experience in a geisha
house?"

"Well, let's get into the proper posture here first,
then I'll give you a synopsis of the sociological and
cultural significance of the geisha," said Carter, moving to the floor mat and sitting down cross-legged at
the small table. "Come on, sit down. I don't know
what you've heard about Japanese geisha houses. But
let me tell you, they offer a unique opportunity to
gain significant insight into the artistic, hygienic, and
culinary aspects of the Japanese culture."

"Yeah, I'll bet they do," muttered O'Donnell, as he
tried to fold his long legs under the table.

"Right. And this one is top of the line. You got to
have connections to even get in here."

"You do?"

"Yeah."

"And we have connections?"

"Absolutely. The mama-san and I are old friends. I
was stationed here in Tokyo before the Korean War
broke out. Come on, relax, Kris; it will do you good.
Rest-and-recuperation leave means forgetting about
the war and fighting MiGs and having a little fun for
a change. Right?"

The tall pilot looked at his friend silently for a
moment, his eyes revealing the troubled emotions

that were churning within. Finally he spoke, in a low, hoarse voice: "Ray . . . I know, and appreciate, what you are trying to do for me, but it's not going to fly."

"Look Kris, all I'm asking you to do is relax and enjoy yourself for an evening. You got to shake this thing, ol' friend, you got to. You nearly got yourself killed on that last mission. Those new MiG pilots are good. They are plenty good. And if you don't get hold of yourself and snap out of this thing, one of 'em is sure enough going to flame your ass."

O'Donnell pulled a pack of cigarettes out of the kimono pocket and fired one with his Zippo. He inhaled deeply and let the smoke roll out in puffs as he spoke. "I know, Ray, I know. But I can't forget her, I just can't get her out of my mind."

"You're not the only guy to ever get a Dear John, and I know it's not easy to get over. But you've got to forget her and get hold of yourself, Kris, or you're not going to make it."

"I'm trying, Ray, I'm trying."

"You ain't trying hard enough. You got to accept the facts: she's married. She married the other guy, Kris. The bitch married the other fucking guy!"

Flashes of anger shot from Kris O'Donnell's narrowed eyes, and a flush moved across his handsome face. "Don't call her a bitch, Ray, just don't!"

As the two pilots sat staring at each other, the sliding wood-and-paper door suddenly opened, breaking the silence in the small room. Two new Japanese girls appeared carrying trays, each with a small decorated porcelain bottle, a tiny teacup, and a steaming towel.

These girls wore traditional floor-length long-sleeved Japanese gowns, with their shiny black hair swept high in ornamented buns. Their movements were quick and efficient, yet carried out with quiet, delicate poise. Kneeling silently beside the two men, they placed the trays on the table and offered the towels.

"This is just a quick cleanup for now. We'll get the, uh, full treatment later," Carter explained rapidly, wiping his hands and face with the hot towel. "Come on, Kris, wipe up," he urged.

Reluctantly, O'Donnell accepted the towel from the girl and followed suit. Watching anxiously, Carter could see the anger on his friend's face gradually soften, but he knew that the turmoil within was still simmering, and he warned himself to go easy. Don't mention the bitch again, at least not for a while. Just keep things light, let nature take its course. And after some sake and companionship . . . yeah. Just let nature take its course, and hopefully . . . "Now they're going to pour us a drink in those little china cups. It's called sake. It's actually a beer made from rice, but it tastes more like a white wine. It's great stuff; they serve it hot. You're going to love it."

As Carter had predicted, the girls removed the used towels, then filled the tiny cups from the contents of the bottles. "Here's mud in your eye," said Carter, picking up his cup and tossing down its contents in one gulp. "Aaah, that's good stuff. Come on, down the hatch, Kris."

O'Donnell took a puff of his cigarette, picked up his cup, and gingerly tasted the sake. He was surprised to find that he liked the taste. He nodded and took a larger sip. "It is pretty good," he admitted.

"Didn't I tell you?" said Carter, pleased at the reaction. "Man, I can drink this stuff till the cows come home. You see, the photosynthesis-produced carbohydrates associated with the fermentation process involving rice is a peculiar phenomenon," he said, breaking into a grin. "And it can sure slip up on you," he added.

"Well, as you know, any kind of alcohol slips up on me, but at least this stuff tastes good," said O'Donnell and tossed down the remaining sake.

"Now you're talking, Lieutenant!" said Carter, mimicking the mama-san's accent. Both pilots laughed, and it seemed to relieve the tension between them.

As they watched the pretty Japanese girls refill their sake cups, O'Donnell asked, "Uh, Ray? Do these girls ever talk? I mean do they speak any English?"

"Not much. Oh, maybe a few words. But they don't need to talk, they just seem to know what you're thinking and what you want. There are some Western girls who could sure take a lesson or two from Japanese girls," declared Carter, watching for O'Donnell's reaction.

"Well, I've heard about geisha houses. But I thought they were just, you know, like whorehouses."

"Old friend, let me tell you: there are whorehouses and there are geisha houses. I've been in both, and I can tell you, never the twain shall meet."

A little skeptical smile eased across Kristian O'Donnell's face as he glanced at his friend. "Then, in consideration of your vast experience, you recommend the geisha over the whore as the preferred therapy for a screwed-up fighter pilot who can't get over being dumped by the girl he loves?"

The blunt question caught Carter off guard, but, after a short hesitation, he composed himself. "Well, let's put it this way: the geisha functions in a far more sophisticated arena than the coarse philosophy involving the prostitute. A whore is a whore. The geisha, on the other hand, is a significant social interfacing in the cultural fabric of Nippon, and profoundly misunderstood in many quarters of Western civilization."

O'Donnell picked up his refilled sake cup and eyed his friend across the rim. "I'll say one thing, Ray: you're a master at verbalizing that bullshit," he said, and downed the contents in one gulp.

Carter looked hurt for a moment, then, recovering, raised his chin and said, "Bullshit? A crude, bovine, term that I predict you shall retract."

O'Donnell smiled. "Could be, but I doubt it. I got to admit, though, this sake stuff tastes good, and it's right pleasant in here," he said, holding out his cup and watching the pretty Japanese girl fill it again.

"Hey listen, you ain't seen nothing yet," assured Carter. "Let me acquaint you with the true facts and the fascinating history of the geisha."

The sake cups held little more than a swallow, but by the time Ray Carter had related his full interpretation of the history and sociological function of the geisha, the swallows had added up to a couple of the small bottles. At this point the serving girls quietly disappeared, and moments later, the mama-san appeared through the sliding door and sat down at the table across from the men. "It good to have you come again to our house, Lieutenant Carter. And welcome to you, Lieutenant O'Donnell," she said with a smile.

"Yeah, and I got to tell you, Mama-san, I sure missed your great hospitality," replied Carter.

The Japanese woman nodded. "Thank you. I have all number-one geisha for you to choose." She then gave two quick claps, and six beautiful Japanese girls, all in different-colored gowns of the same traditional style, moved silently through the sliding door and into the room, their sparkling brocade dresses rustling softly as they formed a line before the two men.

"Take your pick," said the short fighter pilot to the tall fighter pilot.

"Take my pick?" croaked O'Donnell incredulously, his eyes moving over the six girls who stood watching him with shy, demure expressions on their dark-eyed, creamy-textured faces. "Jesus, they're all beautiful. What for am I choosing?"

"The one you choose will serve and entertain you for the rest of the evening."

O'Donnell's eyes broke from the girls, and, after a short search, found and focused on Carter's smiling face. "Uh, serve and entertain me for the rest of the evening?"

"Tha's right, ol' buddy. She's going to prepare your dinner, entertain you, and expose you to all that good cultural stuff I told you about, and all you have to do is pick the one you want to do that. Okay?"

Kris O'Donnell had told himself that, in consideration of the good intentions of his friend, he would stay in the geisha house with him for a while, then leave and go to the BOQ at "Tachi"—the city of Tachikawa, where there was an Air Force facility. He was now aware that it was time to leave. But he didn't feel like leaving now. Despite his conviction that a geisha certainly could not solve his problem, he suddenly no longer cared. He simply wanted to stay.

It was, well, it was nice here. He had a warm feeling inside, and he felt good. Yeah, probably because he was half smashed on sake; that must be why he felt good, mustn't it?

So pull yourself together, O'Donnell, and get the hell out. He swung his gaze back to where the six Japanese girls stood watching him. They were all so beautiful, particularly that delicate little flower on the left end. Her face was like that of an exquisite doll, with flawless features and skin that looked like velvet. Her eyes met his for an instant, and specks of quicksilver flashed from their dark depths.

"Kris, you want first choice or what?"

Kris O'Donnell nodded his head slowly. "Yes . . . I do. I choose the one on the end, uh, the left end."

Ray Carter broke into a smile and nodded. "You got good taste, ol' buddy. Isn't she a doll. My choice is that delicious little lady on the other end. I'm certain she can, uh, cook a great sukiyaki."

The mama-san got to her feet and clapped her hands again, and she and the girls quietly disappeared through the sliding door. "Get set for an unparalleled experience in gastronomic delight," declared Lieutenant Carter, pleased about Kris's decision to stay. Things were working out. Yeah, so far, so good. Now all he had to do was let nature take its course.

Moments later the two selected geishas reappeared. They had changed their clothes into less formal kimonos and brought with them more sake and an array of cooking materials, which they quietly set up on another table that they brought into the room. Working swiftly and efficiently, they alternately poured sake and prepared dinner over a charcoal-fired hibachi.

"They are great little chefs. Oh, some of the sauces are prepared in a regular kitchen. But they'll do most of it right here before you. Look at that! Look at how she did that. And just wait till you taste it. You are about to partake in a transcendental gastronomic experience, unequaled in the annals of culinary pursuits," declared Carter, his cheeks beginning to turn a warm pink from the effects of the sake.

O'Donnell, his cheeks also slightly rubicund, nodded in reply, but his attention was elsewhere. "Uh, Ray, how do we communicate, if they don't speak any English?"

"Oh, they speak a little. But don't worry, she'll communicate with you . . . guaranteed."

"Are they going to have dinner with us?"

"Nope. They have already eaten. Their sole objective now is to serve and please you."

The geishas served the meal in several courses, consisting of exotic appetizers made of both raw and cooked fish in tasty sauces, delicate soups, beef, pork, and chicken dishes, with a variety of fresh vegetables. For the most part, Kris hadn't the slightest idea of what he was eating. But he was hungry, and it was all delicious.

Kanuri, the geisha whom Kris had selected, pronounced her name to him but otherwise spoke little. As Carter had predicted, she demonstrated remarkable perception in sensing his slightest desire. At first she maintained a rather demure poise, smiling and meeting his eyes only in passing. But as the evening went on and the interaction between them increased, her smile warmed, and her sparkling dark eyes began to meet and hold his.

All the dishes were served in small china bowls, using traditional wooden chopsticks. When Kanuri demonstrated how to use the chopsticks, she took his hand, momentarily, in hers. The warm velvet touch of her skin ignited feelings in Kris O'Donnell that both surprised and troubled him.

When the dinner had been completed, the geishas quickly whisked away the cooking equipment and dishes, and the two men got to their feet to stretch their legs and smoke a cigarette. "Didn't I tell you it would be a transcendental gastronomic experience?" said Carter.

"It sure was that," agreed O'Donnell. "I was a little apprehensive about some of that raw fish, but I have to admit, that was some kind of a meal. And you were right about those girls' sensory power. They just know what you want, even before you want it."

"Yeah. And the best is yet to come."

Carter's promise of what lay ahead caused a sudden stir of ambivalence in Kris O'Donnell. He was acutely aware of his unexpected emotional attraction to the beautiful little geisha. But something within was telling him it couldn't be. He loved another. He'd always loved another . . . hadn't he?

Dressed in elaborate theatrical attire, the two geishas reappeared about twenty minutes later. They wore sparkling gowns of bright-colored brocade, and their faces were cosmetically made up to appear as vividly colored masks. Their hair, in convoluted folds, was swept up and held in place by decorative combs. The petite geishas appeared unreal, as if they had been finely made, exquisitely painted dolls.

His ambivalence faded as Kris watched and listened while Kanuri performed an animated Oriental dance. She twisted and rotated her head and body in a series of exotic movements that seemed disjointed, yet each move or gesture was in rhythmic harmony with the haunting sound of a small, stringed instrument played by the other geisha.

The girls took turns, alternately playing the instrument and dancing. Each presentation, although similar in style, was unique. At the conclusion of each performance, the pilots clapped and cheered, and the geishas bowed in quiet recognition. "Have you ever seen anything like that?" exclaimed Carter, after the girls had taken their last bow and retired from the room.

"No, I sure haven't, Ray," said Kris, firing up a cigarette. "That's different from any music or dancing I've ever seen. And as weird as it looked and sounded, it was fascinating."

"I figured you would like it. And I think you're going to like what's next, too," said Carter, smiling.

"Uh, what is next, Ray?"

"The bath."

"The bath?"

"Yeah."

Kris nodded and took a puff of his cigarette. "I do need a bath . . . uh, how do they do that?"

Sounding as casual as he could, Carter said, "Oh, in their traditional way. You'll love it."

Hesitation.

"What is their traditional way?"

"Well, they wash you all up first, and—"

"They wash you? Kanuri is going to wash me?"

"That's right. Then she will put you in this big, sunken bathtub."

"In a sunken bathtub?"

"Yeah."

"Kanuri is going to wash me and put me in the bathtub?"

"Sure, that's the way they do it."

It was quiet in the room for a moment, as Carter pulled a cigarette out of his kimono pocket and lit it.

"Does she get in the tub too?"

"Yep."

Each pilot took a puff of his cigarette.

"What happens then?"

"Then you go to your bedroom. Only it's not like a regular bedroom. There isn't any bed. It's a thick pad on the floor. It's great. You'll love it."

Before Kris O'Donnell could phrase his next question, the sliding door opened again, and the geishas stepped through. All of the makeup on their faces had been removed, and now they wore regular kimonos. Kanuri walked straight to Kris, her delicate white face framed by long waves of glistening hair, which she'd released. She smiled, her teeth showing white in a small, delicate mouth. Her dark eyes, reflecting little specks of dancing light, met his unhesitatingly. Then she reached out, took his hand in hers, and led him through the wood-and-fabric sliding door.

"The only thing I don't like about this place is they don't serve coffee," complained Lt. Ray Carter the next morning as the two pilots, dressed in kimonos, sat cross-legged on a floor mat drinking hot tea. "I have trouble getting my motor going in the morning without my coffee."

With his eyes focused on the sun-kissed garden scene, visible through a large open window, Kris muttered, "Since I don't drink the stuff, I have absolutely no complaints."

Carter glanced across at his friend curiously. "Then, uh, I assume you enjoyed yourself last night?"

O'Donnell pulled his gaze back into the small tea-room where they sat, picked up the elaborately deco-rated teacup, and took a sip. He set the cup down and, ignoring Carter's question, said, "Ray, tell me something. Is Mama-san the head honcho here?"

"Well, yeah. She doesn't own the place, but she runs it."

Kris nodded. "Well, if I wanted to talk to someone about Kanuri, would she be the one?"

"Yeah, sure. Uh, what did you have in mind?"

After a short hesitation, O'Donnell said, "Well, I'm going to get Kanuri out of here."

"You're what?" Carter croaked incredulously.

O'Donnell looked at him and smiled. "I know, I'd never have believed it either. But it happened. And I owe it all to you, ol' buddy."

Trying to keep his voice calm, Carter said, "Yeah . . . ah, just what do you owe me for?"

O'Donnell looked surprised. "Well, you brought me here and I found Kanuri, that's what I owe you for."

Oh, Jesus Christ! Nature had taken its course, all right. And now his friend was out of the frying pan and into the fire! *Now* what are you going do, oh great one, agonized Lt. Ray Carter.

"She is the most wonderful girl I've ever met, Ray. I never realized that a girl could be that way. So warm, so attentive, so loving, she is completely op-posite to . . . uh, well, to other girls I've known."

"Ah, Kris, you gotta remember, now, Kanuri is a professional, I mean that's her business. She is trained to—"

"What's that got to do with it?"

"Well, I mean—"

"Ray, I'm taken with Kanuri. I know that sounds immature and irrational, particularly since, as you know, I was certain there would never be another girl for me, but it happened, and it happened big time."

Carter shifted his legs under the tea table. "I'm glad you discovered there are other girls in the world, Kris. But look. You gotta remember: she is a geisha."

"So? You're the one that said geishas were different. They are cultured, talented ladies. Right?"

Carter could see that he had a problem on his hands. A problem he had created, and he didn't have a clue as to a solution. He'd known before the squadron came to Korea that his friend was so devoted to the bitch that he would never even look at another girl. And the truth was that Kris may have been the only one in the squadron who was surprised when she dumped him. Oh, she was beautiful, all right. Beautiful, spoiled, and selfish.

But Kris was so blindly in love he couldn't see it. Or he thought he was in love, as Carter preferred to think. And his reaction over the geisha was proof that Carter had been right. His friend had finally got a taste of loving warmth that had opened his eyes.

But now what? Well, it was probably a classic case of emotional rebound, wasn't it? Carter cleared his throat and said, "Yeah. I said that. Geishas are refined and talented, but Kris, you don't really know Kanuri. You need to—"

"I know that. But I'll get to know her, and meanwhile, I want her out of here."

Ray Carter knew he was treading on thin ice, but he had no choice. "Okay. You say you want to take Kanuri out of here?"

"Yes."

"She's under contract to Mama-san, you know."

"I'll buy her contract."

Carter nodded. "I'd guess that could be done. But then what are you going to do with her? You sure as hell can't take her to Korea."

Kris hesitated. "I know that. But I can take her to her home, and she can stay there until I finish my combat tour, and then I'll ask to be stationed here in Japan."

Carter pulled out a cigarette, lit it, and blew out a column of smoke. "Kris, do you know that Kanuri feels the same as you do about this?"

O'Donnell hesitated. "Well, she hasn't said it, of course. She doesn't speak much English. But she understands a lot, and I know she feels the same about me as I do about her, I'm sure of it."

"And you're going to take her to her home to wait for you?"

"Yeah."

"Did she tell you she has a home?"

"No, but she must have one."

"Not necessarily. The war left thousands like her without a home, or a family."

"Well if she doesn't, I'll find a place for her to stay and pay for it until I come back."

"And if you don't come back?"

Except for the sounds of chirping birds from the garden, it was silent in the private tearoom for several moments. O'Donnell got to his feet, walked to the open window, and looked at the garden. "I see things a lot different now, Ray. I'll come back, all right."

Carter also got to his feet. "Look, Kris. Before you go any further with this thing, I got to tell you, there are some things that you're not considering."

Kris turned from the window and looked at Carter. "Yeah, what am I not considering?"

"I can appreciate your feelings toward Kanuri. She is a delightful, beautiful girl, and it's hard to imagine that anyone with such tenderness and warmth could, well, you know, do this kind of work. But Kris, she does. She is a geisha. It's a skill. It's what she does. It's her job. And let me tell you, she wouldn't know what you're talking about if you asked her to leave."

O'Donnell stared at Carter. "I don't believe that, Ray. I think she would leave."

"Okay. Before you take this thing any further, would you talk to Mama-san?"

"Sure. I got to talk to her anyway, so why not?"

"All right. You stand by, and I'll go get her," said Carter, pulling open the sliding door and disappearing down the polished hallway.

He returned a few minutes later, with the mama-san in tow. She smiled when she entered the room and bowed to O'Donnell. When they were seated on the mat at the tea table, Carter turned to Kris and said, "I haven't said anything to her yet, so you'll know I haven't stacked the deck." He took a drink of his tea and grimaced. "Mama-san, you just got to get some coffee in this place."

"No can get coffee," she said with a gold-toothed smile.

Carter smiled back at her, then turned serious. "Mama-san, my friend here, he rich. He buy contract and pay you big bonus; take Kanuri away."

O'Donnell glared at Carter, and the Japanese woman glanced at the pilot with a puzzled look. "Why you do that? No can take Korea."

"Yeah, he knows that. He take Kanuri to her home."

The mama-san frowned and shook her head. "Kanuri no have home. All gone. She live here."

Carter and O'Donnell exchanged looks.

"Well, he take her someplace to live."

The mama-san looked confused. "She live here. She no go."

O'Donnell looked suspiciously from the mama-san to Carter. "How do I know she won't go?" he asked crisply.

"Mama-san, you go bring Kanuri, okay?" instructed Carter.

The Japanese woman shrugged, got to her feet, bowed, and shuffled through the sliding door.

"The reason I said you were rich is 'cause I wanted you to see her reaction. I mean it was obvious she would like to pocket some extra yen, right? So there is no incentive for the mama-san to fake this thing. In fact, the incentive for her is the bonus I promised her, so she would logically encourage Kanuri to go. Right? The problem is, the little girl wouldn't know what to do with herself out of her environment. This is all she knows."

"I don't believe that, Ray, that's all. I just don't accept it."

A few minutes later, when Kanuri entered the room following behind the mama-san, Carter could not miss the affectionate look that passed between Kris and the girl, and, for a disturbing moment, he wondered if his strategy was flawed. But he had no choice now. He had to see it through.

She was dressed in a bright kimono that molded her small but perfect figure. This morning her hair was down, falling in long dark waves, accentuating the creamy, exquisite features of her doll-like face. Carter was reminded of one of those beautiful Japanese dolls that were sold in glass containers in the Tokyo curio shops.

When they were settled at the tea table, Carter turned to the mama-san and explained again, slowly, that his rich friend wanted to be Kanuri's benefactor by purchasing her contract so that she could leave the geisha house.

The mama-san hesitated for a moment, then jabbered something at Carter in a mixture of Japanese and English. The pilot shook his head. "No, no, he go back to Korea."

"Ah so," she said, nodding, then turned to Kanuri and made the translation in Japanese.

Carter felt a surge of satisfaction when Kanuri began to shake her head fiercely. But when he saw the look on Kris O'Donnell's face as Kanuri jumped up and ran out of the room, he was reminded of the time back home, when the plow mule had kicked him in the stomach.

Lt. Ray Carter twisted the throttle to the stop position. As the whine of the powerful jet engine subsided, he completed the shutdown procedure and pulled himself up out of the cockpit of his F-86 Sabre-Jet. He climbed out of the cockpit and walked across to the adjacent parking revetment, where another jet pilot was climbing out of his F-86 there at Kimpo air base in Seoul, Korea. "Congratulations, ol' buddy, that was the second MiG you've shot down this week."

Lt. Kristian O'Donnell pulled off his crash helmet and dug a cigarette out of his flight-suit pocket.

"Thanks, Ray. I've got the hang of it now," he said, firing the cigarette.

"Yeah, that you have. I was worried there for a while, because when we came back from Tokyo I was afraid you were in more trouble than ever. But you sure turned it around, Kris."

O'Donnell nodded and took a puff of the cigarette. "I understand some things now that I didn't before, Ray. Oh, I was pretty shook that morning in Tokyo, and it took a while before it all sunk into my thick skull. When it did, I realized that you were right. But let me tell you, ol' friend: what that little geisha did for me not only opened my eyes, she saved my life."

Carter pulled off his helmet and lit a cigarette, as the roar of another jet taking off on the airstrip a few yards away reverberated through the revetment. When the sound had faded, Carter looked up at the freshly painted name on the nose of O'Donnell's Sabre-Jet. It read: Kanuri. "I see you have a new name on your bird."

Kris O'Donnell looked at his friend and smiled. "Yeah. That I have Ray, that I have."

Ray Carter and I were in the same fighter squadron in the Southwest Pacific during World War II. I met him again later, in Korea, and he told me the story of Kris O'Donnell, who went on to become one of the United States' top jet aces. I decided it was best to use fictitious names, but the story is real.

CHAPTER SIXTEEN

Night Mission at the 8055 MASH

In the television series it was called the 4077 MASH, which was fictional. But the 8055 MASH in Korea, which was real, had a lot of similar characters.

The reason I know is that I spent a good portion of my tour of duty during the Korean War at the 8055 MASH. They rotated us pilots and medics every few weeks between the various rescue sites, to balance out the hardship tours.

It was fun to watch the TV program because, generally, I would have a little anecdote to go with the story—particularly when it had something to do with Hawkeye. The real name of the one we called Hawkeye was Dr. Sam Gilfand. He looked a lot like the movie version and was, indeed, a character and a fine surgeon. The *M*A*S*H* writers took some liberties, of course, but a lot of what they wrote was based on real stuff. And that too I know about, because I was in on some of it.

The crazy tricks we played on one another were all in fun and served to break the routine and relieve some of the terrible tension we were all under, particularly those fine doctors and nurses. Sometimes the recipient of a trick would get a little bent out of shape for a few days, but no one really got hurt.

Then one night in the winter of 1953, I was involved in what I perceived as one of those tricks, but it ended up as an exciting, dangerous experience, my most memorable of the Korean War. It nearly got a couple of us killed and set me up for a court-martial.

I had just come from that brutally cold Christmas tour at Ch'o Do Island, and, although it was nearly as cold at the MASH, at least it was in friendly territory and they had a shower and a mess hall. In fact, this story has its beginning one morning in the mess hall. Well, actually it wasn't a hall, it was a GI tent with a wooden floor.

"Whenever I'm here enjoying a gourmet breakfast in this charming café overlooking the beautiful rocks of Korea, I can't imagine why the Army calls it a mess," said Hawkeye that morning, sitting at a long wooden table beside one of the other surgeons, his tent mate. I'm not sure about his name; I think it was Donald. I sat across from them with my element commander, Capt. Chuck Enderton. It was early and cold, and we were all huddled in heavy parkas. There were a few early shift doctors, nurses, and corpsmen having breakfast. No one was talking much, except for Hawkeye; he was always cracking a joke or something. But mostly all you heard was the clank of metal mess trays and the shuffle of boots.

"It isn't hard for me to imagine why it's called a mess," growled Donald, "these powdered eggs look exactly like baby shit. Pass the ketchup."

"You know Don, your problem is you don't have

any imagination. You got to say to yourself: These powdered eggs don't look like baby shit, they look like Russian caviar," said Hawkeye with a grin.

"Whoever heard of sickly, yellowish caviar," replied Donald, shaking out gobs of ketchup over the powdered eggs on his mess tray.

"Like I said, you got no imagination."

Chuck and I laughed, and Chuck said, "Well, Russian caviar it ain't. But I got to tell you fellows, it's a lot better than that C-ration shit we been eatin' at Ch'o Do."

"Correction: You been eatin', Charles," I said, following Donald's lead and dumping ketchup on my powdered eggs. "I ate peanut butter."

"Yuck," groaned Hawkeye. "I like peanut butter, but for breakfast?"

"Kirk eats it for breakfast, lunch, and supper," said Enderton.

"It's that or starve to death on Ch'o Do," I confirmed.

"Aw, you Air Force guys are just used to the good life," put in Hawkeye.

"Speaking of the good life, I got two bottles of Stateside gin. Let's have a party after sundown," suggested Enderton.

"Now you're talking my language," said Hawkeye quickly.

"Hey, Stateside stuff. You got my attention too," said Donald, brightening. "That stuff Hawk makes takes more imagination to drink than I can muster here lately."

"Can I come casual and do we have to wait till sundown?" added Hawkeye.

"Yes to both of the above," replied Chuck with a laugh.

"You guys and this sundown thing. It sounds like something out of a two-bit western flick. I bet the chopper doesn't care if it flies after sundown. How come you do?" asked Hawkeye.

Sometimes it was hard to tell when the surgeon was serious, but I took up the challenge with, "I don't care. It's the Air Force that cares. I'll fly anytime." I caught the gleam in his eye and said to myself: Watch out, he's got something up his sleeve. But about that time someone interrupted, and I forgot about it.

We all lived in pyramidal GI tents right there at the MASH, which was a sort of tent city that could be folded up and moved quickly, if necessary. The Army tried to keep the MASH out of enemy-artillery range, yet as close as possible to the battlefield. That often required some fast moving, and even then it wasn't always possible. There were four of us Air Force pilots in one tent, with our medics and mechanics in tents next to us. Hawkeye and the rest of the surgeons and medics all lived in the same row of tents. The nurses were in a tent complex on the opposite side of the main MASH tent. This was before the unisex military.

The pilots' tent had a direct land-line telephone to the aid stations on the battlefield. They would call us when they had a wounded patient to be picked up in the combat zone. When the call came we flew to the battlefield, picked up the patient, and had him back at the MASH within minutes. It was a tremendous boost to morale and a far cry from the old triage system of World War II, where most of the severely wounded died—if not from their wounds, from the jarring ambulance ride.

That night we held the party in our tent and invited everybody. By the time it was dark outside, the place was packed with just about every surgeon and nurse who wasn't on duty. I was the pilot on alert that afternoon, so I had to wait for it to get dark before I could partake. When I peeked out through the faded Plexiglas window in our tent door and saw the ragged Korean ridges turning dark, I headed for our portable bar (a packing crate) to mix my first drink. Just as I poured the gin into a canteen cup, I heard the alert field phone ring. Enderton happened to be standing next to the phone, so he answered.

I watched him from where I was standing and saw him talking and shaking his head, and finally hanging up the phone. I shrugged it off and went back to what I was doing: mixing some gin with a little canned grapefruit juice. Then I heard the phone ring again. This time I saw Enderton speak for a moment, then, frowning, glance at me and motion for me to come over. I picked up the drink I had just mixed and made my way through the crowded tent to where he was. "What's going on?" I asked.

"I don't know what to think, Kirk. Some lieutenant at the aid station in sector 9G called and says one of his men is bad wounded, and he knows we got somebody brave enough here that will fly after dark to save a man's life."

"What did you tell him?"

"I told him it wasn't a matter of bravery; it was regulations. We can't fly at night because we can't see where we're going. But the guy insisted there had to someone here that would do it."

Hawkeye! I said to myself, remembering his challenge that morning. I looked around, and, sure enough, he wasn't here, which was unusual for Hawk. He was usually the first one to a party. I smiled to myself. I would call his bluff. "If he calls again, tell him your bravest ace helicopter pilot is on his way."

Captain Enderton looked at me skeptically. "What? You can't do that."

"We're being had, Chuck. Just leave it to me," I assured him.

"Okay," Enderton agreed. "It's your game, but you know the orders on night flying."

I smiled. "I know. But just go along with the gag, okay?"

He shrugged and turned back to the nurse he'd been talking to. The field phone rang again. I picked it up. Sure enough, this guy identified himself as a lieutenant at pickup aid station 9G. "You got to come get him!" he pleaded. "He's bad hit in the stomach and he can't make it till morning."

"Sure, I'll come get him," I replied, laughing to myself as I thought of how well Hawkeye had coached this guy, whoever he was, on how to challenge me.

"Oh God, that's great! You will save his life for sure. You know the spot at 9G?"

"I know it," I assured him.

"Great. We'll line up some trucks, and when we hear you coming we'll turn on the headlights, okay?"

"Sure, that will be fine," I said, thinking that Hawk had really thought of all the details. "Say, won't you take some fire from your North Korean friends when they see that light?" I asked, still inwardly laughing.

"Well, if you remember, we're kind of down in a little bowl-like valley, and if we keep the lights pointed down I don't think the gooks will see it."

"Oh, yeah. Good thinking!" I said, chuckling silently. But then my smile dissolved as I saw Hawkeye come through the tent door. He had a nurse on his arm, and it was pretty evident that whatever he'd been doing, it wasn't playing tricks on me. "Are you really serious, Lieutenant?" I suddenly croaked into the field phone.

There was a momentary silence on the other end of the line. "I don't understand," he replied in a cold voice.

"Well, I mean is this all real? You really have someone there that's wounded?"

Another silence, then: "I don't know what kind of a sadistic creep you are. But just what the hell do you think we've been talking about?"

I suddenly felt like I'd been kicked in the stomach. "I'm sorry," I muttered, "sorry." Here I'd thought it was a joke, and it wasn't. It was real. And it was all my fault. I should have known Hawkeye wouldn't play a joke about something this serious. And now I had a real problem.

"Are you going to come and get this man, or are you going to let him die?" snapped the voice on the other end of the field phone.

"Yes. I'm going to come and get him," I heard myself say. I had no choice. There was no way I could turn this man down now, regardless of orders or the consequences. "I'll be there as soon as I can make it.

When you hear the chopper coming, turn on the truck lights," I instructed, and hung up the phone.

Captain Enderton was busy talking to the nurse, so I slipped out the door without anyone's seeing me. There was no point in discussing it with him anyway, because I knew he could only repeat the orders of no night flying. And since I had made up my mind I was going regardless, there was no point in putting him on the spot.

But as I began to think about what I was attempting, I realized it couldn't be done—not alone, anyway. There was no way I could fly the helicopter without being able to see the instruments, or at least the tachometer. In the whirlybird, "Thy rotor RPM is thy staff of life, without which thee shall surely perish." And thee cannot see the rotor tach at night.

I walked down to the medics' tent. They were also having a party and wanted me to join them. I begged off, told them my problem, and asked for a volunteer to go with me. You see, the helicopter requires both hands and both feet to fly: I had to have someone to hold a flashlight on the tachometer.

The medics all looked at me as though I was crazy, but one of them volunteered, and now there was no way I could back out of my commitment. For the life of me I cannot remember the boy's name who went with me that night. And I hate that, because he was certainly a brave young man to do what he did. I can only remember that he was handsome, solidly built, and had bushy brown hair. I think his first name was Roger. Anyway, Roger and I got a flashlight and headed for the helicopter.

The helipad was far enough from the living quarters, and, with everyone partying, I was able to start the chopper engine, warm it up, and lift off before anyone even knew what was going on. Then they all came pouring out of their tents in time to see us lift up from the MASH helipad and disappear into the Korean blackness in the direction of no-man's-land: along the 38th parallel.

The Sikorsky H-5 that I was flying that night had a three-bladed rotor that was powered by a 450-hp Pratt and Whitney R-985 engine. It could carry four passengers, including the pilot, who sat in a single forward seat. When we used the H-5 for medevac, we attached covered aluminum pods to each side, where the patients were carried. The medic rode in the seat behind the pilot. Roger leaned forward from where he sat on the backseat and held the flashlight on the tachometer.

We had covered the flashlight lens with surgical tape, so that only a tiny beam of light shone out to spot the tach. That kept the glare from giving me vertigo, which would have meant certain disaster. I had never before flown a helicopter at night, and it was scary, at first. But after a few minutes I settled down, and the H-5 didn't seem to mind at all that it was flying in the dark.

It was because of the topography that the choppers in Korea could fly right up to the front lines of the battlefield and pick up patients without getting shot down. The terrain along the 38th parallel was a maze of barren ridges with small canyons between them. We flew down in the canyons, below the tops of the ridges and out of sight of the North Korean guns. You couldn't do it with an airplane, but the helicopter worked fine.

However, there was a catch: you had to know

which canyons were friendly and which weren't. Intelligence briefed us every morning on where the MLR (main line of resistance) had moved, from one ridge to another, in the past twenty-four hours. Historians have often referred to Korea as the Battle of the Hills: Porkchop Hill, Old Baldy, Heartbreak Ridge. All were scenes of bloody battles. During the final year of the Korean War, the MLR only moved a few miles one way or the other. But we had to know when it moved and where, or find ourselves in enemy territory and in deep kimchee.

I knew which canyons were friendly that night, but there was no way I could fly them in the darkness. So I decided right off that I would climb the H-5 up to an altitude that would clear all the ridges, and I would have to trust that I could find the pickup point, 9G. Then, when I got close enough for the lieutenant to hear me coming, he would turn on the truck lights, and I could see where to land. But the North Koreans would also hear me coming, wouldn't they? Yes, they would. But with no lights on the chopper, they couldn't see me . . . could they?

I was familiar with the area at 9G, as I had evacuated a patient from there earlier that very day. But on a moonless black night, nothing looked familiar. I did notice, however, that since it was cold and clear the stars were bright, and I could see their reflection on a river that ran parallel to the ridge that I wanted to follow. So I stayed over it and navigated by starlight on the water. Once I had climbed to altitude and set the throttle friction, I could fly without the flashlight, needing only to check my tach and instruments occasionally. This helped my night vision.

After a few minutes of flying my pulse rate slowed

considerably, and I began to feel a little more confident. The bird was purring like a contented kitten, and my eyes were adjusting to the darkness. I glanced back at Roger and gave him a thumbs-up. I couldn't see him very well but he returned my signal, so I guessed he was okay.

Everything went well until we reached the bend in the river where I had to turn north. From there on it was pretty much a guessing game, and I evidently didn't guess well. In retrospect I can't really blame myself too much, because I'd never flown in there except in daylight, and I'd only flown along the bottom of a canyon. The terrain I was looking at now was nothing but black shapes and more black shapes. Within minutes I was totally lost and had no idea which way to turn.

It was awful cold there in the chopper, and, even in the darkness, I could see my breath making white mist. Yet I could feel beads of perspiration popping out on my forehead. I was now getting desperate, just flying this way and that around in circles, hoping against hope that I would stumble onto 9G. And there was no point in looking at my map. It would tell me nothing, since I could see nothing. There was no question in my mind that I was also flying in and out of North Korean territory. Would they suddenly just open fire?

I was no stranger to taking risks, but in this instance I had a young medic who was at my mercy, and I decided I'd better swallow my pride and get the hell out of there. It wasn't right to risk Roger's life any further.

I banked the chopper toward what I guessed was south, and I was about to ask Roger for the flashlight to check my mag compass when I saw the truck lights come on. Twelve o'clock low, at what the Navy would call dead ahead. I went down on the collective and back on the cyclic control sticks in one swift movement, and I yelled to Roger, "Put the light on the tach, quick!"

He leaped forward and zeroed in on the tach. With the truck lights for reference I wasn't worried, now, about vertigo, but I sure didn't want to lose my RPM. I made a beautiful steep approach right down to 9G. There was only one problem: I flew right through the top of a tree. Fortunately it was all shriveled up in winter, and it caused little damage. What upset me was that I'd known it was there, because I had said to someone earlier that day that it might well be the only tree still standing in Korea.

When the Sikorsky's wheels touched down on the Korean earth there at aid station 9G, I breathed a big sigh of relief. I'd done it! I had broken the rules and beat the odds and got away with it! Right at that point I wished I had that glass of gin and grapefruit juice.

I pulled the clutch-engagement lever and let the rotor blades windmill, but I kept the engine running at idle. I didn't want to take a chance on its not starting. As the blades were winding down I pushed the sliding door open, and Roger jumped out to supervise the loading operation, which was our standard procedure. The GIs quickly appeared beside the chopper, carrying the badly wounded patient in a litter. At the same time a battle-weary first lieutenant, dressed in full combat gear, appeared beside me at the door of the chopper. He had a dirty face and there were dark circles under his eyes.

"Thanks, Captain. I know you broke the rules and took a risk, but you've saved the life of a fine soldier. And . . . I'm sorry for what I said earlier."

I nodded as I climbed out of the helicopter. "I had it coming, Lieutenant," I said, as I checked out the H-5 for visual damage from my spatial dispute with the tree.

"Jesus, I thought you were going to crash for sure when you hit that tree," the lieutenant muttered.

"Didn't bother me, I never even saw it. How close are the gooks?" I asked, relieved that I could see no serious damage on the bird.

"Just over that ridge," he said, pointing to a dark shape off in the darkness.

I nodded.

"The patient's on board, sir. We're ready to go," said Roger, climbing back into the helicopter.

"Thanks again, Captain, I owe you one," said the lieutenant, offering his hand.

We shook hands briefly and I crawled back into the pilot's seat of the chopper, strapped myself in, and flipped the rotor-engagement lever. The worst part should be over, I told myself, as the big rotor blades began to gather momentum. I'd simply crank on full power and climb straight up till I was above all the ridges, turn south, and head for the 8055. It should be a breeze.

Within seconds the rotor was up to full RPM, and I was ready to go. I glanced through the front canopy. The lieutenant and his men were all standing around the chopper, with the rotor wash buffeting their winter parkas. Their smudged faces reflected the pale headlights of the half dozen trucks that were parked around the helicopter.

"Here we go, Roger," I shouted as I twisted the motorcycle-type throttle on the H-5 as far as it would go and pulled in full power on the collective. The 450 horses in the Pratt and Whitney engine barked loudly into the black Korean night, and the Sikorsky H-5 helicopter leaped off the ground and climbed skyward like a homesick angel.

Then all hell broke loose. It was like the Fourth of July on Coney Island: glowing red fireballs and explosions everywhere. There was no point in trying to take evasive action: the stuff came from all directions. All I could do was hold full power and hope for the best. The North Koreans were throwing everything they had at me, and I mean everything.

I suddenly realized why. When I'd climbed up from 9G at full power, there had been a stream of fire shooting out of my exhaust stack at least six feet long. The enemy could see it for miles; it made a perfect target.

I could hear the sound of lead and steel piercing the Sikorsky: *Ping! Pow! Plunk!* Then the controls began to feel strange, and at the same time my bird began to shake badly. I could almost feel the helicopter beginning to disintegrate around me. It was slowing down as though all was lost, the sound of the rotors diminishing, RPM decreasing . . . RPM! I was losing my RPM!

"Roger! The flashlight!" I shouted, as I quickly lowered the collective. The beam from the flashlight stabbed the tach, and my heart stopped: the RPM was below the red line. I slammed the collective to the floor and was thrown violently up in my seat, against the shoulder straps. The flashlight went flying across the cockpit as the Sikorsky dropped earthward like a rock.

But then all helicopters drop like rocks when you slam the collective down; it's like suddenly removing your wings. I was pretty sure, at that point, that recovering my RPM before the bird struck the cold, hard Korean earth was another long shot.

But it did recover. I couldn't see the tachometer because we'd lost the flashlight. But I heard that big rotor begin to sing, and I knew I'd made it. I pulled in some collective to stop the rapid descent, and I had it level again when the next episode of the drama occurred.

The North Koreans suddenly stopped firing. I'm not sure why, but they did, and suddenly it was as though I was flying in the bottom of an inkwell. From a sea of red-and-white glare to pitch blackness. It was vertigo time in spades. I don't honestly know how I was able to keep the helicopter level. But I did, at least long enough for my eyes to readjust and pick up the reflecting starlight to give me reference. Strangely, the H-5 seemed to be functioning normally.

Roger recovered the flashlight, and I checked all the gauges, and everything looked okay. I couldn't believe it, because I knew we'd taken a lot of hits; I'd heard them. Nevertheless, inexplicably, the bird was flying like a champ.

All I could figure was that in my anxiety to get away from the ground fire, I had held too much collective for too long and simply bled off my RPM. One thing about those early choppers: when they didn't like what was going on, they'd let you know. They would shake like a hound dog out of water.

The rest of the flight went without incident. I

picked up the river and followed it to the valley where the MASH was, and we landed there a few minutes later in a flurry of activity. The lieutenant had called and told Captain Enderton that we were on our way, and the whole MASH turned out to meet us.

The patient was critical, and we had got him there in the nick of time. After they had operated, he hovered on the edge for several days, but he recovered. Strangely, I never knew his name. But then I flew sixty-nine combat-rescue missions in Korea, and I never knew a lot of their names. It wasn't the man's name, it was saving his life that mattered. It was surely a world apart from what I'd had to do flying fighters in World War II.

"You crazy bastard!" were the first words I heard that night when I stepped down out of the chopper. It was Captain Enderton, but he was grinning and a little flush-faced.

"Any gin left?" I asked.

"Yeah, we still got some. And you're going to need it. You're in deep kimchee, you know."

I nodded. "I figured that. Do they know at HQ?"

"Not yet, but they will, and there will be hell to pay. What possessed you to do it?" he asked, his words slightly slurred.

About that time, Hawkeye walked up and put his arm around my shoulder. "You weren't kidding when you said that sundown stuff didn't cut any ice with you, huh, ace?"

I smiled and looked at Enderton. "I rest my case."

There were two big surprises for me the next morning. Despite an awful gin-and-grapefruit-juice hangover, I went out to the helipad to inspect the battle damage on the H-5 and found not a single bullet hole. I could not believe it. I could have sworn I'd heard bullets striking everywhere. Obviously they hadn't. Despite all that fire the North Koreans had put up, they hadn't touched me. That gave me some hope that maybe I wouldn't be in quite as much trouble for violating orders.

The other surprise came when Chuck Enderton told me that Bill Ryan, our OPS officer, had said that since the H-5 wasn't damaged, he wouldn't report the violation. But if it happened again I was dead. Oh, happiness! I was off the hook!

But I wasn't. A few days later I was ordered to report ASAP to Major Wood, our commander, at K-16 in Seoul. No one had to tell me what it was about. Major Wood was a nice guy, but he could be tough when the occasion warranted it. I knew it was going to be one of those occasions when I entered his office, a sandbagged tent on the east side of Kimpo air base.

"Sit down and read this," he grumbled, returning my salute and handing me a piece of paper.

I sat down on a green, beat-up GI chair in front of his green, beat-up GI desk and looked at the paper. It was a recommendation for the Distinguished Service Cross for one Capt. Richard C. Kirkland AO-749566, for conspicuous bravery in the face of the enemy while saving the life of a wounded U.S. soldier. It had been submitted by the lieutenant at sector 9G.

I just sat there looking at it. "You're to be commended, Captain Kirkland, for saving the man's life," said Major Wood.

I didn't know what to say. "But the next guy who breaks regulations and tries it might not be as skilled, or as lucky. Which do you think it was, Captain?"

I still didn't know what to say, although, in all honesty, I had to admit: "It was mostly luck, sir."

"That would be my guess," said the major.

I nodded.

"There is an old military saying that only a hair separates a citation for valor from a court-martial. In this case I could easily approve either. That was a hell of a mission, and you saved a man's life. But if I approve a citation, I'm condoning breaking the night-flying order. I can't do that, Kirk. As you know, we're doing important lifesaving work here, and I can't afford to have helicopters wrecked and pilots and medics killed trying to win medals."

"I didn't do it to win a medal, Major."

"I know that, Captain."

We were quiet for a moment, as the distinctive sound of a "gooney bird" [C-47 transport plane] taking off filled the tent. When the sound had died away, Wood leaned back in his beat-up GI chair and said, "How is my ol' pal Hawkeye doing? He get any good ones on you lately?"

I looked at Wood and smiled. "Well, sort of, but he didn't realize it."

The major smiled. "He is a character. Well, get your tail on back up there, and give him my regards," he said, dropping the recommendation for my DSC in the trash box beside his cluttered, beat-up GI desk.

I may not have got the medal, but I didn't get a court-martial, either. I thought about it over the years, and really it all came out pretty well.

I had a lot of exciting and emotional experiences in World War II and Korea and the period between them, but the "Night Mission at the 8055 MASH" was certainly the most satisfying. There is something very special about saving someone's life, especially when you know there was no other way it could have been done.

CHAPTER SEVENTEEN

Winged S

When the peace talks finally ended and the shooting stopped in Korea in 1953, I was sent home just in time for Christmas. It was great being with my family again in the good old USA. I was assigned as a helicopter pilot to the 43rd Air Rescue Squadron, 4th Air Rescue Group, at McChord Air Force Base in Washington, where I had flown my first helicopter.

A couple of weeks before Christmas 1955 my squadron commander called me into his office and told me that I had been selected to ferry one of our H-19 helicopters to the Sikorsky factory for modification. I was pleased at the assignment, because in those days we rarely had the opportunity to make such a long flight in the helicopter. It was approximately twenty-seven hundred miles from McChord Air Force Base to the factory in Stratford, Connecticut.

The downside was that it was winter, and the helicopter was not equipped to fly instruments. That meant I'd be delayed by storms, and it could take weeks to complete the trip.

"Sir, I've spent two of the last three Christmases away from my family. I hate to be gone again. Is there any possibility I can wait till after Christmas to make the flight?" I asked.

The major shook his head. "No. My orders are to get it there ASAP."

"ASAP?"

"That's correct."

I could see he wasn't going to bend on a delay, so I went to my second option. "I may have to take a circuitous route to avoid long delays because of weather."

The major looked at me suspiciously for a moment and then said, "Take whatever route is necessary, as long as it gets you there."

The weatherman had told me that I could skirt most of the winter weather by going south—deep south. And that's what I did. I flew the H-19 with my copilot, Lt. Bill Tuttle, and crew chief, T.Sgt. R. T. Hanke, down the west coast of Washington, Oregon, and California. Then we went along the Mexican border of Arizona, New Mexico, and Texas, to the gulf coast, across Florida, and then up the Atlantic coast to the Sikorsky plant in Stratford, arriving three days before Christmas. We had airline reservations for home the next day.

There was a welcoming committee with a big surprise for us at the Sikorsky factory. One of them was a smiling gentleman wearing a black fedora. It was Igor Ivanovich Sikorsky, one of the greatest aeronautical engineers and designers of all time. He had been one of my aviation heros for many years, so it was a genuine thrill and an honor to meet him. He bowed slightly and shook my hand firmly when we were introduced. "Congratulations, Captain Kirkland, on your record-breaking flight," he said.

"My record-breaking flight?" I sort of croaked, uncertain of what he meant.

He was still smiling, his dark, thin mustache turned up at the corners of his mouth. "Yes. Didn't you know?"

I shook my head.

"Your flight of approximately seven thousand miles breaks all helicopter distance records to date that we know of," said one of the other Sikorsky officials standing there.

I found out later the information on our route across the continent came from my daily flight reports to headquarters. But at the time, I had no idea we had broken a distance record. I glanced at my crew, and we all smiled and tried to look like record breakers. Actually, we were too embarrassed to admit that all we'd done was circumnavigate the bad weather so we could get home for Christmas.

"Come gentlemen, we have some refreshments waiting," said one of the others in the welcoming committee.

We were escorted inside the factory to a conference room where there were soft drinks, coffee, and cake.

"What type of problems did you encounter on such a long flight?" asked Sikorsky, as soon as we were seated around the table with our refreshments. I could tell from the way he asked the question that he was genuinely interested in my answer.

We'd had a couple of small problems, which I described for him, like an unscheduled landing in a cornfield when the throttle bell crank sheared. That excited him, and he wanted to know exactly what happened and how we repaired it.

What a fascinating experience it was to be sitting there discussing helicopters with one of the great men of aviation and the man most of the helicopter world considered the father of the helicopter.

Born in Kiev, Russia, on 25 May 1889, Igor Sikorsky decided early that aviation was the love of his life, and vertical flight the passion of that love. His first efforts included a helicopter he designed and built himself when he was nineteen years old. It had a wooden frame and crude rotor blades that were powered by a 25-horsepower Anzani engine. In the backyard of the Sikorsky home on a spring day in 1910, the engine roared and the rotor blades whirled, with Sikorsky at the controls. But all that rose from the earth was a lot of dust.

Despite the failure of his first helicopter, Sikorsky told his father he was certain he could design a helicopter that would fly. But he turned his attention to conventional aviation and within a year had designed and built an airplane with the help of schoolmates from the polytechnic institute he attended. He taught himself to fly the plane and set several world records.

Within two years he had designed and produced six successful airplanes and, after that, the world's first four-engine airplane, the Grand, which also set numerous world records. After the Grand's success, Sikorsky was widely acclaimed in Russia, and personally honored by Czar Nicholas.

But the Bolshevik Revolution forced Sikorsky to flee his homeland and immigrate to America in 1919. His arrival in New York went unnoticed, and he struggled to make ends meet for several years. Then, with the help of a few friends, and parts from a junkyard, he designed, built, and flew his first American aircraft on a Long Island chicken farm in early 1923.

He formed the Sikorsky Aero Engineering Corporation a short time later, moved to nearby Roosevelt Field, and began to design a family of amphibians that would soon make aviation history. His twin-engine, eight-passenger S-38 amphibian was used to pioneer air routes throughout South America, the Hawaiian Islands, and other remote corners of the world.

In 1929 Sikorsky moved his company to Connecticut and became a division of United Aircraft Corporation. There, he met and worked with Charles Lindbergh, and together they ushered in the era of the Pan American Clipper ships that linked the Americas. Sikorsky's next amphibian, the huge S-40, four-engine flying boats, crossed both oceans and carried passengers to the ends of the world.

Throughout the 1930s Sikorsky quietly turned his attention back to his long-held passion for the helicopter. How he convinced management at United Aircraft to allow him to proceed with a helicopter experimental project in 1938, when the depression was causing severe reductions, is a story in itself. It was reported that Sikorsky's rationale to Don Brown, the chief executive at United Aircraft, went something like this:

I believe the time has come when we need to go ahead with vertical lift. To design and build a successful helicopter will require a most serious effort, demanding something more than just reason. It will require intuitive engineering and creative faith, which I believe we possess in our company.

The development of a helicopter is so important to the future of aviation and society, that it becomes our inherent responsibility to understand and pursue it. Admittedly, it is radical, but the helicopter concept is wholly rational, and, like no other vehicle, it will operate without regard to prepared landing surfaces. Therefore it will free us of the serious handicap of airport limitations imposed by fixed-wing aircraft.

Now the helicopter is not competitive with the airplane. It is complementary, and I envision it will bring into the world a whole new means of saving lives.

Don Brown was apparently convinced and gave the green light for the production of the first experimental helicopter, which was to be known as the VS-300 [Vought-Sikorsky experimental aircraft number 300]. A happy Sikorsky returned, after a thirty-year absence, to his first love.

Years later Sikorsky described his thinking when he and his small crew began work on the VS-300. It went something like this:

We knew what we were doing, but we also knew our first guess would not be our last one, so I deliberately made the helicopter more or less as a contraption so we could adjust, remove, or add, as we needed. We could have ordered castings and forgings and specially built gears, etc., but I wanted none of that. The ship would have a welded tube frame and belts for quickly changing

the ratio of rotor speed, and we used gears from a
Mack truck.

His comments on first flight: "In September of
1938, five months after we started, our machine was
ready for first flight. It wasn't much of a flight, but it
was better than my first attempt in 1910. It was very
difficult to control, but I got the VS-300 four to six
inches off the ground for about ten seconds. We considered that a great beginning."

On his learning to fly the VS-300:

It was equivalent to riding a bucking horse, with
little positive control. But over a period of several
months we made numerous changes in the control
system in our search for stability and control, including the use of auxiliary rotors. Finally, we got
it to the point that I could keep it under reasonable
control. But I was somewhat restricted because
management insisted I remain in tethered flight, so
that if I crashed it would be localized. Then one
day when the machine yanked the chain right out
of the concrete, I declared we were free of our
shackles. Besides, I reasoned, the danger is not in
flying through the air but in striking the ground.
Hereafter, I was permitted to seek safety in free
flight.

Eugene Wilson, senior vice president of United Aircraft, described his impression of watching Sikorsky
in one of those early flights in an article in *Reader's
Digest* [Eugene E. Wilson, "The Most Unforgettable
Character I've Met," December 1956]: "He [Igor] sat
there in his business suit and prim fedora on the

'front porch' of his crazy looking craft, looking like a baffled professor trying to remember his notes, and I marveled that he ever learned to fly the thing."

On May 6, 1941, Sikorsky established a new helicopter world record for endurance by remaining airborne in his VS-300 for one hour, thirty-three minutes, and twenty-six seconds. Within a month, United Aircraft received its first government contract for a Sikorsky helicopter, and America's helicopter industry was born.

As we sat there sipping coffee and eating cake, Sikorsky seemed so down to earth, I had the feeling that I could ask him the question that had been on my mind for many years. So I did.

"Mr. Sikorsky, is it true that the VS-300 would climb vertical, fly sideward, and backward, but wouldn't go forward?"

He smiled broadly. "So, you have heard that story?"

I returned the smile and admitted that I had.

"Well, after I had demonstrated the craft to our senior management a couple of times, the president at that time, Mr. Eugene Wilson, said to me, 'Igor, you have shown us a ship hovering over one spot, flying sideways and rearward, but it occurs to me that I have not seen it flying forward. Why is that?' I replied, 'Mr. Wilson, that is a secondary engineering problem which we haven't solved yet.'

"Frankly, Captain, I was getting desperate over that problem, because I could make the machine do everything but go forward. I had about decided to simply turn the seat around and then backward would be forward. But the problem then would be that it wouldn't fly backward, so we had no choice but to solve the problem, which we did by replacing the two rotors with one single center rotor and use cyclic pitch control for stability.

"But there were an awful lot of similar problems which we also solved over a period of time, and now we have helicopters that can do what you just did, Captain, fly seven thousand miles without a major mishap or delay, and can do the important thing I always envisioned the helicopter would: save lives."

"Yes, sir, that they can do. I know."

He looked at me for a moment. "You were in Korea, Captain?"

I nodded.

"Then you wear the Winged S."

I nodded again.

The "Winged S" was the trademark of Sikorsky aircraft. It was also a prestigious gold lapel pen, which Sikorsky initiated and awarded to pilots and crew of a Sikorsky helicopter who had saved a life. I earned mine in Korea, flying a Sikorsky H-5. It flew forward right well.

AUTHOR'S NOTE

Before the Korean War the helicopter was considered to be a novelty with limited value to the general aviation world or the military. That all changed as a result of the remarkable performance of the "choppers" in Korea for both lifesaving and operational applications. In fact, that performance ushered in a whole new era in military tactics.

Between the end of the Korean War and the outbreak of the Vietnam War, rotary wing technology leaped forward, and armed troop carriers and deadly helicopter gunships became formidable weapons on the battlefields of Vietnam. The following two stories are riveting examples of the missions flown by the chopper pilots of that war.

CHAPTER EIGHTEEN

In the Nam Trenches

After we had visited awhile at our lunch table in the Rosslyn Metro Center in Northern Virginia, I knew that John Harris was the one to tell me a Vietnam story. Men who have gone to war and fought in the trenches have a certain distinctive way of talking about it. If you've been there, you know. And I'd been there many times in a two-seat Sikorsky H-5 helicopter over the rice paddies of Korea. John Harris's trench was a twenty-seven-seat Boeing CH-46 over the jungles of Vietnam.

When I began the search for helicopter tales about Vietnam, I was referred to John by a mutual friend, Darryl Riersgard, who was also a decorated Nam helicopter pilot. He modestly suggested that Harris, who is a Marine program director for Boeing in nearby Washington, D.C., had some hair-raising Nam experiences if I could get him to talk about them.

"I have avoided telling war stories for over thirty years. When I heard others drone on about their experiences, I found it boring and self-serving, so I made a conscious decision to move on, not dwell on the past. But as a favor to Darryl, and because you're one of us, I'll open up the ole memory bank and see what comes out," Harris said to me across our lunch table.

John told me some great stories, enough to make a wonderful book, which made it difficult to choose. But I selected one that I felt would provide some gutsy insight into the reality of what the Marine helicopter crews experienced on a day-to-day basis in Vietnam. I created the dialogue, but the story is exactly as John told it.

It was hot and sticky without a breath of air coming through the open windows of the hooch [a small, Vietnamese-style house]. Lt. John Harris lay on his cot dressed in a flight suit with his hands folded behind his head, staring into the blackness and wondering what time it was. He knew the other pilots were also restless as he could hear occasional movements in the darkness. He glanced at the luminous dial on his wristwatch. It was almost midnight.

It would be a miserable, tough mission if they had to go. Outside, there was a muggy overcast with low, scuddy clouds, and the night was as black as the inside of a coal-digger's lunchbox. He and his two helo crews were taking their turn pulling standby night medevac, the most harrowing and dangerous of all helicopter missions in Vietnam. Because of the high-risk factor, night missions were limited to operationally essential or emergencies only. However, more often than not, they would be called out.

The flare of a cigarette lighter reflected off the wall. Harris knew it was Joe Martin, his copilot. Martin was a chain-smoker, even at night between periods of sleep.

Joe also drank a lot of scotch every night—and he probably wanted a shot now, desperately. But he wouldn't . . . not tonight. Not while on medevac standby. Night missions required skill, concentration, and teamwork from every crew member just to survive.

After a while, Harris glanced at his watch again. It was almost 0100 hours. Maybe . . . just maybe, they would make it through the night without a call. God, he hoped so.

God wasn't listening this night, and when the field phone rang a few seconds later, it was like a mortar hitting the hooch. All four pilots were off their cots like a shot. Harris grabbed the field phone. After a silent, frozen moment, listening to the crackling voice from the group-operations bunker, he glanced at the probing eyes and said, "Briefing in five, let's go."

Mumbling a few choice superlatives, the Marines grabbed their Kevlar "bullet bouncer" vests and their .38 pistol belts, and hurried out of the hooch into the sultry night. "I'll wake the crew," said Glen "Smokey" Burgess, the pilot of Medevac Two, the backup helicopter. Although alert quarters were available for the enlisted crew, out of pride, they chose to stay with their bird, sleeping on the canvas seats inside the big CH-46.

A few minutes later, the two helicopter medevac crews stood in the pale light of a portable generator, smoking and fidgeting as a briefing officer told them that a team of Marine infantry "grunts" on night patrol in the jungle had engaged the Vietcong in a firefight and had taken serious casualties. They were now trapped by a superior Vietcong force that was moving in for the kill.

Lieutenant Harris, commander of the two-ship

medevac team, and every one of his crew knew they had drawn a tough, ugly mission. To attempt a medevac in the jungle under enemy fire was high risk anytime. On a black night in lousy weather, it would be something more like suicide. But Harris and his crew also knew that if they failed to perform their mission, fellow Marines would die on this miserable Vietnam night.

Medevac missions were flown with two helos, as the Marines called them. One helo was lead, designated "Medevac One," and a backup, "Medevac Two." If the lead ship was shot down, the backup would rescue the downed crew, or go down in the attempt. But if success was possible on such a mission, it would be with this workhorse helicopter, the Boeing Vertol CH-46, affectionately nicknamed the "Frog" by its crews. But its ungainly appearance belied its exceptional ability to perform and take brutal punishment.

The CH-46 is a tandem-rotor helicopter with three 50-foot-diameter rotor blades at each end of its fuselage. With a gross weight of over 20,000 pounds, it can carry a crew and twenty-four combat-ready Marines. On this mission, the crew consisted of a pilot, copilot, crew chief, two .50-caliber gunners, and a Navy corpsman, who administered medical aid when required, which was often.

"Okay, guys, let's get them in the air," said Lieutenant Harris as he scribbled on a clip pad the geographical coordinates of the trapped Marines, their radio frequencies, and the frequencies of his top cover—two AH-1 Cobra helicopter gunships.

"Good luck," said the briefing officer.

"Yeah. We'll need it," Harris mumbled, hurrying

toward the two darkened shapes on the helipads, where his crew was already scurrying to their assigned positions.

To expedite takeoff, helicopters on standby medevac were given a preflight inspection ahead of time and all checklist items were accomplished down to "engine start." The copilot, Lt. Joe Martin, had already begun that final procedure as Harris pulled himself through the narrow entrance into the cockpit. At a signal from the crew chief that rotor blade tie downs were removed and the area cleared, Harris flipped the start switch and the whine of a General Electric T-58 turbine engine cut the soggy, nighttime silence. A few minutes later, the two Marine CH-46 Frogs lifted off the helipad in tandem and flew away into the blackness.

It was like taking off into an inkwell, and within seconds the helicopter was engulfed in the misting overcast. Harris knew that he had no choice but to fly on instruments until he could get above the clouds where, hopefully, starlight would provide some visibility. After a quick radio transmission to advise the backup pilot of his intentions, he pulled collective to climb power and started up.

The cloud layer was filled with muggy air and the helicopter pitched and yawed as it climbed, causing the instruments to bounce erratically. But after a relatively short flight, they broke out on top of the cloud layer and into a dark but clear sky.

"Thanks for little favors," Harris muttered to himself, then quickly pressed the transmit switch: "You with me, Medevac Two?"

"I'm right off your starboard, Medevac One,"

replied Lieutenant Burgess, pilot of the backup helicopter.

Harris glanced over his right shoulder through the side cockpit window and saw the glow of the backup helo's clearance lights. "Okay, Glen. I make it a heading of 320 degrees for about twenty-five minutes. When we get there, we'll assess conditions and go from there."

"Roger."

Switching to intercom, Harris said, "Take it, Joe, while I recheck these coordinates."

"I got it," replied the copilot, taking the flight controls.

Snapping on a penlight, Harris rechecked his chart. He was confident he could find the coordinate location by using the azimuth and distance off the Danang TACAN [radio aid]. But then how in the world was he going to find the exact spot where the Marines were trapped if it was covered by an overcast? All he could hope for was a break in the clouds.

As they approached the area, Harris called his cover, the two AH-1 Cobra gunships.

"Roger, Medevac One. We're circling the area now, but it's socked in so we can't pinpoint the target," one of the Cobra pilots replied.

"Jesus, now what'a we gonna do?" groaned Martin.

"Firefly, this is Medevac One, do you read?" transmitted Harris, as he put the CH-46 into a wide circle over the area where the trapped Marines, code-named Firefly, were supposed to be.

No answer.

Harris repeated his radio call.

After the third call: "They are either already wiped out or we're in the wrong place," said Martin.

"Lieutenant Harris, I heard something that time. It was real faint but I heard it," said the crew chief over the intercom.

"Firefly, if you're down there speak up!" barked Harris.

This time a reply came, but in a barely discernible whisper: "We're here. . . . We're here, Med One. . . . But I can't talk loud because Charlie's so close we can hear them talking."

"Oh great," said someone.

"Can you hear the helicopters, Firefly?" asked Harris.

"Yeah. We can hear you up there."

"Okay, Firefly. You got any ceiling down there?"

The next transmission was too weak to hear.

"Can't hear you, Firefly."

"Gotta speak low . . . Charlie's real close. . . . It's pitch-black down here . . . can't see anything. Can you make it? They're closing in on us."

"Stand by, Firefly." Harris switched to intercom and spoke to his crew: "This is a real shit sandwich, guys. Our only chance to save those grunts is to try and find a break in the overcast, then drop down under it, and have them talk us into their LZ [landing zone] by sound. We'll be down there alone with no Cobra cover, so we'll take ground fire. It's a long shot but as I see it, the only shot."

"We're ready, sir," replied the chief.

Yeah, they were ready, said John Harris to himself. Not that they had a choice. As the aircraft commander, he made the decision. They went wherever he took them. But John knew those brave men back there at their crew stations would fly that helo to hell with him. Their pride and dedication never ceased to amaze him.

Switching back to transmit, Harris briefed the ground-based Direct Air Support Controller, Medevac Two, and the Cobra gunships of his intentions.

"There may not be any ceiling under the clouds, Medevac One," advised one of the gunships.

Harris knew what the gunship pilot was saying: if there was no ceiling under the clouds, he wouldn't be able to see the trees in the darkness and would probably fly the helicopter straight into the jungle. "Yeah, I know," he muttered on the radio.

"Medevac One, this is Two. You want me to follow you down?"

Harris glanced out at the flashing red anticollision light on the backup helo that was just off his starboard side. "No. You stay above the overcast and orbit with the Cobras. If we don't make it, it'll be your call, Glen."

"Roger."

"Medevac One from Cobra lead. I think I saw a small break in the clouds just this side of that ridge at your nine o'clock position."

"Thanks, we'll check it out," said Harris as he banked the CH-46 toward the dark ridgeline that jutted up from the gray overcast on his port side.

Radio silence for a few minutes.

"There's a hole in the overcast over here all right, and we're gonna go for it. Firefly, do you read?"

"I read you," came the whispered transmission.

"Okay. We're coming down lights out, and if we make it you gotta direct us to you by sound, using clock positions. You got it?"

"Got it."

"All right, good guys," said Harris to his crew. "When the bad guys hear us coming, they're gonna throw the kitchen sink at us. So everybody got your bullet bouncers on?"

The crew all responded in the affirmative, and both pilots rotated their .38-caliber pistol holsters around from their hip so that they covered the family jewels—a habit most Vietnam helicopter pilots practiced.

In the CH-46 the pilots sat in armor-plated seats with "wings" on each side, so they were protected from small-arms fire from the rear, bottom, and each side. The Kevlar "bullet bouncers" protected chest and stomach, which left jewels, arms, legs, and head exposed. The other crew members wore the Kevlar vests but without armor plate; they were significantly more exposed. They accepted this risk as part of their duty.

"It's gonna be black down there, so everybody keep a sharp eye out, and if you see something, sound off. Gunners, don't fire unless I give the order. I don't want to give Charlie a target," instructed Harris.

"Yeah, they can't see us any more than we can see them," added the copilot, switching off all outside navigation lights.

Harris punched his UHF transmit switch. "DAS control, this is Medevac One. We're goin' in."

"Roger, Medevac One, we copy," replied the air controller.

"Okay, here we go," said Harris, pushing the cyclic forward and easing off the collective, which nosed the helicopter into the black hole in the overcast. It was sure enough the black hole of destiny, thought Harris, straining to see something ahead . . . something to get spatial orientation. If he got vertigo all would be lost. Nothing but blackness . . . swirling blackness. . . .

"Trees dead ahead!" snapped the copilot.

Harris saw the dark shapes loom over the nose and pulled collective as he hauled back on the cyclic. The big bird shuddered and pitched up, skimming over the treetops with only inches to spare.

After a moment to let his pounding heart slow, Harris came on the intercom. "Okay. We're here, everyone on your toes and—"

"Medevac One from Firefly, we hear you."

"Give me direction, Firefly."

"I think you're to the north of us."

"Give it to me by clock positions."

"There is a ridge just off our starboard, Lieutenant," advised the crew chief.

Harris glanced out and saw the dim outline in the darkness. "Got it, Chief."

"Medevac One, this is Two. How you doin' down there?"

"We're doin', Two. We're below the overcast. Stand by. Firefly, give me a clock number."

"You're goin' away from us."

"Okay, I'm making a one-eighty," replied Harris, rolling the CH-46 into a bank. Now flying lights out, he must maintain spatial orientation by visual reference to the black shapes below him. This was tricky and demanding flying, and one mistake would plunge the helicopter into the jungle in a deadly crash.

"I can hear you coming back toward us."

"Good, you got the LZ marked?"

"Arely . . . too . . . oss . . . ant . . . ow . . . airs . . ."

"Can't read you, Firefly."

Silence.

"Charlie's too close. Can't use flares," came the weak reply from the trapped Marine.

"Damn, John. There ain't no way you can land in that friggin' inkwell without some kind of marker," rasped Martin over the intercom.

John knew that his copilot was correct. He would be fortunate just to keep the bird flying under these conditions. Trying to land could only result in the loss of the helicopter and six more Marines in addition to those below whose fate, at best, hung in the balance.

"You're going off to the east. . . . Uh, come right, we're at your . . . I think, three o'clock position."

"Correcting right."

Silence.

"Ooo . . . com . . . ight . . . ard . . . uz."

"Repeat your last transmission."

"You're comin' right toward us."

"Okay. But I got to have some kind of reference to land with, Firefly. You have to mark the LZ somehow."

"Ground fire coming up, Lieutenant!" shouted the crew chief. Suddenly the blackness was pierced with lines of glowing fireballs. The Vietcong were firing at the sound of the helicopter, and their tracers were spewing in all directions.

"Gunners, hold your fire!" snapped Harris over the intercom. He could see the Vietcong fire was inaccurate, but if he returned fire his tracers would give them a target. He would hold off firing as long as possible.

"You flew directly over us!" shouted Firefly.

Harris put the helo into a right bank, and, glancing back, he could see the arches of enemy ground fire coming up from the area he'd just passed over. Now he had a bracket on where the grunts were trapped. But it would do him no good, because it was just as pitch-black as everything else.

"Firefly, there is no way I can get to you unless you mark an LZ."

Silence.

"Medevac One, how about if I hold up my cigarette lighter?"

"A cigarette lighter?" said Martin.

"When I hear you getting close I'll hold it up so you can see it, okay?" In a sort of pleading voice.

"I don't think that's gonna work, Firefly."

Silence for a moment. "Medevac One . . . we're in serious trouble down here. We got wounded, and Charlie's moving in fast. We're goners if you can't get us soon."

"Firefly, you sure that's all you can mark the LZ with is a cigarette lighter?"

"We're surrounded by Vietcong on three sides, but there is a clear area between some trees on the one side. I can hold the lighter so it can only be seen from that direction."

A moment of silence.

John Harris took a deep breath. He was faced with an agonizing dilemma. He had his own crew of good men to consider, and to land the CH-46 in the jungle, on a black night, under fire, with nothing to guide him but a cigarette lighter, was madness. But to fly away, condemning those other good men to death, was something he couldn't bring himself to do. He punched the intercom and said to his crew: "You all heard the story. As fellow Marines, we owe it those grunts to give it a shot."

"We're ready back here, sir," came the expected reply from the crew chief, and similar comments followed from the other crew members.

"Okay. Stand by for an LZ landing. Hold your fire till I give the command."

"John, this is Glen. Whatta you gonna do?"

"We're goin' in, Glen. Stand by."

"The ground fire stopped, Lieutenant," said the crew chief over the intercom.

"Yeah. I see it did. Firefly, give me a reading."

"You went off to the south of us. . . . Uh, turn left, I'd guess about your three o'clock position."

Another silence.

"Okay. . . . Sounds like you're headed back toward us."

Maintaining orientation was precarious for the Marine pilot. His only reference was the dim horizon created by the slight difference in darkness between the ground plane and the cloud layer. Now he must make an approach and land in a sea of blackness guided by a cigarette lighter. He was reminded that Navy pilots claim landing on an aircraft carrier at night is the most demanding of all. He'd take that in a New York second over what he was about to attempt.

"You're getting close, Medevac One. Come left a little."

Harris kicked pedal slightly and eased down on the collective and back on the cyclic control, slowing the helicopter's forward speed.

"You're close . . . close," came the whispered advisory.

"I can see trees, Lieutenant. We're about a hundred feet," reported the crew chief hanging out of the crew door.

"Okay, Firefly, light up," instructed Harris.

"My Zippo's on. Can you see it?"

The two marine pilots stared through the CH-46 windshield.

"I see it dead ahead!" barked Martin.

Focusing on the tiny, flickering light in the black world ahead, Harris eased the helicopter forward in a slow gradual decent. "Sound off if you see obstacles!" he instructed the crew.

"Ground fire!" snapped the chief as the darkness exploded in streams of burning fireballs all around the helicopter.

"Stay on the instruments, Joe!" Harris instructed his copilot, knowing that, in this type of blackout flying under fire, engine and rotor RPM and torque could vary dangerously.

Harris felt perspiration run into his eyes as the helicopter shuddered out of translational lift and began its transition to ground effect. "About thirty feet, Lieutenant. Steady as you go," he heard the crew chief say from his precarious perch at the crew door.

"You're over the LZ!" shouted Firefly as the wind from the big fifty-foot rotor blades swept down over the trapped Marines, blowing out the cigarette lighter.

"Move left! Left! We're over a tree!" shouted the crew chief.

Harris felt his heart leap as the controls jerked violently in his hands. He knew the rotor blades had struck something . . . probably a tree. But he'd done that before and knew those big blades could take a beating. Of course, there was a limit to that beating, and when reached, the bird would thrash itself to pieces in a matter of seconds.

"Okay, okay! You're clear, Lieutenant. You can set her down," said the chief.

As Harris fought to bring the ten-ton helicopter to a blackout landing, Martin hit the back-ramp switch. "Ramp going down!" he shouted.

"We're taking hits!" reported one of the gunners.

"Get 'em aboard quick!" commanded Harris.

The grunts, carrying their wounded, scrambled up the ramp and into the helo the second it slammed down, its big rotor blades slicing the jungle growth like giant machetes.

Harris's heart pounded and perspiration stung his eyes as he grasped the controls, maintaining full rotor RPM, ready to pull in everything the engines would give him the instant the crew chief cleared him to go. He cringed from the distinctive hollow sound of lead piercing aluminum. But he knew the helicopter would take a lot of hits and still fly away. The engines and hydraulic lines were protected by armor plating. The rotor, however, was not. A critical hit there and . . .

"All aboard! Go! Go!" shouted the crew chief.

Harris pulled in all the power he could get, and the Frog leaped out of the LZ, its rotor blades slicing and spewing pieces of tree limbs and foliage in all directions as it cut a swath out of the jungle.

"Okay gunners, give 'em a taste of their own medicine!" instructed Harris, and a second later the two .50-caliber guns roared from the cabin of the CH-46, sending a deadly fusillade into the jungle below.

"How you doing down there, Medevac One?" came the voice of Glen Burgess, from the backup helicopter.

"Clear the area, Smokey! We're coming upstairs like a homesick angel!" replied Harris.

"You got the grunts?"

"We got 'em."

"Great job, Medevac One," transmitted one of the Cobra gunships, circling above the overcast.

The CH-46 Marine helicopter popped up through the overcast a few minutes later, and Harris leveled the big bird out, flipped on his navigation and anti-collision lights, and headed for the nearest field hospital.

"How do the controls feel, John?" asked Martin, concerned over the heavy vibrations in the helicopter.

"She's a little rough on the controls. We probably knocked off a few chunks of blade chopping trees, but she'll get us home."

"Okay. You want me to relieve you for a bit?"

"Yeah, you got the controls."

"I got 'er," said Martin.

"Medevac One, this is Control. Understand you made the pickup?"

"That's a roger, Control."

"Good show, Medevac One."

As always, after a mission that brought death so close, the intercom in the Marine helo suddenly became quiet for a few moments while each crew member did his own thing: a silent prayer or just his own private thoughts.

Then, over the intercom, "Lieutenant Harris?"

"Yeah?"

"Uh, this is the chief, sir. You mind if I tell you something?"

"Fire away, Chief."

"I just wanted to say, sir, you've really got your shit together."

John Harris looked across the lunch table at me, there in the Rosslyn Metro Center restaurant. "Ya know, I've thought about it a lot all these years, and I'm still in awe of the unwavering dedication, bravery, and skill of those helicopter crewmen in Vietnam. Day after day in miserable conditions, the maintenance crews kept those choppers flying, and the crew chiefs, gunners, and the corpsmen would crawl in and do their duty on those high-risk missions. Many of them were killed. I didn't know then, and I still don't know, what motivated them. But I do know one thing: they were genuine American heroes."

Harris glanced out the window for a moment, then added: "They awarded me a Distinguished Flying Cross for that mission, and I'm proud of it, even though I've long forgotten the words on the citation. But I'll tell you something, Richard." He hesitated and grinned. "I will never forget those simple words from my crew chief that night. That was the most precious compliment I've ever received and one I'll remember the rest of my life."

CHAPTER NINETEEN

The Game

This is a personal account of the helicopter combat missions flown by U.S. Army pilot Warrant Officer William Q. Kirk on a spring day in Vietnam in 1968. Other than editing and some dialogue translation, this is his story in his words.

Listening to the briefing officer that morning emphasize "shoot anything that moves," I suspected this mission was going to be a rough one—but, then again, most of them were. It was just that some were worse than others, and we T-Birds [our call sign] were playing a rough game. It was called "Kill or Be Killed."

I was the pilot of a Bell UH-1B "Huey" gunship assigned to the 336th Assault Helicopter Company at Soc Trang Army Airfield, South Vietnam. On this particular day, I was the leader of a two-ship fire team that had been assigned to fly low over the LZ [landing zone], where a combat assault operation was to take place. Our job was to reconnaissance the area for any sign of enemy activity and see if we could draw fire. Although that was our normal procedure for this type of mission, I felt that concept was fundamentally flawed. We got shot at enough without asking for it.

The theory was, however, that it was better for us to take fire than the troop-carrier "slicks" [helicopters] that transported the soldiers into the LZ after we'd cleared the way. But the Vietcong wouldn't usually give away their position until the slicks came in because they were juicier targets: they couldn't shoot back, and we could. Sometimes, when their positions were heavily fortified or our gunships were just too inviting a target, we got what we were looking for: big trouble.

After our 0500 mission briefing that morning, my crew and I, designated T-Bird 4, and my wingman, T-Bird 8, trudged to the flight line with our gear and crawled into our birds. Each crew consisted of a pilot, copilot, crew chief, and gunner. The Hueys were armed with fourteen 2.75-inch rockets, seven in each external pod on the side of the helicopter, which I fired, and three thousand rounds of 7.62mm bullets for the machine guns, also mounted on each side, which were operated by the copilot. The crew chief and gunner in the back of the helicopter each had a M60 machine gun with five hundred rounds and a box of grenades. With all that, and a full load of fuel, we were overweight, and it was a struggle to get off the ground, but my wingman and I both managed it and headed off over the jungle. About twenty minutes later we arrived over the AO [area of operation] at 1,000 feet.

I scanned the area and identified the LZ, which was a group of interlaced rice paddies surrounded by jungle. It looked peaceful enough, as all I could see were Vietnamese farmers working their paddies. I called my wingman on the radio and advised that we would descend and do a low-level reconnaissance. I pulled my rocket sight into position in front of me and lowered my bulletproof helmet visor.

"Okay, we're goin' down. Everybody get your protectors on," I said over the intercom to my crew. We wore chest protectors in the cockpit and had armorplated seats. The gun crew wore chest and back armor plates.

"Keep a sharp eye out," I added as I pushed the cyclic forward and nosed the Huey down to the treetops, leveled off, and flew low across the paddies. I could see there were a couple hundred Vietnamese that appeared to be women, children, and old men. They all kept their heads down. Not a one looked up at the helicopter as we flew over. I was aware that my orders were to shoot anything that moved in the LZ, but I could see no threat from these farmers, and opening fire on them would be like slaughtering sheep.

"T-Bird 8, this is T-Bird lead, we're not going to fire on those farmers."

"Don't fire on 'em?"

"That's affirmative. Do not fire."

After zigzagging over the LZ for about fifteen minutes, I called my wingman again: "T-Bird 8 from T-Bird 4, what's your take on it?"

"I don't see any indication of Vietcong, T-Bird 4."

"Neither do I, but I got an uncomfortable feeling. Let's make another pass around before I call Delta 6 with a go for troop insertion."

Delta 6 was the Army colonel in command of the combat assault. He operated from the command-

and-control [C&C] helicopter that orbited 3,000 feet above the AO. Once I gave him a green light, he would then call in the troop-carrier helicopters that were standing by.

As I made one last pass over the LZ, I somehow sensed the Vietcong were there; and my instincts were correct. We were suddenly flying into a sea of fireballs coming out of the trees along the border of the paddies. I guess the temptation was just too much for the enemy gunners.

"We're taking hits!" shrieked my crew chief on the intercom.

I slammed the bird into a bank and keyed the mic: "T-Bird 8, we're under fire from the tree line, get 'em with your rockets!"

My wingman was behind me and in a better position to take out the gun position with his rockets, but he was also under fire and had to bank away.

"T-Bird 8 is hit, and my gunner is wounded!" he shouted.

"Let's get out of here!" I replied and headed away from the trees where the fire was coming from.

We flew out a ways to some open rice paddies to assess our damage. As it turned out, both helicopters had taken numerous hits, but nothing vital and we were operating normally. The gunner on T-Bird 8 had stopped the bleeding of a shoulder wound and reported that he was all right.

I called Delta 6 and advised the colonel I had wounded aboard and was returning to base, but would take out the Vietcong gun position in the LZ before I departed, because I knew exactly where it was.

Although Delta 6 was in command, the fire-team

leader ran the combat assault show, and it was a lot of responsibility. He had to fly the helicopter, read the map, know the enemy locations, understand the friendly locations and their intentions, shoot rockets, and direct the machine-gun fire. He also had to work four radios at the same time: the copilot and crew on intercom, the wingman on VHF, C&C and the transport helicopters on UHF, and the ground troops on FM. He was also responsible for the safety of his crew and the crew of his wingman, reconning and securing the LZ, defining the approach and departure routes for the transport helicopters, providing cover for the slicks during insertions and extractions, evaluating objectives, defining enemy positions and taking them out, and providing cover for the ground troops.

That was a lot of responsibility for a twenty-two-year-old kid, whose world eighteen months earlier had been college parties and girls. I couldn't even have told you where Vietnam was before I got drafted. It's not that I didn't love my country, I just hadn't planned on fighting for it. Well, surprise. Courtesy of my friendly draft board, I was selected to do just that. Preferring flying to walking, I volunteered for helicopter-pilot training and got two months of basic training, nine months of flight school, and an all-expenses-paid trip across the Pacific Ocean.

When I arrived in Saigon and found out what the life expectancy of a combat helicopter pilot was, I immediately volunteered to fly the general. I figured generals didn't get too close to combat. However, much to my dismay, my request was denied, and I was assigned to the transport platoon of the 336th Assault Helicopter Company. After three months of flying troop transports, taking fire and not being able to shoot back, I raised my level of insanity. I volunteered for assignment to the gun platoon. If I was going to take fire, I was going to return fire. Now I wasn't avoiding trouble, I was looking for it. That's what gunship pilots do. It was the game—Kill or Be Killed.

My gunner had thrown out smoke grenades where we'd taken fire, so when we flew back over the LZ the smoke was still visible along the tree line, revealing the Vietcong's position.

"We're goin' in, give it to 'em!" I told my crew on the intercom, then switched to transmit. "Let's take 'em out, T-Bird 8," I said as I started my firing run.

"I'm right behind you, T-Bird 4!" replied my wingman.

The enemy gunners opened fire on us again, but my first two rockets were right on target, and my copilot and cabin gunners shredded the jungle with a fusillade of deadly machine-gun fire. After the third run we had expended our ammunition, but there was no more fire coming our way.

I reported to the colonel at C&C: "Delta 6, this is T-Bird lead, we silenced them, but I suspect there's Vietcong still in there, so mark this area as hot. We're headed for Soc Trang with our wounded and to check battle damage. You'll have to get another fire team to cover the insertion."

"Roger, T-Bird 4. But I need you back here as soon as possible, as we're short on gunships."

"Roger, Delta 6." Then to my wingman: "Okay, T-Bird 8, let's head for the barn."

As we banked away I glanced down at the rice

paddies that had been full of Vietnamese farmers a
few minutes ago. They were all gone. They had been
decoys and could have gotten us all killed. I wondered what I would do the next time I faced women
and children with orders to shoot anything that
moved.

After landing back at Soc Trang, we found that
T-Bird 8 had taken seventeen hits with damage to the
flight controls and fuel cells, so it was grounded. My
bird had taken twelve hits in the tail boom, in the
underside of the fuselage, and in the main rotor
blades, but it was still flyable. I told my crew chief
that I also sensed bullets penetrating right over my
head. He looked but couldn't find any holes. The
guys gave me a hard time about exaggerating the situation. About that time, the crew chief, who had
climbed on top of the helicopter to look at the main
rotor blades again, hollered at me to come up. I
climbed up, and he showed me two bullet holes
above the pilot's seat, about an inch from my head.

T-Bird 8 was assigned another helicopter, and two
hours later both gunships were armed, refueled, and
ready to return to the operational area. We got a replacement for the wounded gunner and struggled
into the air again.

As soon as we were airborne, I checked in with
Delta 6 and he directed me to stand by at a tactical-
staging area that had been set up near the LZ. Another gun team from the 121st Assault Helicopter
Company, call sign "Viking," was on station working with the ground commanders and had covered
the insertion of troop carriers into the LZ without incident.

We landed at the staging area, shut down, and

waited for further direction. The staging area was a plot of earth the size of a football field within a large rice paddy. There are no trees in rice paddies. The temperature was now approaching 100 degrees, the humidity was stifling, and the mosquitoes were hungry. The crew chief and gunner took refuge in the back of the helicopter. The only shade my copilot and I could find was under the tail boom, where we were fair game for all the bugs. Being shot at was almost preferable.

Things were going slowly in the AO. The ground troops were encountering no resistance, but that's par for the course. The South Vietnamese troops didn't look for the enemy very hard. They didn't want to fight. What were they fighting for? Their government was corrupt, their military leaders were inept, their training was inadequate, and they were not paid well. Their objective on a military operation was not to make contact with the enemy if they could help it. But I guess they figured that as long as they were there, they would take advantage of the opportunity to steal the farmer's chickens and whatever other meager belongings they could carry off. Not exactly the way to win the hearts and minds of the people. For most Vietnamese the war was cruel.

After our leisurely lunch of tasteless C rations, we were launched by Delta 6 to assist the ground troops in the LZ. After an hour and a half of searching the jungle for bad guys and laying in a couple of rocket and machine-gun strikes on suspected Vietcong positions, we returned to Soc Trang to refuel and rearm.

Operations called about 1600 and advised us to plan on the slicks arriving at the LZ for troop extraction at 1645. Our T-Birds would be the primary fire team, and the Vikings, the other fire team, would remain in the staging area as backup. After receiving an update on the location of the ground troops and the plan for extraction, my wingman and I launched again and proceeded to the AO. There, I got confirmation from Delta 6 on the LZ and troop locations.

My wingman and I then flew a reconnaissance of the LZ and identified approach and departure routes for the slicks. The extraction would be done with fourteen troop-carrying helicopters, each carrying one "stick" of twelve to fourteen troops.

I made radio contact with the slick leader and gave him directions for landing and departure that avoided suspected enemy areas. As the slicks approached the LZ, my wingman and I took up positions on each side of the formation.

When the transport helicopters had settled into the LZ, T-Bird 8 and I then set up a low-level orbit around the rice paddy. All was well until I noticed a flash off the right side of my helicopter. Then the LZ exploded in a barrage of mortar and automatic weapons.

"We're taking fire! We're taking fire!" screamed the slick leader over the UHF radio, as explosions mushroomed everywhere.

I saw a mortar hit in the middle of one of the troop sticks as they waited to board the helicopter. Several Vietnamese soldiers catapulted head over heels into the air as though they were rag dolls. Now the radio was filled with voices screaming about taking fire, including my wingman, T-Bird 8. My own crew chief and gunner shouted on the intercom that we were taking hits.

"Return fire! Return fire!" I ordered, and a second

later the bird shook as my copilot and gunners opened up with everything they had.

At that moment, Delta 6, who must have been asleep, called for an update briefing on the extraction progress before even listening to his radio, which pissed me off something awful.

"We're under fire! Mortars in the LZ! Get the fuck off the radio!" I yelled at the colonel.

As I scanned the area for the sources of the enemy fire, I saw a slick take a direct hit and explode, spewing bodies and pieces of helicopter in all directions. A piece of wreckage struck the rotor of the nearest chopper and it began to disintegrate. Now I had two transports down, and as I watched, a Vietnamese soldier ran into the tail rotor of a departing chopper, which decapitated him and caused the pilot to lose control. The Huey lurched into the air spinning violently, then plunged back into the rice paddy and beat itself to death, hurtling broken pieces across the paddy, like shrapnel, mutilating everything in its path.

The transports were now trying to take off, with or without troops. But with no gun cover, they were like sitting ducks and taking terrible punishment. The South Vietnamese troops were pinned down in the LZ and offering little resistance. I needed to get them to start firing into the tree lines to curb the enemy gunners, but the radio was clogged with screaming voices and I couldn't get through to the ground commanders.

"Delta 6, scramble Viking! Scramble Viking!" I yelled, hoping my transmission would get through as I needed gunship help, and I needed it fast.

"Let's go, T-Bird 8!" I shouted on the radio as I

spotted a source of fire. "Follow me in!" I added, banking toward the tree line. We swooped down across the LZ, all guns blazing and both of us firing rockets into the trees where I'd seen muzzle flashes.

The two of us were able to curb the Vietcong fire to some degree as the slicks scrambled out of the LZ in all directions, some with troops, many without, all taking fire as they fled. The mortars had stopped, but sporadic automatic-weapons fire continued and a .50-caliber machine-gun nest on the north side of the LZ was murderously effective. Three helicopters were wrecked, and three-quarters of the assault team were still pinned down in the LZ, which was strewn with dead and wounded.

I called the slick leader, and he confirmed that five of his birds got out without damage and were empty.

"Okay, we gotta get our troops out of the LZ before dark or they're in serious trouble. I think you can carry what's left," I told him.

"Unless you can knock out those gunners, and especially the .50s, I'm not gonna take my guys back in there, T-Bird 4," he replied.

"I understand. The Vikings just arrived and are attacking the gun positions as we speak," I replied, watching the Viking gunships make their firing runs on the enemy positions.

"Okay, T-Bird 4, we'll orbit here and wait for your call. We're about five miles south at 1,500 feet," informed the slick leader.

While the Vikings were attacking, I finally managed to get in radio contact with the ground commander. I told him he'd better get his troops to return fire on the enemy LZ perimeter positions if he wanted to get out of there alive. That got his attention, and they got an attack going.

The Viking team had fired rockets and machine gunned the enemy tree line positions but were unable to take out the .50 calibers. I knew that I couldn't extract the remaining troops and our crews without additional casualties if the .50-caliber position wasn't eliminated. I was low on ammo and fuel, but that .50-caliber position had to be taken out.

"Viking lead from T-Bird 4, I'm gonna climb up and make a high-angle rocket attack on the .50s. I can get a better shot that way. I'll call you when I'm in position, and I'd like you to make a simultaneous low-level diversionary attack."

"T-Bird 4, from Viking, we'll try to distract them, but if they catch you coming in like that, you're gonna take a beating."

"Yeah, I know. But we're running out of time, Viking."

"Roger. Call when you want me to go, T-Bird 4."

"Will do. You copy, T-Bird 8?"

"Copy lead. I'm with you, but I don't have any rockets left."

"Okay, T-Bird 8. I've got six remaining. That will have to do it. You cover me with machine-gun fire, and when I fire the rockets, break fast."

"Roger, let's go."

When I reached 1,500 feet above the jungle, I moved into position and asked the Viking lead to begin his attack on the .50-caliber position. The Vietcong began firing at the Viking gunships as I nosed over and started down. I was well into the diving run before I realized there were multiple .50s in the emplacement and a nest of automatic weapons.

I had made a major miscalculation, but I was committed. Red tracers the size of baseballs were coming straight at me. My copilot began firing the machine guns and so did my cabin gunners as I put my rocket sight on the muzzle flashes and fired a pair of rockets. I missed, hitting high. I edged the nose down more and fired another pair of rockets. High again. Damn! Now I could see the faces of the Vietcong gunners, and I knew I was gaining too much speed and getting too close to the enemy position. But I had no choice. I either hit that gun emplacement with my last two rockets or the game was over, and we were going home in body bags.

I pushed the cyclic forward even more, dropping the nose of the helicopter to keep the rocket sight on the target. Suddenly the windshield exploded on the copilot's side. "I'm hit!" he screamed.

The helicopter began to vibrate violently and the cockpit filled with smoke. I couldn't see my instruments, the rocket sight was useless, and I could hardly hold the controls.

"We're on fire, and we're taking hits," shouted the crew chief as the vibrations increased.

I didn't know it at the time but my gunner, who had been hanging outside the helicopter on a "monkey strap" so that he could shoot better, took a hit in his protective chest plate that knocked him clear back into the cabin of the helicopter.

I had to take out those .50 calibers! I was less than 500 feet above the Vietcong guns when I fired my last pair of rockets and pulled off in a hard right bank that made the helicopter shake so bad I nearly lost control.

"You got 'em, T-Bird 4! You got a direct hit!" I

heard somebody shout over the radio as I struggled for control of the helicopter.

After leveling out and reducing power, the vibrations eased off and I regained control. I was relieved when I realized what had caused the violent vibration: retreating blade stall, which had been the result of my exceeding the helicopter's maximum airspeed in the steep dive.

"Where's the fire?" I quickly asked over the intercom.

"We put it out. It was a smoke grenade that took a hit," answered the crew chief.

I breathed another sigh of relief and glanced across at my copilot. He was wiping blood off his face. But it wasn't a bullet wound. It was cuts from Plexiglas fragments when the windshield was shot out.

"Anybody else hurt?" I asked and got negative answers, except our gunner who was hurting from the blow of a .50-caliber round striking his armor plate.

"T-Bird 4, this is Viking lead. Man, I didn't think you were gonna pull out of that dive."

"I didn't either, Viking," I muttered.

"Good job, T-Bird. It's all quiet here now."

"Thanks for the help, Viking," I replied, then called the slicks and told them the LZ was clear for troop extraction.

I climbed to 1,000 feet and assessed our condition. Both T-Birds had sustained extensive damage. We were full of bullet holes, but the engine and transmission gauges looked good. Both birds were flying rough from damaged rotor blades, but they would get us home.

The downed helicopter crews and remaining troops were cleared from the LZ with no further casualties. The dead Vietnamese troops and the three downed helicopters were left behind. An operation would be initiated the next day to recover the bodies and helicopters, but it was not likely that much would be left.

As we headed for Soc Trang, I turned the controls over to the copilot and took a moment to reflect on the day. The sun was setting. It had been a long damn day. I was tired, hungry, and, if I thought about it, scared. I wondered how many times I could survive this shit. Okay, no more reflections. It wasn't healthy. It's the game. Today I won.

Bill Kirk did beat the game. He completed more than three hundred combat sorties in Vietnam, came home, finished college, and flew helicopters in many civil operations. We were together at Hughes and McDonnell Douglas Helicopters for many years, and he is now regional sales manager at Agusta Aerospace Corporation.

AUTHOR'S FINAL NOTE

Although I did not fly combat in Vietnam, my experiences as a war pilot and my many discussions with pilots who did, coupled with historical facts, have convinced me that helicopter pilots and crews in Vietnam faced the most difficult and high-risk flying of all. They were true American heroes.

Don't miss this exciting book
about another outstanding combat pilot
in World War II

AN ACE OF THE EIGHTH
An American Fighter Pilot's Air War in Europe

by Norman "Bud" Fortier

When the skies of Europe blazed with the fiercest
air battles in history, fighter pilots like Norman
"Bud" Fortier were in the thick of it, flying four
hundred miles an hour at thirty thousand feet,
dodging flak and dueling with enemy aces. From
blasting V-1 missile sites along France's "rocket
coast" and the victorious action of D-day to the
critical attacks on the Ruhr Valley and massive
daylight raids on German industrial targets, Fortier
was part of the Allies' bitter struggle to bring the
Nazi war machine to a halt. In describing his own
hundred-plus missions and by including the
accounts of fellow fighter pilots, Fortier recaptures
the excitement and fiery terror of the world's most
dangerous cat-and-mouse game.

Published by Presidio Press.
Available wherever books are sold.